# Introducing Cultural Studies

# Introducing Cultural Studies

## Learning through Practice

**David Walton**

SAGE Publications
Los Angeles • London • New Delhi • Singapore

All sketches courtesy of José Maria Campoy Ruiz

First published 2008

SAGE Publications Ltd
1 Oliver's Yard
55 City Road
London EC1Y 1SP

SAGE Publications Inc.
2455 Teller Road
Thousand Oaks, California 91320

SAGE Publications India Pvt Ltd
B 1/I 1 Mohan Cooperative Industrial Area
Mathura Road, New Delhi 110 044
India

SAGE Publications Asia-Pacific Pte Ltd
33 Pekin Street #02-01
Far East Square
Singapore 048763

**British Library Cataloguing in Publication data**

A catalogue record for this book is available from the British Library

ISBN 978-1-4129-1894-7
ISBN 978-1-4129-1895-4 (pbk)

**Library of Congress Control Number Available**

Typeset by C&M Digitals (P) Ltd, Chennai, India
Printed in Great Britain by TJ International, Padstow, Cornwall
Printed on paper from sustainable resources

For my son, Dan (a constant source of life, energy, affection, humour and fun), and in memory of Dale Thompson (who helped to teach me the meaning of friendship, strength, generosity and support).

# Contents

# Acknowledgements

This book has been a great pleasure to write – partly because I've enjoyed some magnificent support and encouragement. If it seems well thought out and structured – I'm not entirely to blame...

Firstly, I'd like to thank my editor at Sage, Julia Hall, for helping me to get my sometimes fuzzy ideas structured into coherent book form. Thanks, too, for helping to make the book a reality by believing in it and giving it your support. Many thanks go to the 'disappearing' Annie Wilson, who very kindly test read some early drafts of the opening chapters. I'm very grateful to her early encouragement. In the process of writing the book (post-Annie) it evolved in some new and more creative ways. Navigating these changes was made much smoother and enjoyable by the support I received from Lynne Slocombe at Sage. I feel that Lynn is the model of an in-house reader. She read every chapter seeing the book from the inside: that is, reading it from the point of view of the writer's aims. I found all her feedback sympathetic, useful and enormously encouraging. I believe the book has benefited greatly from her observations and comments.

Outside Sage, my most faithful reader has been Emma Hamilton (recent world gold medallist in Hapkido!), who very generously offered, despite her own work and hard training, to read draft chapters, and later agreed to test out and comment on practice exercises. Emma's help has been invaluable. Her criticisms were all constructive, her feedback intelligent, and she proved to be enormously encouraging and supportive (and certainly helped me to believe in what I was doing). She even found me an excellent artist in the shape of José María Campoy Ruiz, her partner. Many thanks go to José who agreed to do the illustrations, taking valuable time out from a very busy work schedule. Despite having detailed ideas about the kind of images I wanted (but lacking the artistic talent to get them down on paper) I was fascinated by how José was able to realize those ideas with such accuracy and yet with such ingenuity. I am delighted by José's interpretations of my original ideas (and the unexpected, but always apposite, details) and it has been a great pleasure negotiating each image with him. I hope readers will agree with me that they make a valuable contribution to the book.

I am grateful to Chantal Cornut-Gentille for encouraging me to pick myself up and get going on a book in the first place and to the Culture and Power group in Spain for providing a forum for debate. Thanks to Lidia Damunt, who originally agreed to do some sketches but owing to the pressures of work had to pull out. Thanks, too, to all those students who have studied on my cultural studies courses. You have often been willing guinea pigs for my pedagogical experiments and delighted me with some very unforeseen results. Thanks to Eva Nicolás Villaescusa for all the moral support. Oh, and thanks to Gurdeep Mattu, at Sage, for helping me to lose a few exclamation marks!

And so it is that the name 'David Walton' tends to function as a mask to disguise the input of many important people. Without them this book would have been a much more difficult and lonely adventure. Finally, it is customary to state that, despite all assistance received, all errors are entirely the responsibility of the author. True – but I'd add that, whatever the merits of this book may be, if I hadn't enjoyed so much help and support you'd be reading a very different and inferior book.

Finally, just before putting the finishing touches to the book, I suffered a serious accident which put me out of action for six months. I'd like to thank my family, friends and work colleagues for helping to put me back on my feet.

# Introduction: A Few Preliminary Notes to the Reader (or, Why read this Book?)

What is heuristic thinking and how can it help me do cultural studies?
What's the point of conjuring up Matthew Arnold's ghost?
What can Humphrey and Bogart tell us about Richard Hoggart?
What have Sherlock Holmes and Dr Watson got to say about the Frankfurt School of criticism?
Who are Ladvi and Vidal, and what can they tell us about Raymond Williams?
What have Dr Jekyll and Mr Hyde got to do with the work of Louis Althusser?
Why might this publication be useful for tutors looking for a book as a source for straightforward exercises to get students motivated to practise cultural studies for themselves?

Just a few things you might learn by reading this book

As large parts of this book are dominated by creative forms of presentation, let's begin by imagining the following situation. You are in a large book shop looking for an introduction to cultural studies. You could be a student about to start a course, or maybe a curious reader who has heard of 'cultural studies' but who wants to know more. You've examined a multitude of titles and they all look interesting. You're not sure which book to try and start to daydream.

You remember that last night you went to see Woody Allen's film *Annie Hall* (1977). A scene comes into your mind where the two central characters (Alvy and Annie) are waiting to see a film. They overhear a man trying to impress a woman with a lot of pseudo intellectual claptrap. Alvy (played by Allen) hears the man mention Marshall McLuhan (one of the writers mentioned in this book). Alvy tells the man he thinks he's talking rubbish and doesn't know anything about McLuhan's work.

The man turns to Alvy and says that he happens to be teaching a course at Columbia University on TV, Music and Culture, so he reckons he knows what he's talking about. Alvy points out that McLuhan is actually in the cinema foyer, and McLuhan, by some happy accident, steps out from behind an advertising board. Alvy has McLuhan confirm that the man has clearly failed to understand his work. Alvy turns to address the camera saying, 'If only life were like this!'

You recover from your reverie and look down at the book you are holding – it happens to be mine. At the information desk you overhear a stranger asking about the same book that you have in your hand. The person who is serving this customer says, 'well, if you're interested, why don't you ask the author? He's standing right over there!' You look round and there I am. You can hardly believe the coincidence, but you use it to your advantage to ask me a series of questions about my book. Here are my replies.

## Who is this book written for?

This book has been written for those who have had little or no contact with cultural studies, or for those who know something about it but wish to *do* cultural studies for themselves (rather than just read about how others have done it). This means that the strategy adopted here is to get readers to learn through practice and to think about and test ideas before moving onto new ones. I've limited the content of this book to ideas that I feel can be put into practice with relative ease. Also, I've written this book imagining that many of my readers' first language may not be English.

## What can I realistically expect from a careful reading of this book?

- To get a basic idea of the historical development of cultural studies, but using Britain as the main focal point.
- To become familiar with some of the most important critics that have been drawn into the British cultural studies tradition.
- To get a concise, reader-friendly, but critically aware, introduction to some of the key concepts that have been used within cultural studies.

- To become conversant with some of the main areas of interest to cultural studies.
- To develop awareness of how theory can be transformed into practice.
- To acquire ways of thinking with important concepts to help stimulate ideas and ask relevant questions in order to develop the skills required to produce well-argued and informed projects (what I call heuristic thinking).
- To see *how* concepts may work in practice from numerous practical examples.

- To appreciate the value of different approaches and, if you follow the numerous practice exercises, to gain the confidence to begin practising simple forms of cultural studies for yourself.
- To recognize how creative critical techniques might help you to understand sources, express ideas and aid learning.
- To have an idea of how you might go about further developing your knowledge and practice skills.
- To receive detailed advice on further reading and study.
- To be given indications, often in a playful way, of what's been left out of the version of cultural studies offered in these pages.

Finally, I hope you will be convinced of the value, interest and relevance of cultural studies.

## This all sounds interesting, but why should I read *this* book? I mean, what special features does it offer to aid understanding?

Well, to start, there are a number of features designed to present the material in a clear and well structured way. Each chapter has a short introduction to explain the basic content and a brief description of your main learning goals. Chapters are concluded with brief summaries, references and advice on further reading. To help you revise, all key ideas appear in bold. You'll also find 'help files' and 'oversimplification warnings'. To further aid understanding, I introduce a limited number of authors and ideas and move from the relatively simple to the more advanced approaches as the book develops. Also, there's a gradual build-up towards greater levels of student independence.

I also demonstrate fully the strategies I recommend to get readers practising cultural studies for themselves at the very first stage of learning (the heuristic thinking mentioned above which is introduced in chapter three). The heuristics, by the way, are tools for generating ideas through asking specific questions, and aids to thinking, interpretation, analysis and research. They have also been designed to help you to structure your thoughts and experiment with ideas. I hope they will help you develop a certain interpretive independence and that, through their use, you will feel confident to think things through for yourself, rather than just examine what others have written. I've designed this book, then, to give readers a few tools to take away with them for future cultural analysis – tools which provide an easy way of getting started. Furthermore, theory is never introduced in isolation from practice. Finally, to make following up ideas easier, I've tried to refer, where possible, to books still in print.

## In what way would you say your book is original?

I use what I call creative critical approaches to introduce much of the theory and give examples of practice. You'll find many dialogues that are intended to make the theory more accessible and there are letters, a chat, and even a form of criticism in the shape of a rap. One of my aims, which I think distinguishes this book from others, is that I encourage my readers to tap into their own creativity to produce cultural analysis. What I try to do is practise what I preach – I don't just recommend creative techniques but give many examples as I go along. Towards the end of the book the creative approach includes playful exercises to help you assimilate the content. For example, in one section I change the names of important writers featured in earlier chapters and you have to see if you can remember who put forward a particular idea. This book works towards the combination of heuristic thinking with creative-critical approaches. I hope to show that the combination of the two can be very effective, engaging, and fun.

## That's all very well, but sometimes introductions set questions that I can't answer! Am I offered any help?

Yes, you'll see that the book is full of sections called 'notes on practice', which are easily distinguished from the main text. These notes serve a number of functions: they offer sample answers to give you an idea of ways you might respond to many of the practice exercises; they offer very detailed advice on how to go about practice, and try to anticipate problems you may have when using the heuristics. So you've got plenty of backup. This book provides a lot of help in the early chapters and encourages readers towards greater autonomy as it progresses, but without abandoning the detailed notes on practice.

A number of strategies have been adopted to motivate readers to respond to the book in an active, and I hope, enjoyable way. By the way, just about all my examples are drawn from popular culture, especially contemporary film, to give what I hope are lively, interesting, accessible and relevant examples. I ought to say, however, that this book does leave significant gaps for you to fill, but always offers advice on how to go about improving your knowledge and skills.

You'll also find the 'oversimplification warnings' mentioned above and, in the earlier chapters, boxes called 'the voice of contemporary criticism' which show how earlier approaches relate to later developments. There are also occasional boxes entitled 'A dialogue with the social sciences' to indicate how the theories may relate to those approaches (which are not the main focus of this book). Another feature I'd like to emphasize is that some of the points are illustrated by drawings to make them more vivid, to help readers understand concepts visually, and to aid memory. By the way, many of the drawings feature the writers mentioned so, through caricature, you'll get an idea of what a writer looked like.

## Hmm, not bad! How about a few *more* details?

I not only provide many original examples of possible practice but show how the ideas introduced may be adapted to new uses and contexts. This means that this book, while rooted in the theories it introduces, does try to make a contribution to the way cultural studies might be tackled (especially at an early stage). I've also tried to inject the book with a certain humour, which I hope will make reading it that bit more lively and memorable. However, I don't think I'll say anymore here because I hope you'll enjoy exploring these features for yourself.

## You mean I have to read your book to find out more?

Yes, that's what I'm suggesting.

## Alright, but I'm not convinced yet. Can you suggest a few strategies for using this book?

Well, let me state the obvious: the ideal strategy is to start at the beginning and finish at the end! The reason is that the early chapters are designed to introduce ideas and themes which will be elaborated as the book goes on. As suggested above, this book progresses from the relatively simple to the more advanced; however, this doesn't mean you can't dip in and explore something that really interests you. Even the more advanced chapters are written using an accessible style, so you should still be able to understand the ideas and experiment with them. Also, the book has been written with numerous summaries and copious references to earlier chapters. This is designed to help you to consolidate your knowledge and practice – if you dip in, or even read the book backwards, these sections give you a taste of what you've missed. If you look at the chapter breakdown (or consult the index), you can negotiate a path of your own. If you're brave and you want a quick, but informed, overview of the entire book, read the last chapter first!

## OK, but what if I don't live in Britain, or don't intend to analyse British culture, is this book still relevant to me?

Yes. While you'll need to adapt the concepts you find in this book to the appropriate cultural contexts of your study, my hope is that the strategies outlined in this book will provide you with useful starting points. You might take into account that the issues the book raises are not the preserve of British culture or the British brand of cultural studies, and that many of the concepts have their origins outside Britain. Also, this book is not obsessively focused on Britain: you'll find that some of the examples and the suggestions in the further study sections refer you to other cultures. The more you read about cultural studies the more you'll notice a certain 'cross-fertilization' of ideas between different cultures. In the practice sections I hope I provide sufficiently broad examples of how to go about using the ideas introduced. But, of course, my references will be limited – I haven't the space or the knowledge to include the whole world! Also, many of the strategies presented in this book have been developed teaching not only Spanish students but many international exchange students from Britain, France, Belgium, Germany and Asia.

## I've been looking at many introductions and it seems to me that defining 'culture' and cultural studies is a very difficult task. What's your approach?

Well, I don't offer general definitions of 'culture' and the identity of cultural studies at the beginning of the book. As suggested above, the approach adopted here has been to assume readers would get a gradual idea of how these might be understood by being exposed to some of the most important contributors to the area and encouraged to experiment with some of the most important concepts and strategies. I focus on these questions in the last chapter when readers are in a better position to consider them.

## How did you decide what to include and what to leave out of the book? I presume you don't pretend to have covered the whole field?

Of course, I'd by lying if I suggested that this book is in any way exhaustive. The idea here is that the exploration of a limited number of authors and ideas is more effective than trying to introduce a lot of material which may overwhelm my readers. I don't offer complete overviews of each theorist – there are many books that already do this admirably, and I indicate those I've found particularly useful in the references and sections on further reading. What I do try to do is to go into enough detail so that the reader gets a fairly good idea of what to expect from a particular author or approach. Inclusion or exclusion of ideas has depended on these questions:

- Is this idea appropriate to an introduction?
- What is a writer actually *doing*, and how does this relate to method?

I ought to state here that I shall no more be describing everything a writer is doing any more than I can discuss all the implications for method. I merely select what I consider to be important and useable concepts from a writer's work and I try to show how these concepts might be applied in practice. Actually, this book has been conceived as a metaphor for cultural studies as a huge, continuing dialogue. But here (the author takes his book and opens a page in his introduction), read this:

### Oversimplification

**WARNING**

It must be kept in mind that the approach adopted in this book is only *one way* of understanding some of the important contributors to British cultural studies (who have tended to have an influence on other cultural studies' traditions). The 'continuing dialogue' created in these pages is not designed to suggest that there is absolute agreement about what constitutes cultural studies. Many historians of cultural studies might question my choices which are based on the aims set out in this introduction.

## One wish?

I hope this book will help to give you the confidence to *practise* simple forms of cultural studies for yourself.

## OK, you've got me interested, but can you give me a little information about the content and organization of the book? But be brief!

I'll be as brief as I can. The first three chapters make up part one of the book ('High Culture Gladiators: Some Influential Early Models of Cultural Analysis'), which collects together, as the title indicates, some early influential versions of cultural analysis that have helped to establish some very important themes in cultural studies. Many of the book's themes will grow out of these chapters. I call the writers included in this part 'high culture gladiators' because they all work with models that give priority to what they regard as high, serious, or quality forms of culture. In this part you'll find things like the ghost of Matthew Arnold and a conversation between Sherlock Holmes and Dr Watson.

The second part (chapters four to six) is entitled 'The Transformative Power of Working-class Culture'. This comprises three chapters which focus on critics who placed great emphasis on the importance and meaning of working-class history, consciousness and culture. In this way they helped to broaden how culture could be defined, interpreted and understood. In these chapters you'll get to read dialogues between Humphrey and Bogart, Ladvi and Vidal, and E.P. and Thompson, to learn about important areas of theory and practice.

The following five chapters (chapters seven to eleven) make up part three, which has been labelled 'Consolidating Cultural Studies: Subcultures, the Popular, Ideology and Hegemony'. This section shows how cultural studies (especially in Britain) reinforced itself as an area. Here subcultures and popular music take centre stage. Growing out of these interests we see how cultural critics revised the Marxist tradition of cultural analysis through engaging with the concepts of ideology and hegemony. This will be done through the exploration of a popular film and dialogues, including one between Dr Jekyll and Mr Hyde.

Part four (chapters twelve and thirteen), has two chapters shaped by the implications of the section title: 'Probing the Margins, Remembering the

Forgotten: Representation, Subordination and Identity'. These chapters are designed to help you think about, and explore, some important themes within feminism. You are then shown, and encouraged, to adapt some simple ideas to the exploration of other areas of subordination. Dialogues and popular film will be used to explain theory and help with practice.

The fifth and final part ('Honing your Skills, Conclusions and "Begin-endings"') is made up of a single chapter, the contents of which are summed up by the title: 'Consolidating practice, heuristic thinking, creative cri-tickle acts and further research'. This section reviews the whole book in terms of the concepts, methods and themes that have been introduced, and also reflects on the identity of 'culture' and 'cultural studies'. Furthermore, it offers advice on how to consolidate and extend research and practice skills (through heuristic thinking and creative criticism) and suggests ways you might synthesize the many ideas explored in these pages.

And by the way, the references are placed at the end of each chapter, rather than at the end of the book, and I've used square brackets to indicate the original date of a publication (where it is different from the later edition I use) – that way you don't get the impression that Karl Marx wrote and published his works in the 1970s.

Well, now you've got this far into the book, why not step inside?

# PART I

## High Cultural Gladiators: Some Influential Early Models of Cultural Analysis

# Culture and Anarchy in the UK: a dialogue with Matthew Arnold

## Introduction

This is the first of three chapters which make up part one of the book, which is developed around the idea of 'High Culture Gladiators: Some Influential Early Models of Cultural Analysis'. Each of the chapters introduces an approach which has been of great interest to cultural studies and which I see as in some way 'defensive' of a particular kind of culture. To begin this survey of high cultural gladiators the chapter you are about to read resurrects the ghost of Matthew Arnold to introduce his enormously influential approach to the definition of culture. It also puts his ideas into historical context by indicating how he responded to social and industrial changes in nineteenth-century Britain. Towards the end of the chapter, you will be encouraged to explore and evaluate Arnold's ideas through practice exercises designed to stimulate creative approaches to cultural criticism. The chapter closes, as will all chapters, with a summary of key points, comments on methodological relevance, and a list of references and further reading.

### *MAIN LEARNING GOALS*

- To understand how Arnold understood and defined culture and why he felt contemporaries were in need of his model of culture.
- To appreciate how Arnold's definition grew out of his reactions to the historical circumstances in which he lived.

- To see how his ideas relate to class and politics.
- To consider Arnold's ideas in a critical but informed way and recognize how these ideas are related to important methodological concerns within cultural studies.

## Matthew Arnold and the culture and civilization tradition

In the following three chapters I shall introduce some basic early models of cultural analysis. I want to do so in a way that will show their continued relevance to contemporary cultural criticism. If these approaches were like a dead language, long forgotten, there would be very little point in resurrecting them here. However, part of the value of being familiar with them is to be found in their importance in historical terms. Knowledge of them helps us to understand how cultural studies has evolved.

As mentioned in the Introduction, I shall not offer exhaustive overviews of each theorist but sift through what I see as some of the key ideas to emphasize how they relate to method. The first two chapters will look at writers whose approaches are usually referred to as the 'Culture and Civilization Tradition' which is, more often than not, the first important context in which concepts of culture are seen to be developed. The third chapter in this section is largely dedicated to the Marxist critic Theodor Adorno, whose work is, in some ways, very different from the other writers in this section. What I see as uniting these writers is their role as 'high culture gladiators' – they all defend and place very high value on what they see as 'authentic' high culture.

To introduce some of Matthew Arnold's ideas I want to use a 'creative-critical act' which, while attempting to reflect Arnold's ideas is, at the same time, an imaginative engagement with them. In fact, I shall use the dialogic form extensively in this book because I believe it can be an effective, lively and user-friendly way of introducing ideas. It is also designed to help you keep in mind that the exposition of other peoples' ideas always involves a certain imaginative engagement with them (regardless of whether they are put forward in dialogic form). A last point before I begin: I will spend more time on Arnold than is customary because I believe Arnold established a number of very important lines of thought that have important implications for cultural studies (you'll have to wait to the last chapter to fully understand why).

## Culture: what it is, what it can do

Matthew Arnold has been in repose since 1888 but as a number of his ideas still interest cultural critics today we have decided to call up his ghost. Luckily, he has agreed to be interviewed by Divad Notlaw.

DIVAD NOTLAW: Now Mr Arnold, in your lifetime you were known as a poet, a social and literary critic, a professor of poetry (at Oxford University), and a schools' inspector. You constantly reflected on the meaning and effects of culture throughout your life and it is this that has left its mark on what we now call cultural studies. Your book *Culture and Anarchy* (1869) has had quite an influence on discussions about cultural value. Now, given that I'm interested in how to do cultural analysis, could you comment on what you were doing in this book?

ARNOLD: I ought to say, to begin with, that I never reflected directly on method but I'll do my best to answer your question. What I proposed was to enquire into **what 'culture really is', what good it can do, and why we need it**. I also tried to establish 'some plain grounds on which a **faith in culture** – both my own faith in it and the faith of others – may rest securely' (Arnold [1869] 1970: 203).

NOTLAW: So, in the first place, you were interested in defining culture. OK, so in your view, what is culture?

ARNOLD: Well, to answer this you might look at the title of my first chapter which is called '**Sweetness and Light**'. Firstly, culture can be related to **curiosity** which is a question of looking at things in a disinterested way and 'for the pleasure of seeing them as they really are' (204–5). But this is only a part of an adequate definition because curiosity has to be linked to a study of perfection. Well (here Arnold hesitates), culture, properly described, doesn't really have its origin in curiosity but in **the love of perfection**: 'it is a study of perfection. It moves by the force [...] of the moral and social passion for doing good' (205).

NOTLAW: (politely but a little perplexed) So, you start by saying that it's concerned with curiosity and then that it's the study of perfection. Why contradict yourself?

ARNOLD: It's simply part of the way I think. Now, before any of you high-powered cultural theorists get hold of me, I ought to emphasize that I saw my approach as simple and unsystematic.

NOTLAW: OK, let's try to live with that. When you say that culture as the study of perfection is motivated by 'the moral and social passion for doing good', you seem to be arguing that culture serves a very important ethical purpose. If we think about this in terms of method, the definition of culture can't be divorced from bringing about positive change.

ARNOLD: That's true; culture realizes a Christian purpose. I believed that culture 'believes in making reason and the will of God prevail' (206).

Culture is sweetness and light. It makes the "best that has been thought and known in the world current everywhere".

Figure 1 Mathew Arnold

NOTLAW (not wanting to offend and thinking, 'Well, he doesn't say much about what reason is or how we can know what God's will is'): Hmm, well, let's move the argument on a little. We know that, in an unsystematic way, you see culture as seeing things as they really are, the study of perfection linked to curiosity, reason and God's will, but let's move on to your next stated aim, what good Culture can do.

ARNOLD: My simple answer is that it can help us achieve ever higher states of inner perfection. It is in '**endless growth in wisdom and beauty**', that is how 'the spirit of the human race finds its ideal'. It is here we find that culture is 'an indispensable aid', this is the 'true value' of culture: it's not 'a having and a resting, but a growing and a becoming, [this] is the character of perfection as culture conceives it; and here, too, it coincides with religion' (208). Yet culture goes beyond religion.

NOTLAW: I'd like to stop you there and say that although I don't agree with everything you say I like the idea of culture as a question of growing and becoming: this suggests that it doesn't have a fixed identity – it is never static.

ARNOLD: But you conveniently forget that I connect it to the question of inner perfection. To help you sum up my argument I would add that culture is: 'a harmonious expansion of all the powers which make the beauty and worth of humanity' (208); it chooses the **best of everything and helps to preserve it**; it helps us to judge correctly (236) and to discover our best self (246) through reading, observing, and thinking (236). In short, culture is a humanizing of knowledge and the **pursuit of perfection** is an internal condition rather than a development of external things or 'animality' (227).

NOTLAW: I would say that here it is necessary to see what you are saying with relation to the historical circumstances of the 1860s. You were attacking what you saw as the exaggerated belief in mechanisms of all kinds, from the factory machine to railways and mechanical ways of thinking associated with science and rational systems of thought like political thinking and theories about the economy. In this sense we could link your work with other British writers like Blake, Wordsworth, Coleridge, Shelley, Carlyle, Ruskin, Morris (to name only a few). In the works of all these writers we see a concern about the increasing dominance of external forms of culture over the inner life.

ARNOLD: Yes, all these writers were responding to and criticizing changes associated with what you now call the Industrial Revolution and, in this sense, we might be called early cultural critics. We were reacting against mere **blind faith in machinery** and the inability to look beyond the machine to the ends to which machinery is put (231).

## Culture: why Arnold thought his contemporaries needed his view of culture

NOTLAW: So, you continued lines of thought already expressed in British culture and which would be continued by other writers like Dickens and William Morris. Is this why, according to you, the British society of the 1860s needed your version of culture so much?

ARNOLD: That is absolutely correct. The industrial society of nineteenth-century Britain was increasingly dominated by external factors, for example: its obsession with material things, unrestricted competition, the making of large industrial fortunes, and forms of dissent in politics and religion. For me, ideal culture was a way of helping humanity to develop in a more balanced way where the inner life is given its proper importance. The role of culture is to bring sweetness and light to everyone, not just a privileged few (although it must inevitably begin with a few enlightened minds). According to my definition, culture acts as a counterbalance to the excessive **materialism** and **utilitarianism** of the industrial age. Now, looking at the world you live in the twenty-first century, I see that you are still arguing over these things.

NOTLAW: Yes, I think you're right, We are still concerned with the *value* of cultural products. Hardly a week goes by where someone isn't complaining about the decline of standards with relation to things like reality TV and mobile phone text messaging ...

ARNOLD (cutting in): Your literary supplements are full of writers insisting on the importance of reading great works of literature instead of dedicating so much time to popular television, films, video games and the internet. If, as I argued, the best does lead to perfection, then it is of the utmost importance for a society to establish the means by which the most exemplary cultural products can be recognized.

NOTLAW: Well, as it happens, in the next chapter some of these issues will be addressed.

ARNOLD (ignoring him): So, fundamental to my view of civilization was **the importance of education**, which, I argued, would broaden the minds of all people, not just the privileged classes. In fact, I was very active in this respect, being an inspector of schools and involved in trying to establish a national system of State education.

### **help** FILE: defining utilitarianism

Many nineteenth-century social critics reacted against the philosophy of utilitarianism. Very simply put, it argues that decisions should be made according to the greatest happiness of the greatest number and with relation to whether the consequences of an action lead to greater happiness or pain. In more general terms, it was associated with an excessively pragmatic approach to life where everything is considered from a practical point of view (for its use) rather than for its value. It is chiefly associated with Jeremy Bentham. However, John Stuart Mill tried to 'humanize' it and iron out some of its theoretical difficulties (see Mill and Bentham, 1987).

NOTLAW: Coming back to method, this means that part of your form of cultural analysis is to be able to recognize the relative value of different kinds of culture, so as to decide which cultural products make a positive contribution to society.

ARNOLD: Yes, of course, if you are going to educate people to reach the ideals of civilized life, you need to decide what it is you're going to teach.

## Arnold, class and politics: Barbarians, Philistines and Populace

NOTLAW: As it is very easy to dismiss a writer's thoughts, and more so when there is a failure to appreciate the historical period in which s/he was writing, I'd like to explore the historical context of your thought. One thing that modern critics have found of interest in your work is how your ideal definition of culture is related to class and politics.

You divided the classes into **Barbarians**, **Philistines** and the **Populace**; could you comment on this for us?

ARNOLD: For me the aristocratic classes were in decline and losing their authority and, anyway, I felt they had to be superseded. These I called Barbarians and were characterized by things like individualism, field sports (physical strength), good looks, chivalry and manners, but all these qualities were external. Their 'inward gifts' were those which came nearest to outward ones; things like courage, high spirits and self-confidence. However, far within, lay sleeping 'a whole range of powers of thought and feeling' which were, for most of this class, completely unrealized (252–3). In this, they also had something of the Philistine in them.

NOTLAW: Yes, for the middle classes I see you coined the term Philistines and described them as 'The people who believe most that our greatness and welfare are proved by our being very rich, and who most give their lives and thoughts to becoming rich' (210).

ARNOLD: That's true but I also saw the Philistines characterized by a practical ability for organization and material development. However, I lamented the Philistine's materialism, dreadful utilitarianism, obsession with machinery and general unreceptiveness or hostility towards the ideals of high culture. I argued that the middle classes, while being important to economic prosperity, had to develop beyond their material obsessions and their narrow-minded individualism.

NOTLAW: Yes, I remember a memorable phrase of yours in your essay 'The Function of Criticism at the Present Time' where you called the English Constitution 'a colossal machine for the manufacture of Philistines' (Arnold, [1864] 1970: 147). There you argued that, given the increasing decline of religion, culture is a civilizing force and criticism one of the chief instruments by which perfection could be achieved. However, coming back to *Culture and Anarchy*, I think the most controversial part of your discussion of class is when you come to the Populace, or what we now call the working class.

ARNOLD: If you want to be accurate, in *Culture and Anarchy* I said that the working class was made up of two groups. One group shared the ideals and characteristics of the Philistines and the other was the 'vast mass' which I referred to as the Populace. The Populace I saw as 'raw and half-developed', a class that had traditionally been hidden by its poverty and squalor. But something angered me about the Populace: by the 1860s it had come out from its hiding place to assert what it saw as an 'Englishman's heaven-born privilege of doing as he likes'. There it was, 'marching', 'meeting', 'bawling' and 'breaking' ([1869] 1970: 254). However, it ought to be remembered that these are dominant characteristics and that each class may display traits associated with the other classes and there will be aliens in every class.

NOTLAW: But you seemed particularly hard on the Populace.

ARNOLD: I was against all their **demands for rights and liberties** which I saw as causing so much social unrest. I saw them as working against civilization, or my model of culture – it was threatening **anarchy**. Once, as I wrote in *Culture and Anarchy* (he quotes from memory):

> The strong feudal habits of subordination and deference continued to tell upon the working class. The modern spirit has now almost entirely dissolved those habits, and the anarchical tendency of our worship of freedom in and for itself, of our superstitious faith, as I say, in machinery, is becoming very manifest. (Arnold, [1869] 1970: 231)

Actually, I saw my view of culture as above class considerations arguing that no single class could be trusted to bring about the high cultural ideals of sweetness and light. The only grounds on which a faith in culture could rest was the **disinterested pursuit of knowledge**, which I saw as above politics and religion. As you may know, the Victorian age was full of people trying to indoctrinate the 'masses' (yes, I used that term (226)). I wasn't necessarily against these debates, but deeply suspicious of them. However, my point was that culture had to work differently – not try to teach down to the level of 'inferior classes' or win them over for sectarian purposes. Culture must be above class if we are '**to make the best that has been thought and known in the world current everywhere**' (226).

NOTLAW: But surely, one class or group still had to dominate to create and preserve your idea of civilization?

ARNOLD: (looking uneasy) Well, yes, the power of the State would have to guarantee 'right reason' over personal liberty. As far as I was concerned, change was not to come from popular revolutionary demands from below; therefore, all disturbances were to be put down by 'the principle of authority' (236).

NOTLAW: Society, then, is to be left in the hands of ... not so much the Philosopher King, but the Culture King?

ARNOLD: (forgetting to answer the question, starts quoting a passage from *Culture and Anarchy* where he starts with 'we' and ends up with 'he')

> [...] – every time that we snatch up a vehement opinion in ignorance and passion, every time that we long to crush an adversary by sheer violence [...] that we are envious [...] brutal [...] that we adore mere power or success [...] that we add our voice to swell a blind clamour against some unpopular personage [...] that we trample savagely on the fallen, – he has found in his own bosom the eternal spirit of the Populace, and that there needs only a little help from circumstances to make it triumph in him untameably' (256).

NOTLAW: Personally, I feel very uncomfortable with your view of the Populace and your nostalgic yearning for subordination and deference, but in terms of what this means methodologically I think this way of looking is very interesting. Stripping away your value judgements, the kind of criticism you are doing here is similar to what we do in cultural studies: you are seeing culture with relation to a broad analysis of different classes in society. Furthermore, you are aware of historical conditions and tensions between classes which may threaten or destroy the bases for the establishment of your ideal view of culture ... (At this point Notlaw realizes that he is talking to himself because Arnold has fallen into a deep sleep.)

Well, reader, let's carry on for moment without him. As suggested above, one problem for many cultural critics is that although Arnold could be sarcastic and critical of other classes (Arnold's sense of irony is not always appreciated) he was especially hard on the working classes. However, despite what many critics regard as Arnold's objectionable political thinking, his ideas have continued to be of interest (as I hope this, and later chapters, will demonstrate). Let's probe Arnold a little more on history.

## Understanding Arnold through political reform

ARNOLD: (Notlaw nudges Arnold, who wakes with start): Who? What? Where am I? Oh, it's you ...

NOTLAW: I was just saying ... Well, never mind. I'd like to return to the question of history.

ARNOLD: (yawning) Must we? Have some consideration for my age!

NOTLAW: Don't worry, we are nearly finished. Earlier you indicated that you reacted against the radical political movements which fought for the rights of those who had no say in politics (we'll be hearing much more about these movements in chapter five on E.P. Thompson). I thought it would be useful to explore this historical background a little further in order to see your ideas within the context of political reform.

ARNOLD: Young man, I'm glad you haven't lost a sense of history. If we just restrict ourselves to the 30 years or so before the publication of *Culture and Anarchy*, the following historical references should prove useful to your readers: the **Reform Act of 1832** and the **Chartist Movement**. But why should I do all the work? How would *you* describe the Reform Act?

NOTLAW: I'd say the 1832 Act attempted to eradicate some of the worst abuses of the British political system and extended the (male) vote (mainly to the moneyed commercial classes and the larger farmers).

ARNOLD: (raising his eyebrows) Those aren't the words *I* would have used. What would you say was its effect?

NOTLAW: Although it satisfied many of the middle classes, the fact that it failed to concede rights to the working classes helped to make those members of the working classes interested in political reform even more discontented than they already were. Hardly surprising, then, that in 1839 the Chartists, the first major working-class reform movement, petitioned parliament for major reforms, including universal male suffrage.

ARNOLD: Yes, but it was, quite rightly, rejected (along with the 1842 and 1848 Charters). All those unruly, violent outbreaks, all that social unrest, pitching civilization towards anarchy – it put the fear of God – or, I should say, the fear of working-class rebellion, into many of us. We saw the decline and historical redundancy of the aristocracy. In its place we saw the rise of democracy, of middle-class power and increasing demands for representation by the working classes. Given these struggles and recent and alarming changes in political life, I saw (as a member of the ruling classes) the need to prepare *all* classes for a future which would guarantee social cohesion and continued cultural development.

NOTLAW: (disturbed by Arnold's words) Although there were riots and some violence, it ought to be said that the Chartist movement was generally peaceful and, in my opinion, wholly justified. What seems to me very unjustified was the violence with which successive governments carefully policed working-class demonstrations and severely punished working-class leaders. Just take a look at the history of reform. In 1867, two years after your *Culture and Anarchy* was published, the Second Reform Act finally conceded the vote to town artisans, shopkeepers and (in England and Scotland) the smaller farmers. It wasn't until 1918 that all men (who were not mentally unfit or criminals) over 21 were given the vote. Upper class women had to wait until 1918 to receive the right to vote and it wasn't until 1928 that all women (who were not mentally unfit or criminals) over 21 were allowed to vote ... (Notlaw realizes, once again, that he is talking to himself because Arnold not only falls into a deep sleep but fades into thin air.)

## Oversimplification

**W A R N I N G**

It is easy to oversimplify Arnold's thought especially when considering his elitist views and general lack of sympathy for radical political movements. However, some moral outrage might be assuaged by the fact that when he proposed reforms in education they were to benefit society as a whole and, if one reads beyond *Culture and Anarchy* (e.g. 'The Popular Education of France' (1861)), the reader finds that Arnold believed that the working classes (the 'masses') had a right to 'expansion and a fuller life' (Arnold, [1861] 1970: 107). Nevertheless, he felt that change could only come in what he saw as an organized and rational way and that meant change from the top down.

If you read over the dialogue above you will see that I have hinted at some of the inconsistencies in Arnold's thought although, in general, I've not offered many criticisms – preferring, at that stage, to let the ideas stand on their own. In the practice sections below, however, you'll find some exercises to help you think through some of the debatable and controversial elements in his writing on culture. I hope these will also help to focus on some of the methodological implications of Arnold's thought while assisting you to develop a critical attitude towards them. In later sections you'll see that many cultural theorists engage in either explicit or implicit debates with a number of Arnold's propositions.

## **practice** EXERCISE 1.1: getting a sense of tradition

Read the following excerpts and see if you can discern how Arnold was extending ideas already present in British culture.

In this first quotation William Wordsworth is recommending his collection of poetry, *Lyrical Ballads*, to the reader (which included some poems by Samuel Taylor Coleridge):

> For a multitude of causes, unknown to former times, are now acting with a combined force to blunt the discriminating powers of the mind, and, unfitting it for all voluntary exertion, to reduce it to a state of almost savage torpor. The most effective of these causes are the great national events which are daily taking place, and the increasing accumulation of men in cities, where the uniformity of their occupations produces a craving for extraordinary incident, which the rapid communication of intelligence hourly gratifies [through newspapers] [...] The invaluable works of our elder writers [...] are driven into neglect by frantic novels, sickly and stupid German tragedies, and deluges of idle and extravagant stories in verse. (Wordsworth, 'Preface to Lyrical Ballads' [1798] 1993: 145)

In 'A Defence of Poetry' Percy Bysshe Shelley describes poetry in the following way (although note that his politics are very different from Arnold's):

> But Poetry [...] wakens and enlarges the mind itself by rendering it the receptacle of a thousand unapprehended combinations of thought. [...] We have more moral, political and historical wisdom, than we know how to reduce into practice; we have more scientific and economical knowledge than can be accommodated to the just distribution of the produce which it implies. The poetry in these systems of thought, is concealed by the accumulation of facts and calculating processes. [...] Poetry is the record of the best and happiest moments of the happiest and best minds [...] Poetry thus makes immortal all that is best and most beautiful in the world [...] Poetry turns all things to loveliness; it exalts the beauty of that which is most beautiful, and it adds beauty to that which is most deformed. (Shelley, [1821] 1993: 761–3)

Thomas Carlyle summed up contemporary life in his 'Signs of the Times' in the following way:

> These things, which we state lightly enough here, are yet of deep import, and indicate a mighty change in our whole manner of existence. For the same habit regulates not our modes of action alone, but our modes of thought and feeling. Men are grown mechanical in head and in heart, as well as in hand. They have lost faith in individual endeavour, and in natural force, of any kind. Not for internal perfection, but for external combinations and arrangements, for institutions, constitutions, – for Mechanism of one sort or other, do they hope and struggle. Their whole efforts, attachments, opinions, turn on mechanism, and are of a mechanical character. (Carlyle, [1829] 1971: 67)

## **practice** EXERCISE 1.2: thinking through Arnold's ideas

1. How does Arnold define 'inner perfection'? Do you agree, and can you see any value in insisting on developing inner perfection as a counterbalance to the outer material world?
2. Try to imagine how Arnold would distinguish between different kinds of cultural products (from any period of history) according to the way he defined culture (this exercise is based on a very useful suggestion for practice in Giles and Middleton (1999: 13–14)). You might organize the lists in the following way:

| | |
|---|---|
| **I**ntimations of Immortality | **T**ina Turner |
| **D**ebussy | **R**eality TV |
| **E**uripides | **A**merican Psycho |
| **A**ristotle | **S**oap operas |
| **L**eonardo da Vinci | **H**ip hop |

You can see that the two columns spell out 'Ideal' and 'Trash' (the latter, by the way, does not reflect what I personally feel is trash). To make this exercise more revealing and fun you might try organizing your material to spell out words which suggest positive, negative or prejudicial attitudes towards certain cultural products.

Now try a third column of items that might complicate a simple either/or way of thinking. That is, can you think of examples of culture which may question the simple distinction between 'high' and 'low' forms of culture? In the following notes on practice you'll find some ideas to get you started.

## **notes** ON PRACTICE: challenging a simple either/or way of thinking

**Dickens' *Hard Times* (1854)**

This work began its life, like many a nineteenth-century novel, in serial form printed in a popular magazine (*Household Words*). At the time of its publication, and after, there was considerable debate about its merits. It is now common to find it on literature courses. Historically, its fate changed from serialized popular fiction to Literature (with a capital 'L').

**Orson Wells' *Citizen Kane* (1941)**

Working within the popular Hollywood system (RKO) Wells' first feature film was a commercial flop. However, again, the film can be regarded as a product of both popular culture and, as it commonly is, a masterpiece of world cinema.

**Michel Duchamp**

As a direct attack on bourgeois art institutions, Duchamp displayed a series of 'readymades' like the wheel of a bicycle screwed to a stool (1913) and a urinal singed 'R. Mutt'

(1917). As predicted, these provoked hostile responses from the art establishment (Arnold would surely have condemned them). However, by the mid-1960s these objects had been absorbed by the establishment they had been designed to shock and defy. They are now on display as important examples of twentieth-century avant-garde art.

3. As a creative critical exercise, you could write a letter to Arnold asking questions about all those things you feel need further explanation. The notes on practice provide you with an example of what you might do.

### **notes** ON PRACTICE: a letter to Matthew Arnold

*You might begin in the following way (imagining you are a contemporary of Arnold's):*

My dear Mr Arnold,

I have, with some profit, read your book called *Culture and Anarchy* and while I feel you do justice to a number of important issues, I feel the book is wanting in some respects. I hope you will forgive me for being so blunt but I write as one who has a strong interest in getting to know your work better.

I feel I should be frank when I say that I have a problem with the idea of high cultural ideals as classless. For example, is it possible to insist on a classless model which relies on State power and the repression of the Populace? What does it mean to be disinterested? How might 'right reason' be defined? Also, *how* would you go about choosing the best that has been thought and written? *Who* would or should decide if there are conflicts between those who have made choices? If there could be agreement on what is the best, how might teaching the 'best' lead to a process of universal perfection? For example, in what ways might listening to Beethoven's Ninth Symphony help to perfect a person? Would knowledge of 'high' culture necessarily lead to perfection? I mean, you could enjoy reading or watching Shakespeare and still be a kleptomaniac, or so mentally unbalanced, that you commit delinquent, violent or murderous acts! You say that perfection may be defined as 'sweetness and light' – a combination of knowing how to behave and 'right reason'. Again, I wonder if it would be possible get wide agreement on these two issues and this would bring us back to politics and State power ...

## Creative-critical practice

The above exercise might be extended considerably and, to do justice to Arnold's work, you might try to anticipate how he would reply. A last comment on this kind of creative-critical practice: this is a technique that can be adapted to taste and can be applied to *everything* you read. In this way you can develop an analytical style in such a way that you entertain yourself in the process. For essay work you might extract the critical, analytical parts and leave the fictive parts behind, unless your tutor is open to a creative-critical approach.

## SUMMARY OF KEY POINTS

This chapter has explored Arnold's definition of culture as the endless growth in wisdom and beauty which helps the human race find its ideal through a critical study of 'the best that has been thought and known in the world'. It has also emphasized what good Arnold thought his version of culture could do and why he believed his contemporaries needed it. Arnold's definition has been seen to have grown out of his reactions to the historical circumstances in which he lived and his scepticism and rejection of libertarian politics. While Arnold claimed that he wished to abolish the classes, his definition can been seen as reactionary because his notion of culture tends to support State repression and sees all cries for political reform as anarchy.

Arnold's importance in methodological terms can be summed up in the following way:

- Like so many cultural theorists, he was concerned about defining culture.
- The definition of culture can't be divorced from bringing about positive change.
- Criticism has to be able to recognize the relative value of different kinds of culture.
- Cultural criticism includes a broad analysis of different classes in society and an awareness of historical conditions and tensions between different classes.
- Cultural criticism includes the idea of resisting what are seen as negative social forces and cannot be divorced from politics.

As we sample different cultural theories we will see that even though many cultural critics differ from Arnold, they will share many of these implicit methodological concerns.

## References

Arnold, Matthew ([1861] 1970) 'The Popular Education of France', in *Matthew Arnold: Selected Prose*. Harmondsworth: Penguin.

Arnold, Matthew ([1864] 1970) 'The Function of Criticism at the Present Time', in *Matthew Arnold: Selected Prose*. Harmondsworth: Penguin.

Arnold, Matthew ([1869] 1970) *Culture and Anarchy, in Matthew Arnold: Selected Prose*. Harmondsworth: Penguin.

Carlyle, Thomas ([1829] 1971) *Thomas Carlyle: Selected Writings*. Harmondsworth: Penguin.

Giles, Judy and Midleton, Tim (1999) *Studying Culture: A Practical Introduction.* Oxford: Blackwell.

Mill, John Stuart and Bentham, Jeremy (1987) *Utilitarianism and Other Essays.* Harmondsworth: Penguin.

Shelley, Percy Bysshe ([1821] 1993) 'A Defence of Poetry' (6th edition), in *The Norton Anthology of English Literature* (Vol. 2). New York: Norton.

Wordsworth, William ([1798] 1993) 'Preface to Lyrical Ballads' (6th edition), in *The Norton Anthology of English Literature* (Vol. 2). New York: Norton.

## Further reading

Brooker, Will (1998) *Teach Yourself Cultural Studies.* London: Hodder & Stoughton. This short, accessible and informative book gives a very concise overview of Arnold's ideas and explores how his work relates to discussions of politics and class. By the way, I adapted my chapter title from Brooker's chapter on Arnold (which is 'Anarchy in the UK').

Storey, John (1998) *Cultural Theory and Popular Culture: A Reader* (2nd ed.). Essex: Pearson Prentice Hall. If you do not have access to Arnold's works you might read the useful excerpts that Storey prints in this reader.

Storey, John (2001) *Cultural Theory and Popular Culture: An Introduction* (3rd edn). Essex: Pearson Prentice Hall. Storey's introduction gives a very clear outline of Arnold's work with relation to an understanding of popular culture. He also, like Brooker (above), explores how Arnold's work relates to politics and class.

Williams, Raymond (1980) *Problems in Materialism and Culture.* London: Verso. In the first essay 'A Hundred Years of Culture and Anarchy' Williams puts Arnold's ideas into historical context and shows how some of Arnold's ideas were still circulating in the late 1960s.

# The Leavisites and T.S. Eliot combat mass urban culture

# 2

## Introduction

We now come to the second chapter of part one on 'High Culture Gladiators' to introduce another early influential model of cultural analysis. In this chapter I will outline the importance of the Leavis circle to the rise of cultural criticism in Britain and explore the importance of its contribution to the 'Culture and Civilization Tradition'. I will also discuss the political importance of the Leavises' account of cultural history and the Leavis circle will be related to trends already established in Arnold's work. Cultural theory will be discussed with relation to important ideas (and implicit methodologies) that have left an enduring mark on cultural criticism. This chapter will demonstrate another possibility for creative criticism and will also look at a number of suggestive ideas about culture in the work of T.S. Eliot. The chapter will be concluded with detailed advice on practice. You will see that the high culture gladiators introduced in this, and the following, chapter were countering what they understood as barbaric forces associated with popular mass culture – contributing to what has become known as the 'mass culture debate' (Strinati, 1995: 10f.).

## MAIN LEARNING GOALS

- To recognize the historical context of the Leavises work and the role of English Studies to the rise of cultural criticism.
- To understand how the Leavis circle contributed to debates about contemporary mass culture and helped to establish forms of cultural criticism focused on popular culture.
- To appreciate the importance of key concepts like discrimination, informed judgements, standardization, levelling down and the devaluation of language and the quality of life.
- To perceive how the training of critical awareness provided a technique for cultural analysis and how the Leavises' work relates to resistance, the raising of consciousness and the moral character of analysis.
- To be aware of how definitions of culture may be considered political, or even instruments of power.
- To understand T.S. Eliot's approach to culture with relation to cultural disintegration and cultured minorities, and to recognize how his understanding of culture resembles an anthropological approach and anticipated later cultural criticism.
- To be able to explore these ideas in (creative) critical ways.

## The historical context and the importance of the Leavis circle to the rise cultural criticism

The question of when British cultural studies began, in the context of humanities courses, often takes the cultural historian back to the importance of the rise of English as a discipline at Cambridge University – that is, in the years following the First World War (Inglis, 1993; Strinati, 1995; Storey, 2001). The new breed of critic at Cambridge, like F.R. Leavis and Queenie Leavis, helped to extend the debates about **contemporary mass culture**. These debates (mediated via literary criticism) were conducted in the lecture hall, in books and, importantly, in the articles published in the journal F.R. Leavis edited, called *Scrutiny*. Indeed, *Scrutiny* became so important that literary and cultural historians talk of the days of the journal as an important 'moment' in the development of British critical/cultural life (Inglis, 1993: 32f.).

From the point of view of cultural studies, the importance of the Leavises and *Scrutiny* can be seen in the way they extended the 'Culture and Civilization Tradition' associated with Matthew Arnold. As we saw in the last chapter, the important debates that grew out of this tradition were concerned with, on the one hand, high literary-intellectual culture and the disinterested pursuit of knowledge and, on the other, anarchy, utilitarianism, materialism and the dehumanizing effects of industrialism. These debates provided the *Scrutiny* writers with an important source of social critique. As we shall see, in this criticism notions of 'high' culture could be usefully deployed in the interests of both analysing what was seen as the damaging effects and tendencies of industrial capitalism and providing cultural antidotes to them.

**Oversimplification**

**W A R N I N G**

Although there was considerable common ground between the academics who contributed to *Scrutiny*, its pages were by no means dominated by acolytes echoing all the ideas and values expressed by F.R. Leavis. This can be seen from one of the most controversial debates that took place between F.R. Leavis and the North American critic, René Wellek. The debate was over the question of whether or not literary critics should be explicit about their use of theory. Wellek (1937) argued that critics, whether aware of it or not, always expressed a theory and therefore should clarify their theoretical position whereas Leavis preferred a 'feeling one's way forward' approach seeing theory as proper to philosophy thus 'queering one discipline with the habits of another' (Leavis, 1952: 213).

In terms of cultural studies, the influence of the Leavises and *Scrutiny* is fundamental to the development of what exploring culture meant in English departments in the British university context. Terry Eagleton has described the importance of the changes brought about by the Leavises to students of English Literature at Cambridge of the 1930s. Eagleton makes the point that in the early 1920s it was by no means clear why English was worth studying but, by the 1930s, 'it had become a question of why it was worth wasting your time on anything else' (Eagleton, 1983: 31):

> English was an arena in which the most fundamental questions of human existence – what it meant to be a person to engage in significant relationships with others, to live from the vital centre of the most essential values – were thrown into vivid relief and made the object of the most intensive scrutiny. (Eagleton, 1983: 31)

Such was the influence of *Scrutiny* on English Studies that 'English students in England today (Eagleton was writing in 1983) are "Leavisites" whether they know it or not' (1983: 31). Although it is possible to question the extent of the ubiquity of Leavisism on the academy (it tends to disguise other tendencies like the American New Criticism and the persistence of the philological tradition), this is still an important point, because many early critics who become associated with cultural studies started out studying and teaching English and often developed their ideas with relation to the debates associated with the Leavises and their circle. Although, quite understandably, the Leavisites are often represented as reactionary elitists (Eagleton, 1983: 30f.), it is important to recognize that, in their day, they were the young rebels – the academic revolutionaries who were destined to leave a significant mark on English Studies. If the term 'the Leavisites' sounds like they were the inhabitants from another planet, in some ways they were! The planet, however, could be said to have been founded by Matthew Arnold, for the Leavis circle were, as we shall see, disseminating an Arnoldian view of class and culture. By the 1930s the Leavisites had definitely landed.

In order to explore some of the most important ideas that have been relevant to the way the Leavisites thought about culture let us imagine a young, intelligent working-class man or woman, living during the late 1930s, who goes to a public lecture where F.R. and Queenie Leavis speak. After the lecture our listener writes to a friend. Using this creative-critical method we can imagine how someone, from a working-class community, might have reacted to the ideas and values being put forward. As I'm referring to some later editions of works written in the 1930s, I'll have to ask you to suspend your disbelief when you see dates of editions from the 1970s.

## Letter to Cecily

*Dear Cecily,*

*You asked me in your last letter if I'd give you an outline of the lecture given by the Leavises that I attended in Cambridge. As I took extensive notes, I'll be able to go into some detail - I've added titles to each part, which I hope you'll find useful. Let's start with the first part.*

***High, organic and mass culture***

*In broad terms the Leavises established a view of culture which was divided into two main categories: on the one hand there were the intellectual and creative works, or what we might call* ***'high' literary culture,*** *and on the other, the pursuits and habits of what they referred to as the ordinary or 'common' people (meaning people like us!). You remember we talked about*

*Matthew Arnold? Well, the first definition was related to Arnold's idea that intellectual, creative culture was something that had to be protected and propagated by an* ***enlightened minority*** *and this would function as a panacea for the ills of contemporary society. I copied down a few of F.R. Leavis's ideas. If you read them you'll get an idea of his rather magisterial tone (by the way he was quoting from a book he wrote with Denys Thompson):*

> *Upon the minority depends our power of profiting by the finest human experience of the past; they keep alive the subtlest and most perishable parts of tradition. Upon them depend the implicit standards that order the finer living of an age, the sense that this is worth more than that, this rather than that is the direction in which to go, that the centre is here rather than there. (Leavis and Thompson, [1933] 1977: 5)*

*I took this to mean that people like you and me must either try to become part of this select group or accept that we are not worthy to have an opinion. It sounded convincing at the time but reading it over again now it all sounds rather 'woolly'. What do you think?*

*However, to get back to the lecture, the second category had a further important distinction that I think you might find of interest. The pursuits and habits of those like us, the 'common' people, were judged according to whether they were the products of* ***organic folk communities*** *or the unfortunate consequences of urban,* ***mass industrial society****. The latter forms were seen as utterly corrupt. This was partly because the processes of industrialization, which forced people to work in factories, were dehumanizing and partly because the kinds of habits and pursuits developed within the communities of industrial workers were considered utterly banal and demeaning. I had mixed feelings about this.*

*On the one hand, I thought about my own family - how my own mother and father (and other family members) have worked in what I would call sub-human conditions. I remember your own poor grandfather who died in a mining accident. And look how much our families have suffered trying to fight for better conditions and higher wages! If it hadn't been for my scholarship to study at university, I'd probably be in a factory by now! This made me feel that at least the Leavises helped to draw attention to some of the degrading conditions of industrialization. On the other hand the Leavises were hardly sympathetic to the working classes with regard to their general way of life or their struggles. Not once did they express any solidarity with our efforts to improve our wages or conditions! But, again, I digress. This brings me on to the second part of my letter.*

## The Leavises and cultural history

*To be honest, I consider the distinction between the organic and forms of debased industrial culture was made possible by what I thought was a*

Figure 2.1 F.R. Leavis contemplates the Leavisite approach to culture

laughable and, to some extent, idealized view of British history. The Leavises argued that everything was different prior to the Industrial Revolution. For example, the world of Shakespeare's contemporaries was one that boasted an organic, vital, common culture; the Industrial Revolution was seen as shattering the unity of a healthy organic, common culture. Mass civilization was characterized by increasing commercialism and declining standards, but minority culture was there to preserve vital cultural standards and values.

I'll never forget Queenie Leavis as she read from one of her works. She reckoned that generations of 'country folk' had lived 'to some purpose' without any other books except their Bible! She said they had enjoyed 'a real social life' and that they had a way of living that 'obeyed the natural rhythm and furnished them with genuine interests'. These turned out to be country arts, traditional crafts, games and singing! What a wonderful vision of our ancestors all dancing and singing to the rhythms of nature, reading the Bible, and spending their spare moments practising traditional arts! What a very neat and convenient view of our forbears – everyone conforming to their role and everybody very much in their place.

I've copied some of her words down for you from her 'Fiction and the Reading Public'. It appears that the 'commoners' of today are dominated by:

> substitute or kill-time interests like listening to radio and gramophone, looking through newspapers and magazines, watching

*films and commercial football, and the activities connected with motor cars and bicycles, the only way of using leisure known to the modern city-dweller. (Q.D. Leavis, [1932] 1974: 209)*

*So, we urban dwellers only dedicate ourselves to trivialities. We don't actually read newspapers and magazines but look through them – I suppose at the pictures! You can see from this that the Leavises associate the* ***consumption of mass culture*** *with* ***passive diversion****. I wondered, while the Leavises were speaking, how they could know what it was that we (the 'commoners') got from newspapers and films etc. and how they could be so confident that we didn't respond in active or critical ways. Here's a little table I drew during the lecture, which I hope will help to sum up what was being said.*

| *The Leavisite approach to culture* | | |
|---|---|---|
| *1. Literary 'high' or minority culture* | *2. The pursuits and habits of the 'ordinary' or 'common' people* | |
| | *Positive* | *Negative* |
| | *Organic, vital, common folk culture* | *Products of urban, mass, industrial society* |

## The voice of contemporary criticism

If you keep Queenie Leavis's list of 'kill-time interests' in mind while reading later chapters, you'll get a good idea of how attitudes towards the consumers of popular culture have changed. You might note that in order to criticize the Leavises' point of view, the writer of 'Letter to Cecily' questions the validity of these universalizing claims, thus anticipating the later chapters on Hoggart, Thompson, Williams and Hall.

*The next section of the lecture was dominated by the themes included in the following title.*

## Discrimination and informed judgements: standardization, levelling down, the lowest common denominator and Americanization

*There were, according to F.R. Leavis, important consequences for the definition of culture here. To counter the worst effects of industrial culture there was a need for society to learn forms of* ***discrimination.*** *He insisted that cultural objects of lasting value had to be chosen by those with the education and training to be able to make informed judgements; hence his insistence on the importance of developing canons of great works.*

### **help**FILE: F.R. Leavis and canons of great works

Leavis's books, *The Great Tradition* (1948) and *Revaluation* (1936), were both concerned with establishing the basis of the literary canons of the novel and poetry. Typical of the criteria that would characterize a great novel were: displaying an open reverence before life, the existence of fine distinctions, high seriousness, a sense of tradition, and the sense that a novel contributed to the evolution of the form.

*In this way the great achievements of culture contribute to the preservation and development of civilized intellectual/creative society. Here, once again, I recognized Arnold's fear that civilization is threatened by the forces of barbarism: in this case the continued spread of mass culture characterized by* ***standardization*** *and what F.R. Leavis called* ***levelling down*** *- referring as he did to his book, 'Mass Civilisation and Minority Culture' (1930).*

*The problem here for the Leavises is that mass culture appeals to* ***the lowest common denominator*** *and thereby impoverishes life. At this point I wondered how a factory worker or manual labourer could be expected to take full advantage of great literary works - and whether or not life might be improved more for the majority by attending to their immediate material needs. But I digress, he went on to argue that this cultural impoverishment is made worse by the increasing* ***Americanization*** *of British cultural life. He was very critical of the importation of American popular culture like Hollywood films, comics and Westerns. And to think, I went to see the gangster film 'Scarface' only last week! This Americanization is made still worse, apparently, by the gradual weakening of the influence, importance and authority of the self-elected cultural minority who attempt to preserve great cultural traditions. By the way, I'm paraphrasing from F.R. Leavis' 'Mass Civilization and Minority Culture' (1930).*

## The training of critical awareness, the devaluation of language and the quality of life

*Once the Leavises had finished their talk, a member of the audience asked if they could give some practical advice on how we might counter the problems of standardization, levelling down and gradual Americanization. The practical answer was the* ***training of critical awareness****. F.R. Leavis suggested we read his 'Culture and Environment' (a book he wrote with Denys Thompson in 1933) he said it gave readers practical advice on how to read what they saw as the debased language of the popular press and advertisements, but in a critical way. He emphasized that* ***debasement of language*** *was not just a question of words but a devaluation of emotions and the quality of life.*

*Well, Cecily, considering our humble origins, it seems that our emotions and quality of life may already be severely debased! Whatever, as I fear I may have bored you with such a long letter, I shall say goodbye hoping that you will at least find it informative.*

*Your very good friend ...*

### The voice of contemporary criticism

This kind of criticism suggested that close (detailed) reading could be transferred from the literary to the cultural text. It is significant that the subtitle of Leavis' and Thompson's *Culture and Environment* was *The Training of Critical Awareness*. This transition is important for cultural analysis not only in terms of method but because it assumed that it was important to be able to read and understand the cultures of everyday life (even if, in this case, it was to point out their demeaning effects and vast inferiority). As forms of cultural studies developed these popular cultural forms would not be rejected by such simple value judgements. Eagleton makes the point that *Scrutiny* 'actually founded such "cultural studies" in England, as one of its most enduring achievements' (Eagleton, 1983: 34). For how Leavis and Thompson suggested criticism should be carried out see the practice section below and for literary into cultural studies see Easthope (1991).

### **practice** EXERCISE: variations on the 'Letter to Cecily'

Take the 'Letter to Cecily' and write your own responses (or the imagined responses of others) to the ideas put forward. Here are some possibilities:

- A concerned contemporary who sees the Leavises' ideas in a very positive way
- A 1930s union official
- A miner or factory worker
- Matthew Arnold's ghost (who looks for continuities with and differences from his own work).

## Resistance, the raising of consciousness and the moral character of cultural analysis

The idea of defending the ideals of 'high' culture from the barbarous forces of industrialism leads to another important strand in cultural studies: **the idea of resistance**. As we saw above, the Leavises (and *Scrutiny* writers) were involved in a **consciousness-raising** project to warn against, and provide adequate training to counter, the worst effects of mass (industrial) culture. The following table sums up the basic ideas.

| Cultured minorities | The masses |
|---|---|
| They cultivate minds through 'high' arts and provide ways of discriminating between great and inferior forms of culture | Enjoy mass culture in a passive or uncritical way with no sense of taste |
| They are involved in consciousness-raising projects | They engage in unthinking consumption |
| They provide training to counterbalance the worst effects of industrial machine culture and set up resistance against the devaluation of emotions and the quality of life | They are lost in the cheap sentimental appeals of popular novels, press, TV and films etc. and are subjected to the dehumanizing forces of industry and commerce |

The Leavises' work can be called 'moral' because of the way it moves from texts to standards and critiques of mass industrial society, and to the extent that forms of resistance and consciousness raising are key ingredients in cultural criticism. In this sense much of cultural studies can be called 'moral' because resistance and the raising of consciousness have become fundamental to reading culture. This is not to say that all cultural critics deliberately set out with this intention, but putting cultural products into a political or ideological context tends to reinforce the 'moral' character of much that is published within cultural studies.

## The Leavises and the 'close reading' of advertisements

For this last section on the Leavises I want to show how some of their ideas are related to practice. In *Culture and Environment* F.R. Leavis and Denys Thompson

(1933: 11f.) gave readers practical advice on how to read what they saw as the debased language of the popular press and advertisements in a critical way. In terms of advertising, they start off by recognizing (through a series of quotations) that it has become a highly specialized branch of knowledge based on market research. In fact, they see it as branch of applied psychology intended to provoke automaton-like responses from the public.

What they suggest is that people might be trained from an early age to recognize how advertisements attempt to appeal to consumers; for example, through simple and obvious appeals to fear. From here they go on to illustrate a whole series of rhetorical strategies that are employed by advertisers. They recommend their readers to ask questions about the aims and functions of advertisements, how much information they actually give about a product and how different strategies affect them.

Leavis and Thompson also suggest that readers consult publications devoted to consumer research, where they can discover the kinds of frauds that are practised on unsuspecting customers. This is a kind of do-it-yourself cultural analysis which not only offers insights into the mechanisms of advertising but is of great practical use in so far that it provides knowledge that can help to expose shady business practices and encourage citizens to protect themselves in an active and critical way. This is a kind of cultural studies which is still relevant and, incidentally, today easier than ever given that the World Wide Web provides more information than ever.

From the point of view of method, Leavis and Thompson were pinpointing an important phenomenon of mass culture; they were seeing it as a form of manipulation which requires interpretation (or '**close reading**'); and they were, through analysis, suggesting ways in which the public may learn to see through advertising and thus resist its power. One consequence of this procedure is that cultural analysis is not simply an exercise in interpretation – it is interpretation with *specific ends* in mind. That is, to make people more aware of questionable practices and to bring about what is seen as positive change. You might be reminded here of Eagleton's (provocative) assertion that the *Scrutiny* group 'actually founded' a certain kind of 'cultural studies' in England.

Although (given the enormous political gulf that separates them), it might seem ludicrous to quote Marx in a discussion of Leavisite criticism, what unites the Leavises and much cultural criticism is Marx's famous statement that: 'The philosophers have only interpreted the world, in various ways; the point is to change it' (Marx, [1845] 1976: 65). Much cultural studies has this in common with Leavisite criticism: consciousness raising is considered an important activity in itself because it may be the first step towards change.

In terms of practice, rather than set up an exercise focused on reading advertisements, here I shall refer you to chapter eleven where there is considerable further discussion on the analysis of advertisements, complete with practice exercises. To begin the practice exercises on the Leavises' work we shall start with a short one to help you explore the question of raising consciousness.

## **practice** EXERCISE: cultural studies as consciousness raising

Look through the abstracts of any cultural studies journal and take note of:

- how far the article might be said to be a form of consciousness raising
- how far it could be said to criticize, defend, or make more complex, our understanding of cultural products and practices.

## **notes** ON PRACTICE: some useful sources

If all the journals which claim to be of interest to cultural studies were taken into account the choice for this exercise would be absolutely enormous. To start you might choose one or more of the following:

*Australian Journal of Cultural Studies*
*Cultural Studies*
*European Journal of Cultural Studies*
*Gender, Place and Culture*
*International Journal of Cultural Studies*
*Media, Culture and Society*
*Theory, Culture and Society*

An alternative is to explore cultural studies websites which often have on-line publications and a host of resources and information. You might try the following which were up and running at the time of writing (each one has many links to other pages but beware, addresses sometimes change):

*Cultural Studies-L Page* : http://comm.umn.edu/~grodman/cultstud/
*Cultural Studies Central:* http://www.culturalstudies.net/
*Voice of the Shuttle's Cultural Studies Page*: http://vos.ucsb.edu/browse.asp?id=2709

### **practice** EXERCISE: getting at passivity

To finish these practice sections dedicated to the Leavisite position, you might think about the question of passivity with relation to entertainment. Here are some questions which may help you:

1. What does it mean to be passive?
2. Even if we question the idea of total passivity, do some leisure activities demand more than others? What's the difference between reading a Disney comic and Dostoevsky? In what ways might one demand more intellectual passivity than another? Is your experience of watching reality TV fundamentally different from watching a piece of drama considered as literature? If so, in what ways? Look at the help file above on 'F.R. Leavis and canons of great works', do any of Leavis' criteria help you? You might come back to this question when you've read the next chapter on the Frankfurt School, where further criteria are offered to distinguish between different kinds of culture.
3. Why might you choose something which does not demand too much from you?

If you don't find answering these questions easy, here's some help.

### **notes** ON PRACTICE: exploring passivity

1. Some of the following definitions of passivity might help you with question one: to be inert, to offer no opposition, to be submissive, to take no active part.
2. Many popular films like *Scary Movie*, or cartoons, like *The Simpsons*, *South Park* or *Family Guy* often structure their plots round all kinds of other narratives, how might this challenge the idea of passive reception? You might think about how far our experience of different cultural forms depends on *how* we look or read.
3. As far as considering why you might choose something which does not demand too much from you, you might consider how work and lifestyles influence what people choose to do in their spare time.

## T.S. Eliot: cultural disintegration and cultured minorities

Going back to the first part of the twentieth century, the poet, dramatist and essayist T.S. Eliot also had an important influence over how 'culture' was understood both within and outside departments of English. Eliot, the third of our 'high culture gladiators', is mentioned in introductions to cultural studies (Turner, 1996 and especially Jenks, 1993) but his work is not often given much emphasis. However, I shall use his *Notes Toward the Definition of Culture* ([1948] 1975) as a useful connection between Arnold and the Leavises and the 'progenitors' of cultural studies explored in chapters four to six (Richard Hoggart, E.P. Thompson and Raymond Williams). Eliot's importance to the 'pre-history' of cultural studies can be understood in the following ways:

- **He continued the debate concerning cultured elites** and their role in upholding civilization (for Eliot, Christian civilization). In this his thinking can be seen as an extension of the Arnoldian tradition but also a challenge to it in terms of the way he does not allow religion to become subsumed into culture.
- **He registered his preoccupation about division and cultural disintegration**. Although this aligns him to some extent with the Arnoldian/Leavisite tradition, Eliot emphasized forms of disintegration at the 'upper group level' ([1948] 1975: 293). According to Eliot, by the seventeenth-century, religious thought and practice, philosophy and art in Britain became increasingly more complex and specialized. This meant that they fell into the hands of specialists and thus became separated from one another. These disconnections resulted in cultural fragmentation which, for Eliot, impoverished culture.

## The voice of contemporary criticism

Fragmentation through specialization has also become an important theme within Sociology (Weber, 1946) and Marxism (Marcuse ([1964] 1986) and Habermas (1981)). It is also relevant to what is known as the 'postmodern condition' (Lyotard, 1984).

- **He put emphasis on the importance of culture as a whole way of life**. One of the things that makes Eliot's ideas relevant is that he defined culture anthropologically. He saw it as 'the way of life of a particular people living together in one place', and this culture is visible in the arts, the social system, habits, customs and religion. However, for Eliot, culture could not be reduced to these categories: these are merely the parts into which it can be anatomized. Each part has to be understood with relation to all the others (Eliot, [1948] 1975: 302). Despite what has been seen as Eliot's elitist emphasis on minority culture (Jenks, 1993: 103f.) and 'extreme right-wing authoritarianism' (Eagleton, 1983: 39), he does, given this anthropological view, offer a wider view of culture which includes everything from religions and literature to Derby day and Stilton cheese. This all-inclusiveness resembles contemporary cultural studies.

## A dialogue with the social sciences

By defining culture in this way Eliot helped to reinforce an anthropological approach to definitions of culture. In many introductions to cultural studies it is not customary to introduce students to the work of Edward Burnett Tylor, but Tylor provided anthropologists with what can be seen as the first persuasive definition of culture as 'that complex whole which includes knowledge, belief, art, morals, law, custom, and any other capabilities and habits acquired by man as a member of society' (Tylor, [1871] 1958: 1). Most dictionary definitions of culture reflect Tylor's and this definition would re-emerge in the work of Raymond Williams (see chapter six) and establish itself as a key approach to understanding culture in cultural studies. For a brief overview of anthropological and sociological definitions of culture see Jenks (1993: 25f.).

- Finally, Eliot asserted that 'the cultures of different peoples do affect each other: in the world of the future it looks as if every part of the world would affect every other part' (Eliot, [1948] 1975: 303). Here Eliot (in the context of 'European culture') saw that cultures are not hermetically sealed from one another: they interact and draw on one another. Methodologically, this notion of '**transnational culture**' is a useful starting point for discussions of **multiculturalism** which complicates cultural identity further by showing how a monolithic cultural identity can be challenged by the circulation of 'other' ethnic cultural identities available within what can be called a 'host' culture. This can also be a starting point for an exploration of any cultural theory that challenges dominant notions of identity. See later chapters, especially chapter thirteen.

## **practice** EXERCISE: working with Eliot's 'transnational culture'

Eliot's prediction that in the world of the future it looks as if 'every part of the world would affect every other part' seems to have been confirmed. There are many ways this might be explored from looking into processes of globalization (how dominant cultures, and especially international capitalism, establishes or enforces its values, beliefs and practices across the world) to how cultures interact with one another. Let's ask a simple question and explore how it might be answered: How might Eliot's idea of 'transnational culture' help us to think about ways in which different cultural forms influence one another?

## **notes** ON PRACTICE: exploring transnational culture with Akira Kurosawa

The Japanese film director, Akira Kurosawa was a great admirer of Western culture, and especially North American films. His love of American film genres and styles led to criticisms in Japan that he was too Western. However, the relation between Kurosawa and Western cinema was not one way: many of his films have inspired directors all over the world. If his films *Stray Dog* (1949), *Yojimbo* (1961) and *High and Low* (1963) drew on detective novels and thrillers and translated them into Japanese idioms, a number of his films have influenced directors in the West. For example, his *Yojimbo* influenced Sergio Leone's spaghetti western, *A Fist Full of Dollars* (1964) and George Lucas acknowledged Kurosawa's *Hidden Fortress* (1958) as an influence on *Star Wars* (1977). Perhaps the most curious case was Kurosawa's *The Seven Samurai* (1954), a film which Kurosawa admitted was very much influenced by the Hollywood western, yet it went on to provide the basic plot structure for one of the most famous westerns of all time, *The Magnificent Seven* (1960).

Kurosawa also drew on writers as diverse as Gorky, Tolstoy, Shakespeare, Dostoevsky, Ed McBain and Georges Simeon, and many film directors around the world have openly recognized Kurosawa as an influence (Richie, 1996). From these references alone we can see how it is unrealistic to see cultures as wholly isolated or self-enclosed. You might also think about other ways Japanese culture has influenced the West (and vice versa) and in what ways the culture you live in interacts (or has interacted) with 'other' cultures.

Here's a final question designed to get you to think in general terms about some of the ideas we have explored with relation to Arnold, the Leavises and Eliot.

## **practice** EXERCISE: culture and power

In order to get a clear idea of how culture may relate to power, you might try to answer the following question. Comparing the ideas of Arnold, the Leavises and Eliot, can you explain very briefly how their definition of culture may be considered political, or even an instrument of power? Try to answer the question for yourself. If you have difficulty, a possible answer is included in the following notes on practice.

### **notes** ON PRACTICE: culture and power

All these writers privileged what *they* regarded as high culture over other cultural forms. Their definitions of culture depended on a privileged elite which put itself above other classes (especially the working classes). The idea of Arnold as a reactionary is reinforced by his opposition to any kind of political change which might result in more rights for the politically dispossessed. Arnold's linking of class war to cultural disintegration and his belief in the necessity of a social elite of enlightened individuals to 'police' culture set the general tone for the work of the Leavis circle and T.S. Eliot. In this way the definition of culture within the Culture and Civilization Tradition can be seen as an instrument of class oppression, and it is in this sense that it can be seen as an instrument of power ...

## *SUMMARY OF KEY POINTS*

This chapter has reviewed the historical context and the importance of the Leavis circle to the rise of cultural criticism, including that focused on popular culture. The Leavisite model of cultural history has been assessed, as have key ideas like the training of critical awareness, the importance of informed judgements, standardization, levelling down, and Americanization. This chapter also outlined Eliot's approach to culture through cultural disintegration and cultured minorities and demonstrated how some of his strategies resemble an anthropological approach to cultural criticism. The last part of the chapter suggested ways that these ideas might be explored in practice.

The Leavis/*Scrutiny* circle's importance in methodological terms can be summed up in the following way:

- Like Arnold, the Leavises linked cultural forms to historical change and mass industrial culture.
- The Leavis circle extended the Culture and Civilization Tradition by developing canons of works and critical practices that would teach discrimination and the training of critical awareness. These provided techniques for cultural analysis linked to the task of raising consciousness. At the same time, their understanding of culture may be considered elitist and an instrument of power. The emphasis on resistance and consciousness raising are strategies which are common to much work in cultural studies.
- Popular cultures like the press and advertising were analysed, valued and understood through 'close reading' (albeit negatively).
- In this way, according to Eagleton, the *Scrutiny* group 'invented' a form of cultural studies.

Metholologically, Eliot is interesting because:

- His discussion of fragmentation through specialization reflects this kind of thinking in sociological and Marxist cultural criticism.
- He helped to reinforce an anthropological approach to definitions of culture.
- He offered a wider view of culture which included everything from beliefs and literature to holidays and eating habits.
- He saw that cultures are not hermetically sealed from one another: they are *transnational*, interacting with and drawing on one another.



## References

*A Fist Full of Dollars* (1964) dir. Sergio Leone.

Eagleton, Terry (1983) *Literary Theory: An Introduction*. Oxford: Blackwell.

Easthope, Anthony (1991) *Literary into Cultural Studies*. London: Routledge.

Eliot, T.S. ([1948] 1975) 'Notes Toward the Definition of Culture' in *Selected Prose of T. S. Eliot*. London: Faber.

Habermas, Jürgen (1981) 'Modernity – An Incomplete Project'. *New German Critique*, (Winter).

*Hidden Fortress* (1958) dir. Akira Kurosawa.

*High and Low* (1963) dir. Akira Kurosawa.

Inglis, Fred (1993) *Cultural Studies*. Oxford: Blackwell.

Jenks, Chris (1993) *Culture: Key Ideas*. London: Routledge.

Leavis, F.R. (1930) *Mass Civilisation and Minority Culture*. Cambridge: Minority Press.

Leavis, F.R. and Thompson, Denys ([1933] 1977) *Culture and Environment: The Training of Critical Awareness*. Westport, CT: Greenwood Press.

Leavis, F.R. (1936) *Revaluation: Tradition and Development in English Poetry*. London: Chatto & Windus.

Leavis, F.R. (1948) *The Great Tradition: George Eliot, Henry James, Joseph Conrad*. London: Chatto & Windus.

Leavis, F.R. (1952) *The Common Pursuit*. London: Chatto and Windus.

Leavis, Q.D. ([1932] 1974) *Fiction and the Reading Public*. New York: Folcroft.

Lyotard, Jean-François (1984), *The Postmodern Condition: A Report on Knowledge*. Minneapolis: University of Minnesota Press.

*Magnificent Seven, The* (1960) dir. John Sturges.

Marcuse, Herbert ([1964] 1986) *One-Dimensional Man: Studies in the Ideology of Advanced Industrial Society*. London: Ark.

Marx, Karl ([1845] 1976) 'Theses on Feuerbach', in *Ludwig Feuerbach and the End of Classical German Philosophy*. Peking: Foreign Languages Press.

Richie, Donald (1996) *The Films of Akira Kurosawa*. California: University of California Press.

*Seven Samurai, The* (1954) dir. Akira Kurosawa.

*Star Wars* (1977) dir. George Lucas.

Storey, John (2001) *Cultural Theory and Popular Culture: An Introduction* (3rd edition). Essex: Pearson Prentice Hall.

*Stray Dog* (1949) dir. Akira Kurosawa.

Strinati, Dominic (1995) *An Introduction to Theories of Popular Culture*. London: Routledge.

Turner, Graeme (1996) *British Cultural Studies: An Introduction* (2nd edition). London: Routledge.

Tylor, Edward Burnett ([1871] 1958) *Primitive Culture: Researches into the Development of Mythology, Philosophy, Religion, Art and Custom*. Gloucester, MA: Smith.

Weber, Max (1946) 'Science as a Vocation' in *From Max Weber: Essays in Sociology*. Oxford: Oxford University Press.

Wellek, René (1937) 'Literary Criticism and Philosophy', *Scrutiny*, March.

*Yojimbo* (1961) dir. Akira Kurosawa.

## Further reading

For detailed accounts of the development of the new degree in English at Cambridge see Inglis cited above (1993:32f.) and for a brief discussion of Eliot's politics see Eagleton cited above (1983:39f.).

Baldick, Chris (1983) *The Social Mission of English Criticism*. Oxford: Blackwell. Baldick describes the rise of English, the importance of the Leavises and the *Scrutiny* group linking their work to the values that lay behind it.

Doyle, Brian (1989) *English and Englishness*. London: Routledge. A book which explores how English Studies relates to national identity.

Foucault, Michel (1980) *Michel Foucault: Power/Knowledge. Selected Interviews and other Writings 1972–1977*. London: Harvester Wheatsheaf. In one of the practice exercises I asked you to think about Arnold, the Leavises and Eliot and how their ideas may be related to culture and power. Michel Foucault is a key writer for critics interested in these relationships. Although Foucault's work can be very complex for the beginner, these interviews present Foucault's ideas in a more accessible, conversational style and demonstrate how different forms of culture relate to power.

Mulhern, Francis (1979) *The Moment of 'Scrutiny'*. London: New Left Books. Like Eagleton and the other writers mentioned here, Mulhern is interested in the historical moment of *Scrutiny* with relation to its ideological affiliations.

MacDonald, Dwight ([1957] 1998) 'A Theory of Mass Culture', in John Storey (1998, see references above. This is another approach often mentioned in introductions to cultural studies that offers positive readings of folk art and 'High' culture and a negative view of mass commercial culture.

Steger, Manfred B. (2003) *Globalization: A Very Short Introduction.* Oxford: Oxford University Press. In the section on Eliot I mentioned globalization in a very generalized way. Although this reference is a very basic introduction to the topic, it offers a useful overview of some of the main issues that have been raised with relation to this concept stressing, as it does, not only the economic aspects but the political, religious, cultural, environmental and ideological. It also contains a useful annotated bibliography.

Storey, John (2001, see references above). Storey's second chapter offers a particularly effective critique of the Leavises' ideas and the politically objectionable values that stood behind them, while appreciating their historical importance – and without doing too much of a hatchet job on them.

# Adorno, the Frankfurt School and the 'Culture Industry'

3

## Introduction

This is the third and final chapter dealing with 'High Culture Gladiators'. Here I shall review some of the work of the Frankfurt School putting the main emphasis on Theodor Adorno. I shall start by introducing the historical context in which the ideas of the Frankfurt School were introduced and go on to discuss an enormously important idea in Adorno's writing: that of the culture industry. As my main aim is to focus on method, I shall show how writers like Adorno interpreted popular music (in this case, jazz) by drawing on and uniting the work of Marx and Freud to create a highly distinctive form of criticism.

Adorno will be presented as a (Marxist) high culture gladiator to show how his approach can be seen to extend, and challenge in very significant political ways, the Culture and Civilization tradition. Adorno and Max Horkheimer's negative reading of Enlightenment rationality will be illustrated with relation to Adorno's discussion of jazz. This chapter will be concluded by relating Adorno's way of working to what I've called the 'hypodermic needle' model of analysis. In the practice sections, detailed advice will be given on working with Adorno's ideas by applying them to an analysis of hip-hop, which will include examples of, and advice on, how to do creative criticism and how to assess analysis. The latter will be illustrated through a rap on Adorno. The ideas will be introduced through a conversation between Sherlock Holmes and Dr Watson.

## MAIN LEARNING GOALS

- To appreciate the historical context in which the Frankfurt School developed its ideas.
- To understand the concept of 'the culture industry' as model and method.
- To be aware of how Adorno's method united Marx and Freud to offer negative critiques of mass popular culture.
- To appreciate the points of contact and difference between Adorno's approach and Leavisism.
- To recognize that Adorno's negative view of mass culture is made possible by his positive notion of 'authentic' art.
- To be aware of how the products of the 'culture industry' can be seen to depoliticize and disempower those who consume them.
- To see how Adorno and Horkheimer linked Enlightenment thinking to the rise of fascism.
- To appreciate how these forms of interpretation work in practice.

## Adorno and the Frankfurt School

After the death of Sir Arthur Conan Doyle, Sherlock Holmes and Dr Watson have been enjoying a little freedom and dedicating themselves to activities other than detective work. Watson is sitting in a comfortable leather armchair in 221B Baker Street enjoying a glass of sherry and listening to Holmes playing the violin. Watson has recently taken an interest in cultural studies and has asked his friend and mentor to introduce him to some of the ideas put forward by the Frankfurt School. Holmes, who is of course an expert (and has already lectured Watson on Arnold and the Leavises), finishes the piece he is playing. He stuffs his pipe and takes a chair opposite Watson. Here is a transcript of their conversation.

WATSON: So, my dear Holmes, tell me something about this famous Frankfurt School. I suppose you're going to tell me it's all quite elementary?

HOLMES: Sorry to disappoint you, but on the contrary, the ideas can be quite complex. Thus, I shall not try to introduce you to all the writers of Frankfurt School but focus on two of its members – Max Horkheimer and Theordor Adorno, putting most emphasis on the latter. As you may know, they were prominent members of this School, which united a group of Jewish writers who were affiliated to the Institute for Social Research at the University of Frankfurt (later known as the Frankfurt School of Critical Theory).

WATSON: (politely interrupting) But before you continue, tell me something about the historical era in which they developed their ideas.

HOLMES: It was roughly the same as the Leavises: they began to make an impact in the difficult inter-war period of the 1920s and 1930s. Those members of the School who survived the Second World War continued to write after it.

WATSON: Why is the historical context so important?

HOLMES: You might take into account that this historical context was not only important to the kinds of criticism they practised but also to *where* they produced it. The rise of Hitler and Nazism in the 1930s forced them out of Germany and the School had to move to the University of Columbia in New York. This happened in 1933 but by 1949 the Institute had re-established itself in Frankfurt. As you'll see later, the rise and inhumanity of Fascism was something that left a deep imprint on their thought, and their contact with the United States exposed them to forms of popular culture which, again, left a strong impression, given that they found it manipulative, trivial and harmful.

WATSON: You've pricked my curiosity! But before we move on, who were the other writers in this School?

HOLMES: Apart from Adorno and Horkheimer there were critics like Leo Löwenthal, Walter Benjamin and Herbert Marcuse.

WATSON: But isn't the contemporary theorist Jürgen Habermas also associated with the School?

HOLMES: True! Well done, Watson!

WATSON: So, what united these critics and why are they important to cultural studies?

HOLMES: The first thing to keep in mind is that the different writers cannot be reduced to a single approach. The case of Benjamin is particularly interesting. However, they *were* united by their belief in, and commitment to, **Marxism**. They are important names partly because they helped to establish the terms in which popular culture could be discussed (and often denounced or dismissed) by critics on the left. One of the things I shall try to get you to see is how some of the ideas associated with the Frankfurt School related to (and differed from) the values and assumptions found within the Leavisite approach. Let me now turn to Theodor Adorno.

## Oversimplification

**W A R N I N G**

Even though Adorno is represented here as a 'high culture gladiator', it must be remembered that he was, politically speaking, very distant from the Leavis circle (see below). Also, his contribution will be reduced to a number of influential ideas which do not reflect the full extent or complexity of his work, or the difficulty of his style.

## Adorno and the culture industry

WATSON: So, how would you say Adorno has contributed to *how* cultural studies has been practised?

HOLMES: I would say in how he described mass popular culture as a product of the '**culture industry**'. He claimed that products of the culture industry can be seen as anything produced for mass consumption (the press, music, film, TV etc.).

WATSON: (raising an eyebrow) Why call these forms products of the culture industry? He makes it sound like they were produced in a factory!

HOLMES: That's not a bad way of expressing his approach. He argued that, motivated by profit, industrial capitalism merely produced **formulaic and utterly predictable forms of popular culture** which functioned to **pacify the masses** and encourage them to adjust to the 'humiliating conditions' of their lives. The effect of this was to make them conform to the system and resign themselves to these conditions. Not only were the masses rendered politically impotent but were impoverished materially emotionally and intellectually. In short it depoliticized its victims (Adorno, 1991: 143f.). I refer to *The Culture Industry* here, although these ideas are developed in many contexts in Adorno's work, including his collaborative effort with Horkheimer, *The Dialectic of Enlightenment* (Adorno and Horkheimer [1947] 1972: 125) where the authors discuss what they see as the banality and predictability of popular film.

WATSON: Would it be true to say, then, that he saw entertainment produced within capitalism as rather sinister?

HOLMES: I would agree. Adorno's way of analysing mass culture can be visualized in the following way (Holmes doodles on a piece of paper and hands it to Watson – see Figure 3.1 following).

## The Frankfurt School and popular music: Marx and Freud, all jazzed up

WATSON: (frowning) I think I'm beginning to get the main ideas, but can't you give me a concrete example and show how his ideas link to method?

HOLMES: A rather tall order, Watson! Now, to see how these ideas work in practice we can look at an essay written by Adorno in the early 1960s called 'Perennial Fashion – Jazz' (Adorno, 1990). In this essay, based on ideas developed in the 1930s, Adorno provides the arguments that typified his argument against the products of the culture industry. So you can appreciate the basic steps of his (implied) method I'll represent his arguments in a highly simplified way (once again, Holmes begins doodling and Watson, unperturbed, helps himself to some more sherry. Holmes hands his work to Watson for approval).

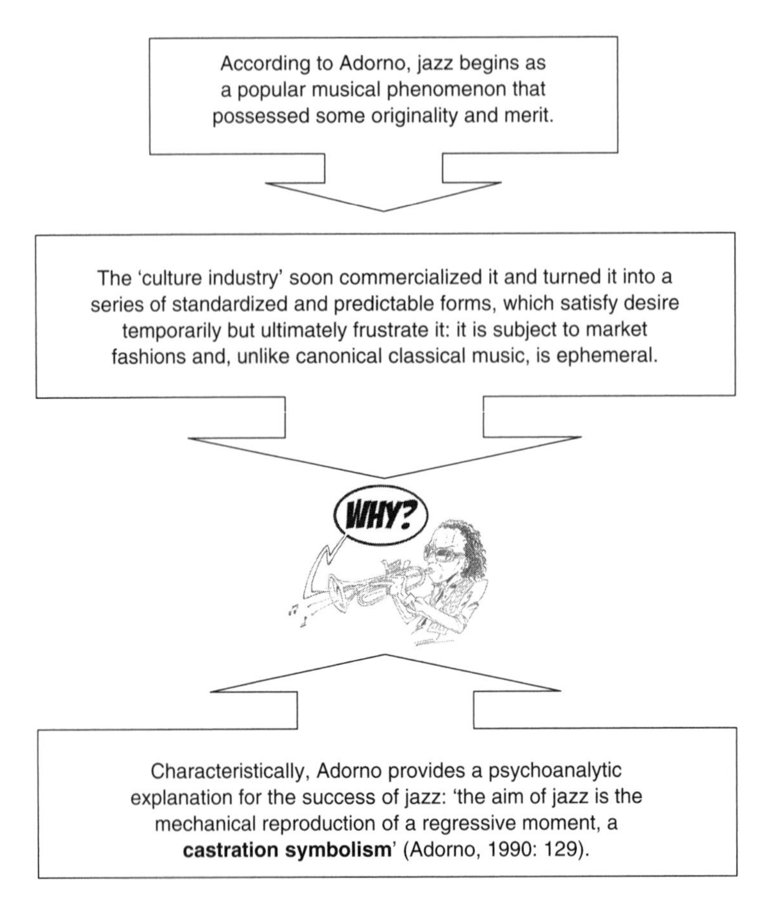


Figure 3.1 The basic steps of Adorno's argument against the products of the culture industry

HOLMES: (continuing) What Adorno is saying here is that the reduction of musical expression to standardized, predictable forms **disempowers** jazz musicians and fans alike – they do not genuinely express themselves in a spontaneous artistic way (although you will need to read the whole essay to understand all the implications of the argument).

## Adorno, Freud and the castration of the audience

WATSON: What's all this 'mechanical reproduction of a regressive moment' and 'castration symbolism'? Had this fellow Adorno been reading Freud?!

HOLMES: An excellent point, my dear Watson. What can make these arguments difficult for readers who have not read Sigmund Freud is that this way of interpreting

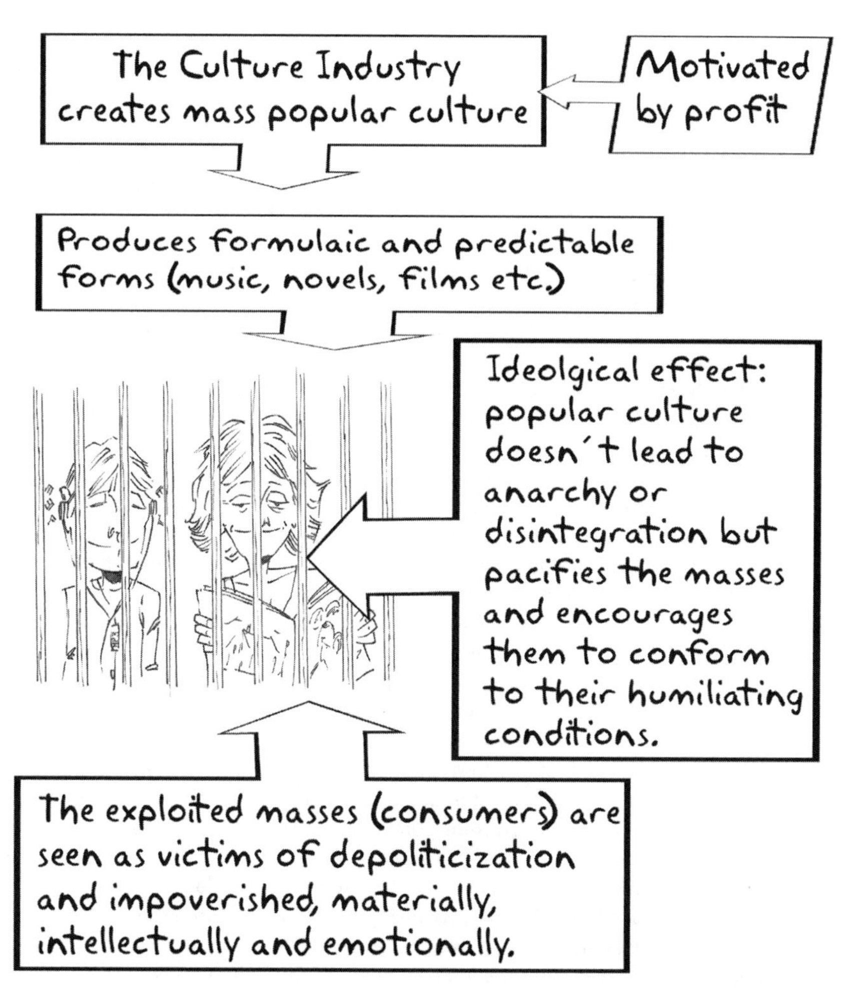


Figure 3.2 Drawing on Adorno's work, here's the classic Frankfurt position on mass cultural forms. See Theodor Adorno, *The Culture Industry: Selected Essays on Mass Culture* (1991) and his collaborative effort with Max Horkheimer in The Dialectic of Enlightenment ([1947] 1972).

culture reflects **the fusion of Marxism and psychoanalysis**. Interestingly, while the essay is inspired by Marxism, Adorno never actually *cites* Marx. The way I put the case here (in order to make clear how Adorno relates to Marxist thought) it sounds rather more 'preachy' than in Adorno's work – Adorno learnt from Marx and Engels but did not seem to feel the need to show his credentials by quoting his sources at every opportunity.

WATSON: (with polite impatience) OK, he drew on Marx and Freud, but what on earth did he mean by 'the aim of jazz is the mechanical reproduction of a regressive moment, a castration symbolism'?

HOLMES: Have patience, my dear Watson. Put very simply, Freud argued that in infancy the psyche passes through phases of development, i.e. the oral, anal and genital. To develop into an adult each person has to learn to suck and control the functions of anus and genitals. For Freud, the newborn child learns how to imbibe sustenance through sucking at the mother's breast (let's ignore the fact that this may not be the case for many children). The oral phase (the mouth–breast relation) is seen by Freud as an ideal state of fulfilment where mother and baby are indistinguishable in the child's primitive consciousness. Not only this, but suckling is *not only* a question of nourishment, babies will suckle without drawing milk – simply because it is pleasurable. Thus, he was able to talk about infant sexuality (Freud, [1917] 1973: 355).

WATSON: Ah yes, it's all coming back now. I remember the scandal Freud caused in polite circles!

HOLMES: (ignoring him) Let's imagine the following situation. The first months of your life have been characterized by sucking at the breast, being the centre of attention, digesting milk and excreting it until one fine day you have to learn to drink from a bottle. Up to now, life has been dominated by what Freud called '**the pleasure principle**'. It is the withdrawal of the pleasure of the breast that is the first sign that the child does not control the world around it and 'reality' makes itself known. You start to grow and begin to learn some language. One day you are about to do what comes naturally in your nappy and ... 'Whoahhh – STOP THAT NOW!' You look up in amazement. You have that 'but-why-can't-I-carry-on-like-I've-always-done?' look on your face. But now you're in the world of rules, regulations and prohibitions. You've got to be the master of your own bowel and sphincter. Later, used to being able to touch ANY part of your body, the genitals become out of bounds – you can't derive any (public) pubic pleasure from stimulating them. That's it, from here on it's all controls and responsibilities – and those early freedoms slip away. You are now being subjected to what Freud called the '**reality principle**'.

WATSON: (staring in disbelief) But what's all *this* got to do with Adorno's reading of jazz?

HOLMES: Worry not, my dear Watson, all will be revealed! Freud argued that adults who were unable to cope with the pressures, responsibilities and stresses of their lives had a tendency to regress back to earlier phases (like the oral) where they could relive the ideal maternal relation of pleasurable warmth, protection and nourishment. Jazz, according to Adorno, has as its object this regression back to an infantile phase which effectively pacifies the listener rather like the breast does the baby: the reality principle is replaced by the pleasure principle. This is one way that his work relates to psychoanalysis. But I must insist, Watson, that I'm simplifying Freud's ideas here and I am deliberately ignoring the incestuous, Oedipal implications of them. This is largely because Adorno's argument doesn't depend on them – Adorno being interested in how psychoanalysis can assist political readings of culture.

WATSON: (on the end of his seat) Yes, but how on earth does he work in the idea of castration?

HOLMES: Very simply put, Adorno draws on Freud's idea that some male neuroses are based on the fear of losing the genitals (literally having them cut off). This symbolism is one where the male loses his masculinity, meaning his strength.

WATSON: So, women are immune!

HOLMES: Not at all. If males can suffer from the castration complex, females can suffer from what Freud called 'penis envy' (Freud [1917] 1973: 360f.) – a concept that has not exactly endeared itself to many feminist critics. But I digress. To Adorno, becoming a jazz fan (whether you're male of female) is like being initiated into a fraternity where you share not only the degraded music but a sense of impotence: you are introduced into 'a community of unfree equals'. Jazz, in its predictable monotony, becomes like a drug where jazz aficionados are so accustomed to the 'drivel' they are fed that they can't give it up (Adorno, 1990: 126). In short, musicians and fans alike are enfeebled – castrated.

## Marx and Freud united

WATSON: (a little scandalized) But I always thought that many jazz musicians and some of the audience were outsiders. I actually see them as rather rebellious!

HOLMES: Adorno was aware that jazz descended from potentially rebellious music like African slave songs but argues that 'it is no less certain that everything unruly in it was from the very beginning integrated into a strict scheme, that its rebellious gestures are accompanied by the tendency to blind obeisance' (Adorno, 1990: 122). What Adorno seems to be saying here is that to be a jazz rebel is ultimately to be a thoroughgoing conformist. The jazz enthusiast is a victim: a compulsive consumer consuming sameness disguised through fashion as variety. The castrating effect carries over to any potential challenge jazz may pose to society. Any asocial forces are, through the standardizing conveyor-belt approach to the music, charmed away.

## Adorno and the distinction between authentic and mass culture

WATSON: I hope you'll forgive my frivolity, Holmes, but if we strip away the Marxism and psychoanalysis, I think I hear echoes of Arnold and the Leavises here.

HOLMES: Yes, but let's be a little more specific. Like the Arnold/Leavisite tradition, Adorno's ideas are based on a distinction between authentic and inferior forms of culture. However, as indicated above, there is an enormous difference in the politics behind this distinction.

WATSON: So, what distinguishes great, authentic culture from mass culture for Adorno?

HOLMES: Why not get yourself another drink and I'll sketch out the differences for you (Watson does what he says, returns and decides to puff on his pipe until Holmes is ready). Here (he hands a sheet of paper to Watson), take a look at this. Drawing on Adorno's essay 'On Popular Music' (reprinted in Storey, 1998), the following table outlines some of the main differences between authentic and mass culture.

| *Great, authentic art or culture* | *Mass culture* |
| --- | --- |
| 'Serious' music is organic where the detail expresses the complex whole and is not based on predictable formulas | It is predictable, formulaic and stereotypical – each song gives the illusion of being different but is only another version of the established pattern |
| It offers genuine aesthetic and intellectual fulfilment | It only provokes desire and false dreams (e.g. wealth, adventure, passionate love, power). It is sensationalist and sentimental |
| Utopian ideals are expressed in it opening up the possibility and promise of a better the world | It is conservative and centres thinking on the immediate present rather than focus the mind on the future and on possibilities for improvement and change |
| It provokes imaginative responses and challenges the audience/reader and does not inspire escapism | It is escapist and requires no real effort (inspires passivity) – the socio-psychological function of popular music is psychological adjustment to the status quo – popular music is a kind of 'social cement' which denies or stifles the critical faculties |
| Danger! The culture industry assimilates, depoliticizes and drains authentic culture of its revolutionary potential by incorporating it into itself, an idea given great emphasis in the work of a later Frankfurt critic, Herbert Marcuse (e.g. *One-Dimensional Man*, 1964) | |

What Adorno is saying here is that the reduction of musical expression to standardized, predictable forms disempowers jazz musicians and fans alike – they do not genuinely express themselves in a spontaneous artistic way.

Figure 3.3 Adorno, the culture industry and disempowerment

## Adorno as (Marxist) high culture gladiator

HOLMES: Looking at this table, I hope it is clear how 'castrating' popular mass culture was for Adorno and most of his colleagues. However, there are significant differences between his way of understanding the *effects* of mass culture and the way Arnold and the Leavises understood it. According to Adorno, the masses are not to be feared because they may overturn the existing political system and social arrangements but quite the opposite! They are seen as the victims of a culture industry that renders its consumers politically and intellectually anaesthetized to the miserable conditions of their lives. The passive resignation that working under capitalism achieves during working hours, mass culture extends and intensifies through the leisure activities of the culture industry (Adorno and Horkheimer, [1947] 1972: 142).

WATSON: But I must insist, I still see some resemblance between Adorno and the Leavises!

HOLMES: Politics aside, I agree – there are some resemblances between him and the writers in the Culture and Civilization Tradition. Adorno is a member of a small beleaguered troop fighting for survival against what is seen as the dangerous forces of modern (mass) cultural barbarism. For Adorno, Arnold and the Leavisite tradition authentic art is powerful and transformative: it has the power to awaken critical awareness and offer genuine intellectual and aesthetic pleasures. What distinguishes it from the Culture and Civilization view is that through offering alternative visions for a better future it can actually serve to awaken the masses to *rebel against* subordination, injustice and inequality.

### Oversimplification

**W A R N I N G**

It is a mistake to think that there is only *one* form of Marxist criticism – even though Marxists are inspired by Marx and Engels' revolutionary ideals. See the chapters on E.P. Thompson, Antonio Gramsci and Louis Althusser for further examples of the tradition. As suggested earlier, even those within the same 'School' didn't necessarily agree on every issue. The idea that art can promote the revolutionary purposes of Marxism unites many Marxists like the German playwright Bertholt Brecht and the contemporary critics Jürgen Habermas and Fredric Jameson (see further reading).

WATSON: Is there anything else that distinguishes Adorno's work from that of the Arnold/Leavisite tradition?

HOLMES: You might notice that Adorno uses the term '**barbarism**', but in a way that is distinct from the earlier writers. Writing against those who confuse popular song with modern art he states that anyone who 'mistakes a triad studded with "dirty notes" for atonality, has already capitulated to barbarism' (Adorno, 1990: 127). Barbarism here does not refer to the unruly behaviour of the masses but to the economic tyranny of the culture industry.

## **help** FILE: Adorno, 'dirty notes' and atonality

'Dirty notes' in jazz are those which stand outside the standard or expected scale patterns (especially flat thirds, fifths and sevenths – very characteristic of the blues). Atonality, to put it as simply as I can, is associated with classical composers like Arnold Schoenberg. This is where traditional tone centres and harmonic structures are abandoned for music which is tonally ambiguous and doesn't seem to belong to any key. If these ideas make no sense, you might start by listening to music composed by Mozart, Vivaldi or Beethoven and then listen to Schoenberg's Piano Concerto (1942). You'll probably find it harder to whistle to Schoenberg's piano concerto. You might also explore works by Anton Webern or Alban Berg.

## More barbarism: the Frankfurt School and Enlightenment rationalism

WATSON: An interesting twist on the idea of barbarism!

HOLMES: Yes, but barbarism doesn't end there. In Adorno's collaborative effort with Horkheimer, *The Dialectic of Enlightenment* ([1947] 1972:125) they not only discuss what they see as the banality and predictability of popular mass cultural forms but what they thought of as the barbarism resulting from the **rationalizing tendencies of the Enlightenment**.

WATSON: (surprised) What? Barbarism and the Enlightenment! Wasn't it supposed to bring reason to bear on the social and intellectual world?

## **help** FILE: A short detour into the Enlightenment

The Enlightenment, sometimes known as 'The Age of Reason', is associated with a number of very influential trends in seventeenth- and eighteenth-century thought (although the boundaries are rather hazy). Rebelling against traditional, authoritarian forms of thinking and social control, writers like Voltaire, Diderot, Montesquieu, Locke, Kant and Franklin (to mention only a few) argued that progress with regards to science and the social-political world should have its basis in reason. Reason, organized knowledge and scientific thinking were to transform the world for the betterment of all humanity – something which involved overthrowing the ancient tyrannies of ignorance, religion (often associated with superstitious belief), and the monarchy (see further reading).

Figure 3.4 The cultural extreme of Enlightenment rationalism

HOLMES: Yes, it's often understood in this way. However, the first thing to be clear about here is what they think of as **Enlightenment thinking**. Adorno and Horkheimer link Enlightenment rationalism with the catastrophic rise of the Fascists and the inhuman tragedy which was the Holocaust (the mass extermination of the Jews in Nazi concentration camps). Let's see how the argument works. In Enlightenment thinking reason became the dominant force which objectified nature. Reason replaced mythological (non-rational) thinking and then became dominant as rationalization (so dominant that it became a new kind of myth). The rational mastery of nature was eventually extended to human beings who become objects for the most terrible exploitation.

## The voice of contemporary criticism

Attacks on reason and the Enlightenment have been important to much contemporary (but notoriously difficult) cultural criticism. See the work of Jean-François Lyotard, Michel Foucault, Jacques Derrida and Jürgen Habermas where reason is politicized and, like in the *The Dialectic of Enlightenment*, is no longer seen as necessarily positive or innocent. For further information see Cahoone (1996) in the section on further reading.

WATSON: (a little dismayed) Reason, then, far from realizing the humanitarian dreams of the Enlightenment thinkers, actually works in favour of the forces of **totalitarianism** and facilitates the highly efficient and inhuman death camps of the Nazi regime? I never thought I'd see the Enlightenment understood in this way.

HOLMES: You might also be surprised to learn that Adorno also connected the products of the culture industry with authoritarianism. He asserted that syncopation (the dominant form of jazz rhythm) achieves 'musical dictatorship' over the masses in such a way that it 'recalls the usurpation that characterizes techniques, however rational they may be in themselves, when they are placed at the service of irrational totalitarian control' (Adorno, 1991: 125–6). For Adorno, the exaggerated behaviour of jazz enthusiasts recalls 'the brutal seriousness of the masses of followers in totalitarian states, even though the difference between play and seriousness amounts to that between life and death'. Here I'll read a section of his work to you (taking up his copy of *The Culture Industry*):

> While the leaders in the European dictatorships of both shades raged against the decadence of jazz, the youth of the other countries has long since allowed itself to be electrified, as with marches, by the syncopated dance-steps, with bands which do not by accident stem from military music. The division into shock-troops and inarticulate following has something of the distinction between party elite and the rest of the people. (Adorno, 1991: 128–9)

WATSON: (taken aback) So, enjoying your favourite popular music, from this point of view, means that you are unwittingly being subjected to the kinds of dangerous manipulative techniques used to dominate the masses!

HOLMES: Yes, from this point of view it might be said that there isn't much distance between your dance steps and the Nazi goose step. But that is enough for this evening. I have a gentleman coming with a particularly interesting case that intrigues me ...

WATSON: My dear Holmes, don't tell me you're getting back into detective work. What a pity, you'd make such a good teacher ...

## Adorno and method: the 'hypodermic needle' model of analysis

Let's leave Holmes and Watson in Baker Street and carry on without them. By now you may feel that there is much that is questionable in the way Adorno analyses mass popular culture. However, although many critics have found much to criticize in these examples of the work of the Frankfurt School, there are still many who find these ideas valuable and relevant to contemporary debates focused on popular culture. Adorno's and Horkheimer's critical practice can be described as a kind of 'hypodermic needle' model of analysis because all forms of popular mass culture inevitably have the effect of drugging the consumer into a state of submission and political weakness. This can be seen as the theory's greatest strength and weakness, something that will be explored in the sections on practice.

## Preparation for critical practice: the culture industry model as a method

To start, I shall present the bare bones of what we've been looking at above and reduce it to a number of methodological steps. This way, it's possible to experiment with the ideas to see how useful they might be to the world you live in. It is important to remember that these steps do not represent the full complexity of Adorno's and Horkheimer's thought. To mistake a simple exercise of this sort for what goes on in their criticism would be to parody their work (which, incidentally, can be a valuable exercise). Actually, the way I'm going to ask you to practise this exercise will border on parody - but it will be parody with a pedagogical point. However, the rationale for this exercise is that it should help you to see the relevance of the ideas and, at the same time, appreciate some of the most questionable assumptions that stand behind them. This brings me to the idea of heuristic thinking.

## Heuristic thinking and practice

From now on, I shall not only ask you to think about the ideas introduced but design a series of 'heuristics' to help you to think *with* the new concepts that we are going to explore. I have designed these heuristics as:

- something designed to help you learn through practice
- a tool for generating ideas by asking specific questions
- a set of concepts to aid thinking, independent thought, interpretation, analysis and research
- an aid to help you structure your thoughts and experiment with ideas
- in short, they are designed to help you **practise** cultural studies for yourself.

The idea here is to help you to develop a certain interpretive independence early on in your studies. The heuristics are designed to get you used to thinking with concepts and reading for strategies, rather than just absorb the content of what you read. Once you've absorbed a set of strategies you can test them out on anything that interests you to see which ones are the most productive in any given interpretive situation. They will also give you a position from which to assess what others have written.

Here's a heuristic to help you appreciate and explore some of the basic methodological steps of Adorno's analysis of jazz:

- pick a popular form of culture
- recognize its cultural context and possible origins (Adorno was aware that jazz was linked to the blues and slave songs)
- emphasize its formulaic and predictable conventions
- describe its psychological, economic, ideological and political effects (using as a background ideas related to Marxism and psychoanalysis):

  1. *Psychological effects*: the cultural form offers temporary satisfaction and is escapist but is largely empty and ultimately leads to frustration and disempowerment (castration).
  2. *Economic effects*: the constant promise and frustration of satisfaction, plus the dictates of fashion, plunge consumers into a vicious circle of consumption which perpetuates the culture industry and those profiteering from popular culture.
  3. *Ideological effects*: impoverishes consumers intellectually and emotionally and helps to adjust consumers to the status quo.
  4. *Political effects*: strengthens the inequalities of capitalism, pacifies consumers, and renders them politically impotent.

- finally, ask questions about how the form of popular culture chosen may link to the rise of totalitarianism or dangerous forms of rationality.

## **practice** EXERCISE 1: working with the culture industry heuristic

As a first exercise, take any popular form of culture (you might look at music, television, film, video games, magazines, newspapers, fiction) and subject it to this process of analysis. I would recommend you choose something you like (the reason has to do with the next practice exercise). The following notes are designed to help you get started.

## **notes** ON PRACTICE: hip-hop as a product of the culture industry

Let's take a manifestation of contemporary music which has now become enormously popular and lucrative, hip-hop. Following the methodological steps above (and following them in a fairly mechanical way), it is possible to arrive at the following interpretation. Why follow the steps in a mechanical way? The simple answer is so that you can assess the main assumptions behind this approach. For the sake of concision, I'll just sketch out a possible interpretation. I ought to make clear from the start that I have nothing against hip-hop – I am playing Devil's advocate.

- The recognition of its cultural context and possible origins:

We would have to relate the phenomenon to capitalist forces and recognize that it is an extension of other styles of music from traditional West African (the oral tradition of the griots) to African-Western styles like spirituals, ragtime, the blues, jazz, rhythm and blues, soul, reggae and Jamaican DJ dances (and this doesn't exhaust all the possible links).

- Emphasize its formulaic and predictable conventions:

It's possible to argue that after the innovative styles associated with Clive Campbell (Kool Herc), Grandmaster Flash and Afrika Bambaataa the music, despite its often oppositional political stances, was commercialized. Once 'Rapper's Delight' by the Sugarhill Gang (1979) had broken through selling 500,000 copies (statistic taken from Haskins, 2000: 126), it could be said that hip-hop was ripe to be drawn into the culture industry – its principal reason for existence now being to fill the pockets of record company executives. It might be recalled that Ice Cube claimed that the 'real pimp is the motherfucking record companies' (in Goldstein, no date: 48). One might say that if techniques like scratching, backspinning, sampling, snapping, dubbing, punch phrasing etc. were once at the cutting-edge of music they have been so assimilated that they can now be heard on everything from *Public Enemy* to songs entered for the much maligned Eurovision Song Contest.

- Describe its psychological, economic, ideological and political effects (using as a background ideas related to Marxism and psychoanalysis):

*Psychological effects*: according to this point of view hip-hop only offers temporary satisfaction and escape from the stresses and difficulties of contemporary life in late capitalism but, despite its claims to be rebellious, it inevitably leads to frustration and disempowerment (the castration effect) for its listeners. Rappers (whether listeners or performers) may play the game of being social rebels but are, ultimately, disempowered conformists.

*(Continued)*

*(Continued)*

*Economic effects*: the constant promise and frustration of satisfaction, plus the dictates of hip-hop fashion (we've had everything now from Gangsta rap to Christian rap), helps to maintain the vicious circle of consumption which feeds the culture industry and the profiteers behind it.

*Ideological effects*: rap impoverishes consumers intellectually and emotionally and helps to adjust the rap fans, through the ritual of consumption, to the existing social and political arrangements.

*Political effects*: it strengthens the inequalities of capitalism, pacifies consumers, and renders them politically impotent.

- Finally, ask questions about how the form of popular culture chosen may link to the rise of totalitarianism or dangerous forms of rationality:

It could be argued that highly commercialized hip-hop has achieved a 'musical dictatorship' over the masses in such a way that it 'recalls the usurpation that characterizes techniques, however rational they may be in themselves, when they are placed at the service of irrational totalitarian control' (Adorno, 1991: 125–6). Rap fans are unwittingly being subjected to the kinds of dangerous manipulative techniques used to dominate the masses.

Now, you might feel that some of this makes sense and/or, you may even be offended by this analysis. If you are offended I hope you will be stimulated to focus on why you disagree with the idea of all popular culture being branded in the same way. If you're not a hip-hop fan, you might imagine the same kinds of things being said about your favourite form(s) of popular culture. How would you respond to these claims? It is worth considering that while many arguments may be put forward to contradict these views, it does not mean that the ideas are not of considerable value – the problem is in being able to establish the extent, truth or accuracy of the claims.

## **practice** EXERCISE 2: assessing your analysis

Once you've experimented with the heuristic, you can then assess your own analysis to consider the strengths and weaknesses of the approach. Now let's consider a number of questions concerning the use of this methodology:

- What do you think are the main assumptions behind this approach?
- In what ways did you find this way of thinking useful?
- How well do the ideas adapt to the contemporary world?
- Having analysed something that interests you personally, did you object to some of the conclusions Adorno might have drawn?
- If you feel there are weaknesses in this approach, how would you define them?

## **notes** ON PRACTICE: Rappin' on Jazz – Perennial Fashion

Here I'm not going to answer all the questions I've posed above but, through a piece of creative criticism, suggest some ways in which the ideas explored above might be useful, if questionable. I'll also hint at some of the assumptions behind the ideas. Here, as I've been using hip-hop, I've written a short rap where I'm putting myself in the position of a rapper who tries to take up a critical but appreciative attitude towards the method we have been exploring. You might try extending this rap for yourself and/or rewrite it to apply to other popular forms. If you do, you'll find that it can serve as a useful mnemonic (memory) device to remember the basic concepts and your attitudes to them. This is a technique which is particularly useful at examination time. Try it.

*Rappin' on Jazz – Perennial Fashion*

Hey, Mr Adorno, I've read your dissertation
And it's sent me into a state of agitation.
I reckon some of your thinking is right on
about the commercialization of the jazz song.
And I reckon just about anyone can see
how it's just another victim of the culture industry.
But all that stuff about inevitable castration
and your disempowerment, it's an oversimplification!
You know everything there's to know about consumption?
All those effects! Your political, your economical,
Your ideological, your psychological,
It may be methodical but it's based on assumption!

This may not be def – have some compassion!
We're rappin' on jazz – perennial fashion!

Jazz can be formulaic, it can reinforce the status quo
but it ain't as simple as it looks, so how do you know?
You got some of it right but there's a lot you miss,
have you listened to absolutely everything there is?
You got your Armstrong, your Parker, your John Coltrane
your be-bop, your free jazz, you reckon they're all the same?
Look at Miles Davis, he never looked back
and he made many Afro-Americans proud of being black.
But even if early 60s jazz was formulaic, dissidence was rife
to know the music, you gotta know the way of life.
Jazz culture crossed over into politics and religion
some demanded change, and some ended up in prison.

(Continued)

*(Continued)*

This may not be def – have some compassion!
We're rappin' on jazz – perennial fashion!

So, you telling me they were all castrated fools?
Scratching their names up on prison walls?
Some had vision, a different world in their sights
where jazz was part of a cry for back rights.
For some it was merriment, for others experiment.
You had your dogmatists, activists, evangelists,
islamists, pacifists, revolutionists,
unionists, humorists, satirists,
commercialists, romanticists, emancipists,
those with silk gloves, others with iron fists.
All this difference, it makes me weary,
can it really be summed up by your theory?

This may not be def – have some compassion!
We're rappin' on jazz – perennial fashion!

Just in case you've not come across the term 'def', it means great or cool. I also refer to Louis Armstrong, Charlie Parker, John Coltrane and Miles Davis, who were all considered highly innovative musicians in their time. Be-bop and free jazz both revolutionized jazz – the first by about the mid-1940s, the second by the end of the 1950s, early 1960s. If you'd like to follow up some of these movements see Tirro (1993) and Townsend (2000).

## **practice** EXERCISE 3: further development

Another exercise you might try is to go through this rap to see what kinds of points I'm making, then develop them and see whether or not you are in agreement with them. You could begin as follows:

1. The rapper accepts that Adorno's analysis is valuable and relevant (I agree/disagree).
2. But sees it as an oversimplification (your reaction).
3. Did Adorno know all there was to be known about *how* jazz fans and musicians lived jazz culture? That is, how can he know how different people responded to jazz? (your reaction).

*(Continued)*

A final point, Adorno assumed that he knew what he was talking about when he wrote about jazz and I've assumed that I know what I'm talking about when I use words like 'rap' and 'hip-hop'; however, the question of what these forms *actually* are is often far from clear. Many so-called jazz musicians reject the term 'jazz' preferring to call what they do 'improvised music'. If you look at the first chapter of *The Cambridge Companion to Jazz* you'll see that it's dedicated to one thing, the word 'jazz' (Cooke and Horn, 2002). The conclusion? While there are dominant conventions, there is no absolute agreement about what the music is, or even was. This is complicated by the fact that jazz, like most living forms of culture, is not static but dynamic and thus subject to constant revision.

## SUMMARY OF KEY POINTS

As the practice sections serve to rehearse the main content of this chapter, I shall sum up Adorno and Horkheimer's contribution by focusing on their importance in terms of method. Linking what has been emphasized in Adorno's work back to the Arnold/Leavisite tradition it is possible to see that they have a number of methodological features in common:

- Like the Arnoldian-Leavisite tradition Adorno linked cultural forms to historical change and mass industrial culture, and his theories were dependent on the importance and superiority of complex, authentic works of art which can change society for the better.
- Implicitly, critical theory demands forms of discrimination and can be seen in terms of the training of critical awareness.
- Popular cultures (products of the culture industry) are analysed, valued and understood negatively as formulaic and predictable.
- Forms of resistance and consciousness raising are key ingredients in the critical theory practised by Adorno.
- Decisions about cultural value are still dependent on a minority - but in Adorno's case, Marxist intellectuals.

The Frankfurt contribution goes beyond the earlier debates insofar that:

- Through a synthesis of Marxism and Freudianism, the masses are not represented as a threat to civilization but 'barbarized' by the culture industry - as disempowered, manipulated and depoliticized victims.

*(Continued)*

*(Continued)*

- Authentic art is not there to be passed *down* to the masses in such a way that the masses are absorbed into a 'civilized' and civilizing tradition but to rouse them in such a way that they can challenge the system upon which the culture industry thrives.
- The Frankfurt School's discussion of culture is not beyond politics; in fact, it is, unlike the Leavisite approach, self-consciously political. The culture industry is politically corrupt because of the way it favours industrial capitalists and exploits, represses and impoverishes the lives of the proletariat.
- Adorno extends his criticism to condemn Enlightenment rationality: Enlightenment thinking, rather than realize humanitarian dreams, ultimately led to Nazi totalitarianism and the death camps.

## Oversimplification

**W A R N I N G**

If you read the sections concerning methodological relevance in the summaries of key points in this book, you might get the idea that I am arguing that the history of cultural criticism is a series of smooth transitions within a coherently evolving tradition of cultural analysis. *This simple conclusion should be avoided.*

Much contemporary cultural criticism has been very critical of the idea of history is an uncomplicated progression of events or states. The question of continuity is complex because while it is possible for writers to self-consciously refer to one another (the Leavises to Arnold, Adorno to Marx and Freud) the construction of history, lines of thought, movements etc., are also the result of choices, linked to ways of organizing and making sense of different phenomena. As Stuart Hall once wrote, in 'serious, critical intellectual work, there are no "absolute beginnings" and few unbroken continuities', cultural studies growing out of 'significant *breaks* – where old lines of thought are disrupted, older constellations displaced, and elements, old and new, are regrouped around a different set of premises and themes' (Stuart Hall [1980] in Munns and Rajan, 1995: 195). For further discussion of cultural studies and identity see chapter fourteen.

## References

Adorno, Theodor W. (1990) *Prisms*. Cambridge, MA: MIT.

Adorno, Theodor W. (1991) *The Culture Industry: Selected Essays on Mass Culture*. London: Routledge.

Adorno, Theordor W. and Horkheimer, Max ([1947] 1972) *The Dialectic of Enlightenment*. New York: Herder and Herder.

Cooke, Mervyn and Horn, David (eds) (2002) *The Cambridge Companion to Jazz*. Cambridge: Cambridge University Press.

Freud, Sigmund ([1917] 1973) *Introductory Lectures on Psychoanalysis*. Harmondsworth: Penguin.

Goldstein, Dan (ed.) (no date) *Rappers Rappin*. Chessington, Surrey: Castle Communications.

Hall, Stuart ([1980] 1995) 'Cultural studies: two paradigms', in J. Munns and G. Rajan *A Cultural Studies Reader: History, Theory, Practice*. London: Longman.

Haskins, James (2000) *The Story of Hip-Hop*. London: Penguin.

Marcuse, Herbert ([1964] 1986) *One-Dimensional Man: Studies in the Ideology of Advanced Industrial Society*. London: Ark.

Munns, Jessica and Rajan, Gita (eds) (1995) *A Cultural Studies Reader: History, Theory, Practice*. London: Longman.

Storey, John (ed.) (1998) *Cultural Theory and Popular Culture: A Reader* (2nd edition). Essex: Pearson Prentice Hall.

Tirro, Frank (1993) *Jazz: A History* (2nd edition). New York: Norton.

Townsend, Peter (2000) *Jazz in American Culture*. Edinburgh: Edinburgh University Press.

## Further reading

Brecht, Bertolt (1964) *Brecht on Theatre: The Development of an Aesthetic*. London: Methuen. A collection of notes and theoretical writings which illustrate how Brecht saw revolutionary potential (or the lack of it) in dramatic forms.

Benjamin, Walter (1973) *Illuminations*. London: Fontana. Unfortunately, I haven't been able to dedicate space to Benjamin's contribution but he deserves close reading. This book collects together a number of his key essays. Buck-Morss (1977, see below) provides a useful discussion of Benjamin's work.

Buck-Morss, Susan (1977) *The Origin of Negative Dialectics: Theodor W. Adorno, Walter Benjamin and the Frankfurt Institute*. London: Routledge. This book gives a solid outline of the Frankfurt School's approaches, putting particular emphasis on the work of Adorno and Benjamin.

Cahoone, Lawrence (1996) *From Modernism to Postmodernism: An Anthology*. Oxford: Blackwell. Given the difficulty of defining the Enlightenment, it would a good idea to read short passages from some writers associated with it. This anthology includes some very useful sections dedicated to seventeenth and eighteenth-century writers associated with the Age of Reason and the introduction to the first section offers a useful overview of Enlightenment issues. This collection also includes short excerpts by Jürgen Habermas and Fredric Jameson in which they argue that art can promote the revolutionary purposes of Marxism. It also contains excerpts by writers who challenged the ideals of the Enlightenment – see the sections dedicated to Jean-François Lyotard, Michel Foucault, Jacques Derrida and Habermas.

Freud, Sigmund (see references above). For a basic introduction to Freudian theory, including regression see Freud's 'Some Thoughts on Development and Regression Aetiology' which, despite the technical sounding title, is written in a fairly accessible style (Freud, [1917] 1973: 383f.).

Morley, David (1980) *The 'Nationwide' Audience*. London: BFI. I've adapted from Morley the idea of the Frankfurt School's model of mass media as 'hypodermic'. The opening sections of Morley's study make very useful reading given that they put this 'hypodermic' model into the context of the way audiences have been understood by critics interested in popular media like television.

Rose, Gillian (1978) *The Melancholy Silence: An Introduction to the thought of Theodor Adorno*. London: Macmillan. Another useful source to understand the history of the Frankfurt School and, in particular, Adorno's massive contribution.

Storey, John (2001) *Cultural Theory and Popular Culture: An Introduction* (3rd edition). Essex: Pearson Prentice Hall. Storey offers a comprehensible and broader overview of the Frankfurt School than the one I offer here.

If you want to follow up Rap styles of music with relation to commerce and innovation, you might begin with one of these titles (or Haskins see references above):

Neal, Mark Anthony and Foreman, Murray (eds) (2004) *That's the Joint: The Hip-Hop Studies Reader*. London: Routledge.

Perry, Imani (2005) *The Prophets of the Hood: Politics and Poetics in Hip Hop*. Durham, NC: Duke University Press.

Quinn, Eithne (2004) *Nuthin' But a 'G' Thang: The Culture and Commerce of Gangsta Rap*. New York: Columbia University Press.

# PART II

## The Transformative Power of Working-class Culture

# From a Day Out at the Seaside to the Milk Bar: Richard Hoggart and Working-class Culture

## Introduction

This is the first chapter of the second part of the book on 'The Transformative Power of Working-class Culture'. The writers introduced in the three chapters of this part contributed to cultural studies by placing great emphasis on the importance and meaning of working-class history, consciousness and ways of life.

Through a dialogue, this chapter will begin to look at the transformative power of the working classes. I will begin with a brief consideration of the importance of Richard Hoggart's contribution to cultural analysis, his working-class background and the historical context in which his work was written. Once these preliminary issues have been dealt with I shall outline how Hoggart's description of a day out at the seaside illustrates an implicit method that is capable of giving insights into the tastes, behaviour, language and common practices of a particular working-class community. I shall also indicate how Hoggart's way of describing the working class reflects approaches in the social sciences and show how, through his description of Teddy Boys, his positive notion of working-class culture breaks down with relation to contemporary mass popular culture. At the end of the chapter I will emphasize Hoggart's methodological relevance and the importance of working-class forms of cultural adaptation and resistance.

## *MAIN LEARNING GOALS*

- To appreciate the historical context in which Hoggart was writing and what relation his writing has to mass literacy.
- To see that Hoggart's approach to cultural analysis is not dominated by a view of culture as exemplary works but the culture of everyday life.
- To be conscious of how Hoggart's approach to cultural analysis is dependent on offering an 'insider view' of traditional working-class life, in such a way that it could be understood as rich, meaningful and valuable in itself.
- To understand *how* Hoggart went about understanding the working-class community in which he was brought up and how this might be practised as a method.
- To be aware of how Hoggart's distinction between pre-1930s working-class culture and contemporary mass culture affected how he valued different aspects of working-class taste and how his criticism both reflects and departs from the work of the Leavises and Adorno.
- To grasp the positive role of working-class adaptation and resistance.

This chapter will be mediated through the voices of Humphrey and Bogart (the relevance of my choice of names should become obvious about half way through the chapter). Humphrey has to write a piece on Richard Hoggart but doesn't know much about him. For that reason he visits an old friend of his, Bogart, who has agreed to introduce him to Hoggart's work. Their conversation takes place in a quiet bar in a working-class district somewhere in Leeds, England.

## The importance of Hoggart's contribution and his working-class background

HUMPHREY (after asking after his friend's health): Well, let's get down to business. To begin, can you give me an idea of Richard Hoggart's contribution to cultural studies?

BOGART: Well, Hoggart's life, for the purposes of his contribution to cultural studies, is usually reduced to two very important things:

1. The publication of his book, *The Uses of Literacy* (1957).
2. His role as founding director of the Birmingham Centre for Contemporary Cultural Studies (1964).

For the sake of convenience, I'll begin with the second point first. One of the institutional contexts which most helped to establish a distinctive cultural studies identity in Britain was the Birmingham Centre for Contemporary Cultural Studies (hereafter I'll refer to it as the 'Birmingham Centre'), and it was Hoggart who established himself as the Centre's founding director in 1964 (a post he was to retain until 1969).

HUMPHREY: What was so important about the Birmingham Centre?

BOGART: The Birmingham Centre provided an important institutional context in which scholars could be trained and in which something like a cultural studies group identity could evolve. It wasn't the only centre, though. However, I shan't go into more detail here as I believe the author who is responsible for our existence will mention the Birmingham Centre's work in later chapters.

HUMPHREY: So, tell me something about the importance of Hoggart's *The Uses of Literacy*.

BOGART: The publication of *The Uses of Literacy* in 1957 helped to establish Hoggart as a major voice in discussions of the media and popular culture. Let's begin by considering something which is often missed out of introductions to Hoggart's work: what is the significance of the title? The answer has a lot to do with the general historical context of Britain as an industrial nation and **the extension of obligatory education in Britain**.

## **help**FILE: historical context

By 1870 (the date of the Forster Education Act) many in the political and business world believed that Britain's prosperity was partly dependent on an educated working class. From that date a whole series of reforms gradually attempted to expand compulsory education. With greater literacy, came the possibility to exploit this ever-growing reading public (which had been growing steadily before this with relation to the middle classes). By the time Hoggart came to write *The Uses of Literacy* large numbers of the industrial working classes were able to read and it was possible to talk about common tastes in working-class reading. In fact, Hoggart provided a useful summary of working-class reading habits in his last chapter ([1957] 1958: 318f.). If you think back to chapter two you may remember that Queenie Leavis was also interested in the reading habits of the middle and working classes, entitling one of her books *Fiction and the Reading Public* (1932). The next chapter on E.P. Thompson will also give you an idea of the importance of working-class reading habits – in this case the interest shown in radical political works.

BOGART: (waiting patiently for the reader to finish the help file) Hoggart was interested in *how* mass literacy impacted on the lives of working people: that is, how people used this ability and whether it was being used for positive or negative ends. In short, the task he set himself was to study how the 'appeals of the mass publications connect with commonly accepted attitudes, how they are altering those attitudes, and how they are meeting resistance' (Hoggart, [1957] 1958: 19). However, as you'll see, his book actually goes beyond the uses of literacy to consider many other aspects of working-class culture, including the fact that the working classes, despite the mass media, still drew on oral and local tradition.

HUMPHREY: So what did Hoggart actually *do* in this book?

BOGART: I would argue that the first important thing he does in *The Uses of Literacy* is to reflect on how the working classes may be defined. He argued that to be working class included having a sense of group identity, sharing certain kinds of tastes, interests and common ways of speaking (e.g. urban accent, phraseology, dialect etc.), wearing similar kinds of clothes, receiving an education in working-class schools, doing similar kinds of work, and paying for things in small instalments. However, the 'working class' is not a water tight concept because there could be some overlap between the richer working families and the lower middle-classes. Hoggart was also aware that different working-class groups often distinguished themselves from others (who could be 'posh' or 'rough' etc.). This makes defining the working classes rather more difficult than it might seem.

HUMPHREY: Interesting ... but the book must be enormous! Is it an entire history of the working class?

BOGART: Not at all! Hoggart limited his observations to his experiences of the urban North of Britain – especially the Leeds of his childhood. He concentrated on the working-class culture of the 1920s and 1930s and compared it with the contemporary mass culture of the 1950s. Hoggart intentionally limited his book excluding references to 'the purposive, the political, the pious, and the self-improving' not because he didn't appreciate them but because 'the appeals made by the mass publicists are not primarily to their kind of minds' (23). This means that his observations on, and definitions of, the working class were governed by a very specific context: his sense of historical continuity and change with relation to patterns of consumption. He expressed one of the main arguments of his book in the following way (here, handing Humphrey a copy of *The Uses of Literacy*), take a look at this quotation:

> [...] the appeals made by the mass publicists are for a great number of reasons made more insistently, effectively, and in a more comprehensive and centralized form today than they were earlier; that we are moving towards the creation of a mass culture; that the remnants of what was at least in parts an urban culture 'of the people' are being destroyed; and that the new mass culture is in some important ways less healthy than the often crude culture it is replacing. (24)

## A day at the seaside: making working-class life meaningful A view from the inside

HUMPHREY: But what special qualifications did Hoggart have to give his readers insights into working-class culture? I mean, the Leavises described it but very much as outsiders.

BOGART: In this context I'd want to emphasize that Hoggart was brought up in a working-class family in Leeds, so was able to give an 'insider view' of working-class urban life, consciousness, culture and experience. In *The Uses of Literacy*, he offered detailed descriptions, and discussed the meanings of, everyday events – everything from going to Working Men's Clubs to a day out at the seaside. This emphasis on personal experience would not be relevant were it not for the fact that it gave readers of *The Uses of Literacy* the possibility to assess what a view of working-class life actually *meant* to a particular community. An often-quoted example is the following description of a day out to the seaside, which, in its fine attention to detail, gives an idea of quite how well Hoggart observed and understood the class he was representing:

> [...] the 'charas' go rolling out across the moors for the sea, past the road-houses which turn up their noses at coach-parties, to one the driver knows where there is coffee and biscuits or perhaps a full egg-and-bacon breakfast. Then on to a substantial lunch on arrival, and after that a fanning-out in groups. But rarely far from one another, because they know their part of the town and their bit of beach, where they feel at home. [...] They have a nice walk past the shops; perhaps a drink; a sit in a deck-chair eating an ice-cream or sucking mint humbugs; a great deal of loud laughter – at Mrs Johnson insisting on a paddle with her dress tucked in her bloomers, at Mrs Henderson pretending she has 'got off' with the deck-chair attendant, or in the queue at the ladies' lavatory. Then there is the buying of presents for the family, a big meat-tea, and the journey home with a stop for drinks on the way. If the men are there, and certainly if it is a men's outing, there will probably be several stops and a crate or two of beer in the back for drinking on the move. Somewhere in the middle of the moors the men's parties all tumble out, with much horseplay and noisy jokes about bladder capacity. The driver knows exactly what is expected of him as he steers his warm, fuggy, and singing community back to the town; for his part he gets a very large tip, collected during the run through the last few miles of the town streets. (147–8)

## **help** FILE: a few tips on Hoggart's use of words

It is important to take into account that Hoggart is writing about a particular working-class community in Leeds in England between the two World Wars. Because his way of writing reflects both the period and the community, some of the words may not be familiar to you (especially if English isn't your first language or you weren't born in Britain). Here are some definitions you may find useful:

'**Charas**' is short for charabanc, an old word for a motorized carriage, now a bus or coach

**Road-houses**: pubs or inns on a major road where travellers could stop to rest and have something to eat and drink

**Bloomers**: women's long (almost knee-length), loose-fitting knickers: the subject of much British seaside humour.

Figure 4.1 A day at the seaside

HUMPHREY: Now I think I can see part of his relevance to cultural criticism. Here is a work, then, written *about* the working classes by a man *from* the working classes who could draw on valuable personal knowledge to challenge the rather more simplistic versions of working class culture offered by Leavis and the *Scrutiny* circle.

BOGART: Exactly! As Graeme Turner has stated, Hoggart's personal experience gives an air of 'authenticity' to his depiction of working-class life (Turner, 1996: 44). Ah, I hear a voice! It is some advice to the reader! It says: 'As a preparation to a discussion of how Hoggart's approach relates to method, you are advised to do the following practice exercise'.

## **practice** EXERCISE 1: A day at the seaside

Look at the long quotation above and consider the following questions:

- What indications are there in this passage that suggest Hoggart understood how this small community functioned as a group?
- How does the passage give insights into forms of behaviour, language and common practices?
- How would you describe Hoggart's tone here? For example, what mood does he evoke? Here are some terms you might consider:

  distant, intimate, sympathetic, critical, humorous, suspicious, judgemental, understanding, fault-finding, tolerant

- If we follow Graeme Turner in seeing the passage as having an air of 'authenticity', what features might suggest that it is an accurate, trustworthy and faithful portrait?

As a backup exercise you might consider the following questions:

- Do you consider yourself as a member of a particular class?
- If you do, try to outline the kinds of attitudes, values, customs, language and tastes that seem to you to typify the class.
- If you do not, or you can't decide, try to explain why.

## **notes** ON PRACTICE: Hoggart's method and the importance of *The Uses of Literacy*

AUTHOR: How did you two get in here?

HUMPHREY: I don't know, but now we're here we might as well carry on. But tell me, Bogart, does Hoggart discuss the method he adopts?

BOGART: The answer is no, Hoggart doesn't focus directly on it. However, if you've thought over the last practice exercise I think you may have noticed that Hoggart is able to enter into the more intimate details of the day out. Hoggart doesn't only know about what *happened* but he gives indications that he knows:

- what the typical rituals are of a sea-side trip (he knows about a particular working-class way of life)
- how the travellers are perceived by others (he is aware of attitudes towards the working class)
- what kinds of things are likely to be enjoyed and what will raise a smile (he shows knowledge of working-class tastes and its sense of humour)
- how the community expresses itself linguistically (he is familiar with working-class forms of speech)

HUMPHREY: (sounding slightly smug) And yet one should admit that Hoggart's view is only one way of looking – I mean he was an educated male and could hardly speak for everyone in the community ...

BOGART: True! But it is in providing these detailed forms of understanding that Hoggart is able to give a portrait of a particular working-class community that has this 'air of authenticity'. Here I have only quoted one passage but one of the things that makes *The Uses of Literacy* so relevant to changing ways of perceiving and understanding popular culture and working-class life is that Hoggart offered a very broad depiction of the community he knew so well. We might say that just as the Leavises applied the methods of close reading to mass culture, Hoggart offered close readings of popular music, newspapers, magazines and fiction, *but without necessarily condemning them in the process*. In fact, working-class life could be 'a full rich life' (as the title of one of his chapters announced).

HUMPHREY: Is this, then, his most significant achievement?

BOGART: I would say it is one of them; however, Graeme Turner sees Hoggart's most significant achievement in that he was able to demonstrate:

- how various aspects of public culture were interconnected. That is, the reader can see how pubs, working-men's clubs, magazines and an interest in sports contributed to a way of life
- and how these aspects related to the structures of an individual's private, everyday life expressed in family roles, gender relations, language patterns, and the community's understanding of 'common sense'.

In short, 'Hoggart describes working-class life in the prewar period as a complex whole, in which public values and private practices are tightly interwined' (Turner, 1996: 44).

HUMPHREY: And one might add that Hoggart offered a less restricted conception of culture.

BOGART: Yes, that's one of the ways Andrew Tudor described the significance of Hoggart's work (Tudor, 1999: 41). All these observations tend to be borne out even if readers only concentrate on Hoggart's final chapter, which gives insights into things like the ways working-class life is organized, attitudes, education, leisure, reading habits and change – all considered with relation to increasing literacy.

### A dialogue with the social sciences

Hoggart's way of understanding working-class life is reminiscent of approaches associated with the social sciences like Anthropology and Ethnography.

### Anthropology

We saw, when reviewing T.S. Eliot, that fundamental to an anthroprological approach was to view culture as 'that complex whole which includes knowledge, belief, art, morals, law, custom, and any other capabilities and habits acquired by man as a member of society' (Tylor, [1871] 1958: 1). It is possible to see Hoggart as seeing the working-class community he describes in terms of a complex whole; however, while Hoggart's study goes some way towards this way of thinking, he does not claim to be using the intellectual tools of Anthropology. See chapter six on Raymond Williams for more discussion of culture as a complex whole.

### Ethnography

Another way Hoggart borders on approaches associated with the social sciences is that it resembles, to some extent, ethnographic techniques. Put very crudely, ethnography is associated with the scientific description and understanding of races and cultures. In this sense, Hoggart's work doesn't count as Ethnography insofar as he doesn't make any claims to be practising it and made no claims about being scientific. However, again, what he *did* does relate to ethnographic technique. One of the techniques that researchers within Ethnography have at their disposal is participant observation where researchers mix with a community and try to win its trust in order to give an 'insider view'. Hoggart, in effect, practised a form of participant observation only he was *already* a member of the community he chose to represent, which gives him a great advantage over academics trying to integrate themselves into a community.

Clifford Geertz (1973: 19f.) explains that the ethnographer 'inscribes' social discourse (s/he writes it down) and turns it into an account and thereby 'rescues' it for interpretation. I would argue that this is precisely what Hoggart did. From the ethno-methodological perspective associated with the work of Harold Garfinkel (1967), Hoggart probed the kind of everyday knowledge that is usually taken for granted within a community and reflected the social practices which constantly reaffirm collective life. Hoggart, then, without claiming to be a social scientist, is relevant to some sociological approaches to the understanding of groups in society. For a brief overview of ethnomethodology see Jenks (1993: 126).

## Hoggart and 1950s mass entertainment

HUMPHREY: So Hoggart was really quite exemplary in his definition of working-class life and culture? He seems to have taken cultural analysis considerably further than Adorno and the Leavises.

BOGART: Yes, but his book still shared much in common with the way those earlier critics understood and valued mass culture. You may remember how F.R. Leavis and Denys Thompson divided the culture of the 'common people' into two types: (1) traditional organic and (2) mass (consumer) culture – valuing the one and disapproving of the other. Hoggart also divides working-class culture into two categories:

1. the older (pre-1930s) working-class culture of his youth
2. and the Americanized mass entertainment of the 1950s.

To explore this distinction let's focus attention on Hoggart's attitudes towards a certain kind of 1950s youth culture. To begin with, let's have a look at the way Hoggart described the 1950s phenomenon of the milk-bars. Here (handing *The Uses of Literacy* to Humphrey), this is what I consider to be a key passage (Humphrey takes it and reads the following):

Like the cafés I described in an earlier chapter, the milk-bars indicate at once, in the nastiness of their modernistic knick-knacks, their glaring showiness, an aesthetic breakdown so complete that, in comparison with them, the layout of the living rooms in some of the poor homes from which the customers come seems to speak of a tradition as balanced and civilized as an eighteenth century townhouse [...] the 'nickelodeon' is allowed to blare out so that the noise would be sufficient to fill a good-sized ballroom, rather than a converted shop in the main street. The young men waggle one shoulder or stare, as desperately at Humphrey Bogart, across tubular chairs.

Compared even with the pub around the corner, this is all a peculiarly thin and pallid form of dissipation, a sort of spiritual dry-rot amid the odour of boiled milk. (Hoggart, [1957] 1958: 247–8)

BOGART: (continuing) Hoggart is referring here to the Teddy Boy culture that was taking hold in Britain. He notes that 'boys between fifteen and twenty' wear drape suits (the Teddy Boy fashion) and slouch – a kind of lazy or stooping walk he associated with Hollywood films. Hoggart speculates that most of these youths are of inferior intelligence and therefore more vulnerable to 'the debilitating mass trends of the day' (248–9). While they aren't typical of the working class, he fears they are a portent of the future.

## **help**FILE: a few more tips on Hoggart's use of words

**Milk-bar**: the meaning is clear from the context but the milk-bar is important historically because during the 1950s young men and women in Britain had to be 18 to be able to drink alcohol (legally). This meant that the under 18s, if they wanted to explore the new rock'n'roll culture in bar-like places, had to resort to places like the milk-bars

**Knick-knacks**: showy, vulgar objects used for ornamentation rather than practical use

'**Nickelodeon**': an old word for a juke box – a slot machine with a series of buttons which could be used to select and play records

The **Teddy Boys** were named this way because they adopted a particular style of dress associated with the Edwardian period (referring to the reign of Edward VII of Great Britain (1901–1910)). As you can see from the rock 'n' roll singers and bands of the 1950s, this style included wearing close-fitting jackets, pointed shoes ('winkle pickers'), bootlace ties and what became known as 'drain-pipe trousers'. As a short form of Edward is 'Ted', this was adapted to create the term Teddy Boys (later known as 'Teds')

HUMPHREY: (cupping his hand to his ear) Hark! I hear our author's voice calling for another practice exercise...

## **practice** EXERCISE 2: Rockin' in the milk-bar

Referring to the above quotation, answer the following questions, which are related to the ones we used for the day at the seaside quotation. (In the following notes on practice I offer some possible responses but try to answer the questions for yourself first.)

- What indications are there that Hoggart understood how the Teddy Boys functioned as a group?
- Does the passage give insights into forms of behaviour, language and common practices?
- How would you describe Hoggart's tone here? To answer this you might look at Hoggart's choice of adjectives and descriptive phrases. Given these choices, what mood does he evoke? Here are some terms you might consider: distant, intimate, sympathetic, critical, humorous, suspicious, judgemental, understanding, fault-finding, tolerant

## **notes** ON PRACTICE: dealing with the questions

- If you agree with me, I think you'll find that Hoggart's view positions him very much as an outsider. Instead of giving the effect of being involved in 'participant observation' he seems far removed from the group he is describing and makes no effort to see things from the Teddy Boys' perspective.
- He tries to give insights into forms of behaviour but seems alienated from what he describes.
- This is reinforced by his choice of language. The milk-bars are dominated by 'nastiness', 'knick-knacks' and 'glaring showiness'. Music 'blares out' and Hoggart reads what he sees around him as 'desperately thin' and 'pallid' and a symbol of 'spiritual dry rot'. Even the boiled milk seems unattractive with its 'odour'.
- The tone he adopts, rather than being intimate, sympathetic, tolerant and understanding (as in the day at the seaside passage), is distant, narrow minded and judgemental.

## Hoggart and the shoulder waggling barbarians

HUMPHREY: So, from a contemporary point of view, while Hoggart is significant, he had his shortcomings?

BOGART: Yes, but we all have our defects! But you are right and Hoggart's chapter titles are very revealing in terms of the way he read contemporary mass culture. As mentioned earlier, to pre-1930s working-class culture Hoggart gives the title 'The Full Rich Life'; to 1950s youth culture he offers titles like 'Invitations to a Candy-Floss World' and 'Sex in Shiny Packets'. It could be argued that Hoggart was more able, and wrote with much more subtlety, when describing the complexity and functions of working-class culture prior to the 1930s. However, his alienation, scepticism and what seems like a certain fear of contemporary (mass) 1950s youth culture leads him to reject it rather than try to understand its complexities.

HUMPHREY: Yes, he seems to tar all the Teddy Boys with the same brush – they are all seduced by the clichéd screen persona of Humphry Bogart and reduced to a band of unthinking shoulder wagglers! I can see that Hoggart's representation of mass youth culture allies him to some extent with the Leavisites and the work of some of the Frankfurt School writers like Adorno and Horkheimer.

BOGART: Yes, there are a number of useful comparisons we might make here. Hoggart, like Adorno and the Leavises, lamented the products of the culture industry and saw the consumer of contemporary mass culture as 'hedonistic but passive' (Hoggart, [1957] 1958: 250).

HUMPHREY: From what you've said I'd say that if the Leavises would have the consumers of mass culture return to a culture rooted in pre-industrial society, Hoggart would have them hold on to traditional working-class culture. That is, before they became corrupted by things like Hollywood films, rock 'n' roll and radio soaps!

Figure 4.2 Hoggart and the post-1930s working-class culture

BOGART: That's right. For Hoggart, the 'barbarians in wonderland' (193) were transforming working-class life into a form of empty hedonism where having 'a good time' is valued above all else.

AUTHOR: I'm sorry, gentlemen, but I'd like you to move on to a discussion of working-class resistance because I plan to revise and compare some of these ideas in chapter seven.

## Hoggart and working-class resistance

HUMPHREY: Hold on a moment, I'm a bit confused. Didn't Hoggart claim that the new breed of barbarian is 'hedonistic but passive'? Now our author is talking about resistance!

BOGART: Well, to understand this it's important to recognize that Hoggart thought of passivity with relation to the newer mass entertainments – when he talked about resistance he was referring to more traditional working-class ways of thinking and behaving. He rejected the idea of seeing the more traditional working classes as mere passive victims of mass popular culture. However, I would argue that there is a certain ambiguity in Hoggart's *The Uses of Literacy*, which tended to reflect both his allegiance to and fear for the working classes. On the one hand, he felt that competitive commerce would represent a real threat to traditional working-class culture (he indicates the following passage to Humphrey, who still has the book in his hand):

> Inhibited now from ensuring the 'degradation' of the masses economically [...] competitive commerce [...] becomes a new and stronger form of subjection; this subjection promises to be stronger than the old because the chains of cultural subordination are both easier to wear and harder to strike away than those of economic subordination. (243–4)

On the other hand, Hoggart never quite let go of the idea of **active resistance**, insisting that many people in the working-class community interpreted popular songs in their own way and adapted them to their own tastes, actually *improving* them in the process. This means that the working classes are 'less affected than the extent of their purchases would seem to indicate' (231). In fact, early on in *The Uses of Literacy* Hoggart asserted that working-class resistance, though not articulated, is positive rather than passive and that the working-classes 'have a strong natural ability to survive change by adapting or assimilating what they want in the new and ignoring the rest' (32). However, as Storey states, Hoggart failed to go into much detail on the question of *how* the working classes make forms of culture their own (2001: 40).

HUMPHREY: Hmmm, odd how those who inhabited the milk-bars seemed to have lost this vital spirit of resistance!

BOGART: Quite! But I have a feeling that our author will be taking up these questions in the following chapters.

## **practice** EXERCISE 3: reading with resistance

Before reading the summary of Hoggart's contribution you might try the following exercise:
Go back to the previous chapter on Adorno's critique of jazz and my 'Adornoesque' critique of hip-hop and reread them. You might reflect on the following points:

- How Adorno's critique might be revised with relation to the idea of active working-class resistance (my Rappin' on Jazz – Perennial Fashion should give you some ideas to start with).
- Having completed this first exercise, which is designed to help you appreciate the value of Hoggart's ideas, you might think about how Hoggart would have responded to jazz or hip-hop. Would *he*, given what you've read so far, have appreciated the possible points of resistance in these musical styles?
- There are a number of differences that distinguish Hoggart's approach from that of Adorno – some things are added, some lost. Look at the summary of key points sections and evaluate the different approaches making clear where you feel Hoggart could have learnt from the writers of the Frankfurt School, and vice versa.
- John Storey has written that the 'real weakness' of *The Uses of Literacy* 'is its inability to carry forward the insights from its treatment of the popular culture of the 1930s into its treatment of the so-called mass culture of the 1950s' (Storey, 2001: 40). How well do you feel this sums up both the strengths and weaknesses of Hoggart's book?

## *SUMMARY OF KEY POINTS*

This chapter started out by emphasizing Hoggart's role in helping to establish a tradition of cultural analysis in Britain and the historical context in which *The Uses of Literacy* was written. Hoggart's description of a day at the seaside has been used to show how he gives an informed, 'insider view' of the working classes. The chapter has also reviewed Hoggart's negative attitude towards post-1930s mass culture and discussed the importance of active resistance within working-class communities. Although Hoggart did not reflect directly on method, his methodological relevance can be summed up as follows:

- He linked cultural forms to historical change and mass industrial culture.
- He argued that working-class life was 'a full rich life' and that the traditional working classes take an active role in making, choosing and adapting culture.
- These ideas concerning the importance and value of working-class life distance him from the general assumptions behind Adorno's critique the Culture and Civilization approach.

- However, in so far that he argues that newer mass entertainments are numbing, Hoggart's approach resembles the work of the Leavises and Adorno.
- His rejection of the idea that the working classes were passive victims of mass culture helped to challenge earlier views and introduce the idea of active resistance.
- Hoggart defined the working classes from the inside and gave insights into how a working-class community functioned as a group (in terms of behaviour, language use, taste, humour, common practices etc.) and explained what these factors *meant* to the working-class community.
- From the point of view of the social sciences, Hoggart's work is uneven: when discussing pre-1930s working-class culture he seems to act as a privileged participant observer, when discussing 1950s mass entertainment he has a rather more narrow-minded and distanced view.
- Finally, as Storey has indicated, what makes Hoggart's approach different from that of Leavisism 'is his detailed preoccupation with, and, above all, his clear commitment to, working-class culture' (Storey, 2001:43). This point is enormously important to the way cultural analysis has been broadened within cultural studies and it provides a convenient bridge between the work of Hoggart and E.P. Thompson - the subject of the next chapter.

## References

Garfinkel, Harold (1967) *Studies in Ethnomethodology*. Englewood Cliffs, NJ: Prentice Hall.

Geertz, Clifford (1973) *The Interpretation of Cultures*. New York: Basic Books.

Hoggart, Richard ([1957] 1958) *The Uses of Literacy*. Harmondsworth: Penguin.

Jenks, Chris (1993) *Culture: Key Ideas*. London: Routledge.

Leavis, Q.D. ([1932] 1974) *Fiction and the Reading Public*. New York: Folcroft.

Storey, John (2001) *Cultural Theory and Popular Culture: An Introduction* (3rd edition). Essex: Pearson Prentice Hall.

Tudor, Andrew (1999) *Decoding Culture: Theory and Method in Cultural Studies*. London: Sage.

Turner, Graeme (1996) *British Cultural Studies: An Introduction* (2nd edition). London: Routledge.

Tylor, Edward Burnett ([1871] 1958) *Primitive Culture: Researches into the Development of Mythology, Philosophy, Religion, Art and Custom*. Gloucester, MA: Smith.

## Further reading

Corner, John et al. (eds) (1991) 'Studying culture: reflections and assessments. An interview with Richard Hoggart'. *Media, Culture and Society*, 13. A very useful and accessible dialogue which should help to clarify Hoggart's ideas.

Easthope, Anthony (1991) *Literary into Cultural Studies*. London: Routledge. When describing a day out at the seaside, Hoggart mentions how Mrs Johnson caused loud laughter by tucking her dress into her bloomers. This coincides with much typical British seaside humour. Easthope's book offers some interesting insights into bawdy British humour with relation to seaside postcards.

Hartley, John (ed) (2007) 'Special Issue: The uses of Richard Hoggart'. *International Journal of Cultural Studies* 10.1. This special issue is devoted to discussing Hoggart's contribution and influence on contemporary cultural studies. This is a very useful retrospection.

Hoggart, Richard (1970) *Speaking to Each Other (volume 1): About Society*. London: Chatto and Windus. This is a collection of essays which will give you further insights into Hoggart's way of understanding society.

Hoggart, Richard (1995) *The Way We Live Now*. London: Chatto and Windus. If you get really interested in Hoggart you might compare these reflections with his earlier observations and analyses in *The Uses of Literacy*.

Strinati, Dominic (1995) *An Introduction to Theories of Popular Culture*. London: Routledge. Another concise overview which puts Hoggart's work into the contexts of debates on mass culture and growing fears about the Americanization of culture (27f.).

Turner, Graeme (1996, see references above). Turner offers a very concise and useful overview of Hoggart's work and influence and gives a sense of how Hoggart fits into a developing tradition of British cultural studies. He also dedicates a little space to the impact *The Uses of Literacy* has had on British culture (47).

# E.P. Thompson and Working-class Culture as a Site of Conflict, Consciousness and Resistance 5

## Introduction

This is the second chapter on 'The Transformative Power of Working-class Culture'. By way of a series of dialogues, it will introduce you to the historian E.P. Thompson's *The Making of the English Working Class*. I will begin by discussing Thompson's general aims, the particular way he chose to define the working class and how his Marxist background influenced his approach. I will then look at how Thompson traced the formation of working-class consciousness. This will involve looking at the role of religion, the state of eighteenth-century politics, the history of popular revolts, and radical politics. The idea is to show, through description and practice exercises, how these contexts, added to forms of repression, helped to polarize British society in such a way that by the beginning of the nineteenth century it was possible to talk about the existence of a working class.

An eye will be kept on *how* Thompson constructs his history and readers will be encouraged to be aware of Thompson's methodological significance and his engaged attitude towards the history he tells. The chapter will be concluded with a discussion of how Thompson's method relates to what is known as 'culturalism'.

## MAIN LEARNING GOALS

- To understand what Thompson understood by the 'making' of the working class.
- To appreciate how Thompson offered a vision of the working class that put this class at the centre of historical change, rather than on the periphery.
- To see how Thompson helped cultural historians to focus on the culture of political radicalism and consciousness as key ways of defining the working class.
- To become aware of how the working class can be understood as an active agent of change.
- To recognize *how* Thompson went about the writing of history.
- To see how Thompson fits into the approach known as 'culturalism'.

## Preliminaries: the working class and filling historical gaps

To introduce you to E.P. Thompson's work we'll be listening to a dialogue between two people. By some strange coincidence they happen to be named E.P. and Thompson. E.P. is a young man who is studying cultural studies and beginning to take an interest in politics but doesn't know much about working-class history (although he fancies himself as a bit of a radical). He's recently been alerted to the work of E.P. Thompson and decides to arrange a meeting with a studious friend who is a teacher, and whose name happens to be Thompson, and who, coincidentally, is writing a book about E.P. Thompson. They meet on a sunny day in London's Highgate Cemetery (they stroll about near where Karl Marx is buried).

E.P.: So, who was this Thompson guy – and can you explain his relevance to cultural studies?

THOMPSON: (a little shocked at E.P.'s tone) A tall order! But I'll answer the first part of your question here and the second part as we go along. Thompson was one of the most important marxist historians of his generation and, although he is usually mentioned in introductions to cultural studies, it is worth noting that he saw himself as a historian.

E.P.: So, what should I read to get an idea of his work?

THOMPSON: Although a prolific writer, the study that has made the biggest impact on cultural studies is his *The Making of the English Working Class* (1963) ...

E.P.: (interrupting) OK, so what did Thompson try to achieve with this book?

THOMPSON: Well, in brief terms, the answer is that he attempted to trace **the formation of the working class between the years 1780 and 1832**.

E.P.: Why is that such a big deal?

THOMPSON: (ignoring his choice of language) One reason why Thompson's study has become fundamental to the development of cultural studies is because he tried to **explore the common interests, experiences, preoccupations and struggles of the working classes**.

E.P.: (softening up a little) Hmm, sounds interesting ... OK, another question: I've read a little Richard Hoggart, how did Thompson's book go beyond the kinds of questions that Hoggart set himself to answer?

THOMPSON: If you've read *The Uses of Literacy* you'll know that Hoggart intentionally limited his study by excluding 'the purposive, the political, the pious, and the self-improving' ([1957] 1958: 23). If this is seen as a gap (not necessarily a weakness) in his work, then one way of looking at E.P. Thompson's contribution is to see it as a way of filling this gap.

## The working class in the 'making' and the making of working people into a class

THOMPSON: (continuing the last point) As you may know, one thing that Hoggart did was to offer a **definition of the working class**. Well, Thompson in *The Making of the English Working Class* addresses the same question, but we'll see that his answer to the question, while related to Hoggart's, goes beyond it.

E.P.: In what way?

THOMPSON: Let me answer this by saying that Thompson begins his book by explaining that the working class is the product of **active struggle**. He says that his book has a clumsy title but that it serves its purpose because the idea of the **making of the working class** means that 'it is a study in an active process, which owes as much to agency as to conditioning'. The working class, he goes on to say, 'did not rise like the sun at an appointed time. It was present at its own making' (Thompson [1963] 1968: 8).

E.P.: Yea, I like that – but why does he use the term 'working class' rather than 'working classes'?

THOMPSON: A good question. Of course, he realized that the working class is really a collection of many different kinds of worker from the simple labourer to skilled artisan. However, Thompson deliberately used the term 'working class' in order to affirm the uniqueness of individuals united by **common experiences and struggles** in such a way that they unite behind a common identity in conflict with other groups opposed to their own. Describing the working class being 'present at its own making' is to see it as a collectivity: it's an **active agent**. Instead of being understood as a class lost in a history made, principally, by kings, queens, important politicians and military leaders etc. (other classes), it's a historical force in itself.

E.P.: Now, *that* I really do like!

THOMPSON: Very simply put, if we were to pose a question about what it was that Thompson was *doing* in *The Making of the English Working Class* the answer would be *practising a kind of deliverance*. As he outlines in his preface, he was seeking to rescue members of the working class, especially radicals, from 'the enormous condescension of history' (12). This rescue operation introduces a note of **political radicalism** informed by Thompson's Marxist background and training, situating the working class with relation to **growing political consciousness**. There are a number of factors here which I feel are worth emphasizing for what they suggest in terms of methodology and practice. To explore these let's start with a point Thompson made on page four of his book. Well, look, I just happen to have the idea written down with a little cartoon a friend of mine sketched for me. It's for a book I'm planning (with a flourish, he shows it to E.P.):

Figure 5.1 Class as a relation

THOMPSON: (continuing) Look at the drawing. If we see each person as a representation of a class you can get an idea of how Thompson understands class: it is a *relation*. From the point of view of method, this means that it doesn't make much sense to isolate one class without showing how its existence is dependent on, and in conflict with, other classes.

E.P.: Am I right in thinking that this means that classes can't exist in isolation?

THOMPSON: Precisely. Thompson expressed it like this (I just happen to have committed the point to memory, word for word):

> And class happens when some men, as a result of common experiences (inherited or shared), feel and articulate the identity of their interests as between themselves, and as against other men whose interests are different from (and usually opposed to) theirs. (8)

THOMPSON: (continuing) In short, Thompson understood class as (and I quote from memory) 'a historical phenomenon, unifying a number of disparate and seemingly unconnected events, both in the raw material of experience and in consciousness' (8). And this, my dear E.P., means that *we cannot expect history to be a convenient and seamless narrative*.

## Oversimplification

**W A R N I N G !**

If you look back at one of my oversimplification warnings (in chapter three on Adorno) I stated that much contemporary cultural criticism has been very critical of representations that suggest that any kind of history is an uncomplicated progression of events or states. Thompson, in *The Making of the English Working Class*, gives a practical example of how a reconstruction of working-class history is dependent on following up forms of radicalism which flared up and died (or achieved different levels of intensity) at different moments. This means that we cannot necessarily expect history to resemble a constantly flowing river.

E.P.: (adds, with a smirk on his face) This, no doubt, is an important factor in terms of method? **Class has to be seen historically, it cannot be understood by stopping it dead and anatomizin it without recognizing its processes of development.**

THOMPSON: (looking at E.P. in disbelief and disappointment) Why, yes! You took the words right out of my mouth! This is precisely one of Thompson's points.

E.P.: (looking pleased with himself and about to get up to go) Good, so is that it then?

THOMPSON: By no means – there's much, much more! Listen, E.P., and I will pluck, from my prodigious memory, a quotation which will help to clarify Thompson's ideas and demonstrate how his approach is related to Marxism. (He looks at Marx's tomb and declaims in actorly fashion):

> The class experience is largely determined by the productive relations into which men are born – or enter involuntarily. Class-consciousness is the way in which these experiences are handled in cultural terms: embodied in traditions, value-systems, ideas, and institutional forms. (8)

THOMPSON: (continues) This means, that **class is something connected to common experience and consciousness and this is identified with the dominant relations of production**.

E.P.: (trying to anticipate what Thompson is going to say) And all this demonstrates Thompson's affiliation to Marxist forms of analysis in which the material relations of production (who governs, who exploits, who is governed and who is exploited in this arrangement) are seen as fundamental to an understanding of history and culture?

THOMPSON: (with a look of disappointment) Er, yes (brightening up) but I am now going to impress you with another quotation I've committed to memory (from page 11 of Thompson's book) which will give an idea of the historical scope of Thompson's

Figure 5.2 Thompson gives E.P. the benefit of his prodigious memory

study. It will also illustrate the importance of how an understanding of class relations are intimately bound up with **history as a form of antagonism**; another important ingredient of the Marxist conception of history:

> For I am convinced that we cannot understand class unless we see it as a social and cultural formation, arising from processes which can only be studied as they work themselves out over a considerable historical period. In the years between 1780 and 1832 most English working people came to feel an identity of interests as between themselves, and as against their rulers and employers.

THOMPSON: (refusing to let E.P. speak) As Thompson insisted, this ruling class 'was itself much divided, and in fact only gained in cohesion over the same years because certain antagonisms were resolved (or faded into relative insignificance) in the face of an insurgent working class' (11). And this leads me to an observation that is not always brought out in introductions to Thompson's contribution. What Thompson is arguing here is that the ruling capitalist class was not anything like a homogeneous group prior to the emergence of the working class. This kind of thinking helps us to realize that *all* classes are complex formations that come about through conflicts of interests rather than simple entities that somehow exist in a historical vacuum.

**help**FILE:

For more on class as a complex formation see chapter ten on Antonio Gramsci.

## Thompson and the working class as a 'revolting' class

THOMPSON: Thompson argued, then, that a working class *and* a ruling coalition were emergent between 1780 and 1832.

E.P.: OK, so what enabled Thompson to arrive at these conclusions?

THOMPSON: The answer is that Thompson observed historical change in such a way that he could detect patterns in relationships, ideas, and institutions which would indicate the formation of a working class. This took the shape of – to offer only the briefest summary:

- recounting the popular revolts which influenced the English Jacobin agitation at the end of the eighteenth century (Part One of his book)

- describing the particular experiences of workers during the Industrial Revolution and giving 'an estimate of the character of the new industrial work-discipline, and the bearing of this on the Methodist Church' (11) (Part Two)
- and narrating the story of plebeian radicalism (like Luddism) with relation to working-class consciousness and political theory (Part Three).

E.P.: What's Jacobin agitation, Methodism and Luddism?!

THOMPSON: Well, I just happen to have some information written down for my new book (he hands E.P. a page from it which makes up the following help file).

## **help**FILE: Jacobin agitation, Methodism and Luddism

**English Jacobin agitation**: the name 'Jacobin' was given to political radicals or revolutionaries who demanded and worked for political reforms, often inspired by the Jacobins of the French Revolution. The historical origin of the term 'Jacobin' goes back to the members of a radical democratic club established in Paris (in 1789, the year of the storming of the Bastille). The reason why they were called Jacobins is that the club was established in an old convent of the Jacobins, who were Dominican friars.

**The Methodist Church**: this was an evengelical protestant movement founded by John Wesley in the eighteenth century which attracted large numbers of poor people who found in it the promise of self-improvement and salvation (through strict discipline). Thompson argued that if the Methodist Church could be understood to be positive in some respects it also, among other things, served to weaken the poor from within by adapting them to strict forms of work-discipline (through the practice of submission) and even served as an apologist for child labour (390). In this and other senses Methodism worked directly against the political interests of the poor and in favour of the industrial capitalists. The Methodist repression of possible radicalism and tendency to channel all passion into guilt and public confession led Thompson to describe the Methodist Church as 'a ritualized form of psychic masturbation' (405). A final point: we should be careful not to confuse the Methodists with all representatives of the church: as Thompson shows, the relation between the church, repression and radicalism was complex.

**Luddism**: describes the British textile workers who (between 1811 and 1816) were involved in rioting and machine-breaking. This was a result of seeing their livelihoods severely threatened by the introduction of machines and the factory system of production. As Thompson noted with great succinctness: 'Luddism ended on the scaffold' (540). The movement is believed to be named after Ned (Edward) Ludd an eighteenth-century Leicestershire workman who was known as a machine breaker and who became a popular hero.

E.P.: Thank you, most helpful. But *how*, according to Thompson, did the working class manifest this sense of growing class consciousness?

THOMPSON: His history of the development of working-class consciousness showed how working groups, towards the end of the eighteenth century, fought for what they saw as their rights by setting up institutions through which to express their ideas. This involved things like (he hands E.P. another section from his book):

- the establishment of popular movements to protect or improve wages and traditional ways of life
- demands for social and political rights
- complaining about increasing exploitation, rising food prices and taxes
- the organization of meetings
- and the printing of radical newspapers and journals

E.P.: And what conclusions might be drawn from this?

THOMPSON: One important conclusion is that radical working groups are seen as **active agents of change**, not just pawns to be moved around in a larger historical game It is important to remember this idea of working people involved in forms of meaningful action where they take things into their own hands, because it is this idea of agency that would distinguish writers like Thompson from later approaches associated with structuralism (see below).

E.P.: (in an incredulous tone):
You said earlier that Thompson traced the formation of the working class between 1780 and 1832, but surely there were signs of a working class before the end of the eighteenth century?

THOMPSON: Yes, Thompson was not ignorant of the fact that British history was full of conflicts between the ruling classes and the poor before this period. If you will permit a pun, one might see the working class as a 'revolting' class in so far that it manifested itself through revolt, but at the same time made itself offensive to the ruling classes. It was this 'revolting' condition that led to the fact that by 1832 the working class had consolidated itself to the point that its presence was 'the most significant factor in British political life' (11).

## The industrial context

E.P.: That's all very well, but what was the historical context for the emergence of the working class from the end of the eighteenth century? I mean, why then?

THOMPSON: The context for the significant growth of an emergent and recognizable class was the developing economy associated with the Industrial Revolution where large sectors of the working population found their lives radically changed or threatened by new processes of production (like the Luddites). This was made worse by the political situation. In England in 1792 there was what we might call only the most primitive 'democracy', which hardly deserved the name (plutocracy – government by the wealthy – would, perhaps, better describe it). It was characterized by widespread corruption, bribery and injustice, and was dominated by hereditary monarchy, the traditional rights of the great landowners and the Anglican Church. But take a look at this (Thompson hands E.P. a few sheets of paper): it's a little practice exercise I've designed for my new book. (E.P. takes a look at it.)

## **practice** EXERCISE 1: Defining 'democracy' in the late eighteenth century

In a brief introduction of this kind it is not possible to go into much detail but a short practice exercise might help to give an idea of what passed for 'democracy' in Britain in the later eighteenth century. Look at the following definitions and decide what kind of democracy was operating in England in 1790s.

In the counties only those who had more than a certain amount of land could vote. In the boroughs the right to vote depended on some of the following factors:

- 'Pot-wallopers': a householder who could vote solely on the grounds that his fireplace was large enough for a cooking pot.
- 'Burgageholders': householders who could vote simply because their houses carried ancient voting rights.
- Those who paid 'scot and lot': householders who could vote because they paid certain ancient taxes.
- Some boroughs were known as 'nominating boroughs' in which the whole estate was owned by just one man who had the right to name the parliamentary candidate.
- There was also the 'rotten borough' where very few people lived but had the right to one or more Members of Parliament. Then there were boroughs where a large number of people lived but where there was only one MP or where there was no political representation at all.

Although the working-class movement known as Chartism (see chapter one on Arnold) stands outside the general limits of Thompson's book, if we look at its demands we can get an idea of what was lacking in British politics before, during, and after its existence (given that the movement failed). In 1838 Frances Place drafted the People's Charter which demanded:

| | |
|---|---|
| **The universal right for men to vote in elections** (note women, even within the radical working-class movements, were not generally deemed fit to vote) | Responding to the fact that working men had absolutely no voting rights whatsoever |
| **Voting by secret ballot** | Responding to the fact that votes were cast in public which allowed for all kinds of coercion |
| **Annual parliaments** | This was an attempt to force politicians to respond quickly and effectively to voters' interests for fear of being voted out in the following elections |

| | |
|---|---|
| **Equal electoral districts** | This was designed to counter the corruption and injustice of the rotten boroughs |
| **Payment of MPs** | This would allow members of the poorer classes to become MPs, even if their income was very low |
| **Abolition of the property qualifications for MPs** | Again, this was to enable poorer members of the community to become MPs and break the domination of the landed classes |

## Corresponding Societies, pain, Paine and repression

E.P.: Hmm, I didn't realize 'democracy' was such a flexible word! Right, is that it? I'm getting hungry.

THOMPSON: Hard luck, you asked me to talk about Thompson and I insist on doing his work some kind of justice! Later, if you don't interrupt to much, I may share my sandwiches with you. Now I would like to discuss an aspect of Thompson's book which I feel isn't always given much emphasis, and that is *how* he conveys the sense of suffering of working people. Thompson did not give the impression of being a dispassionate historian uninvolved in the history he was writing. Many readers find his book deeply moving, not only with relation to the content of the story he tells but with relation to his choice of documents to back up the points he makes. It is this aspect which helps the modern reader to understand the enormity of the rebarbative history he recounts. (Handing E.P. another wad of papers), have a look at another practice section I'm planning for my book, which includes some advice on how to answer the questions. (E.P. has a look through it.)

### **practice** EXERCISE 2: Thompson, child labour and the writing of history

Read the following extract from a section where Thompson is reviewing the question of child labour and answer the questions at the end of it. The following notes on practice will give you some tips, but try to answer the questions for yourself first.

A minister of unidentified affiliations declared:

> If there was one place in England that needed legislative interference, it was this place, for they work 15 and 16 hours a day frequently, and sometimes all night: Oh! – It is a murderous system, and the mill-owners are the pest and disgrace of society. Laws human and divine are insufficient to restrain them [...].

He related the story of a boy whom he had recently interred who had been found standing asleep with his arms full of wool and had been beaten awake. This day he had worked 17 hours; he was carried home by his father, was unable to eat his supper, awoke at 4 a.m. the next morning and asked his brothers if they could see the lights of the mill as he was afraid of being late, and then died. (His younger brother, aged nine, had died previously: the father was 'sober and industrious', a Sunday school teacher.) The Anglican curate here gave his unreserved support to the limitation of child labour:

> I have seen the poor in this valley oppressed, I have thought it my duty to expose it ... I am bound, from the responsible nature of my office, to bring it into contrast with the liberal and kindly truth of the Gospel. ... And where oppression is exercised it generally falls most heavily upon those who are least able to bear it [...].

As a consequence of his sermons – and of personal protests to the masters – the mill-owners had cursed and insulted him and his daughters in the streets. (382–3) (All elliptical points outside square brackets are Thompson's.)

- How well do you think Thompson uses his historical source with relation to the content of the history he recounts?
- In what ways does Thompson encourage the reader to identify with the history he tells?

## **notes** ON PRACTICE: some advice on answering the questions

You might consider the following:

- The fact that the events are not mediated through the working-class community but an Anglican minister.
- The minister's role in the community.
- The inhumanity of the owners and the extremity of the case.

- The age of the victims.
- The character of the dead boys' father.
- The treatment of the minister and his daughters for having tried to expose the injustice, exploitation, cruelty and oppression.

E.P.: Moving stuff, but I hope you don't think I'm going to answer any of those questions!

THOMPSON: I know you too well to expect you to do any work. Now, to give you a further idea of the narrative Thompson constructs I'm going to tell you about his treatment of what were known as the **Corresponding Societies** and then talk about a man named Thomas Paine.

E.P.: So, what were the Corresponding Societies? And why bother telling me about them? Can't we forget what sounds to me like a boring history lesson?

THOMPSON: (feigning outrage) Listen, you impertinent blockhead, the *point* of exploring these societies is that they help Thompson to give historical substance to the rise of working-class radicalism. Now, in England, at the end of the eighteenth century, working men (tradesmen, shopkeepers, mechanics etc.) began a series of societies or clubs like The London Corresponding society, which was founded in 1792. What these societies were asking for was social and political reform – like the Chartists after them, the simple right to vote. The societies grew – and along with them working-class consciousness (Thompson names 29 different societies across the length and breadth of England and there were others in Scotland).

E.P.: (anticipating Thompson) So, we can say that by the end of the eighteenth century it looked as if some progress was being made: radical ideas were being channelled through organizations and institutions. Things were certainly looking up!

THOMPSON: Well, yes, it may have looked that way. But let's talk about Thomas Paine before we get too enthusiastic. At the beginning of the 1790s Thomas Paine published his *The Rights of Man* (1791–92) – for Thompson 'a foundation-text of the English working-class movement' (Thompson, [1963] 1968: 99) and one of the most important books ever to be published in terms of working-class political radicalism. In this book Paine asserted the rights of all men, who were not incapable or criminal, and attacked the Monarchy and rulers. He saw the latter as (among other things) unjust, unfair, unprincipled, unseeing, unfeeling, unreasonable, undemocratic and, in short, unacceptable. Not only this, but they were cruel, greedy, lazy, exploitative and inhuman. Just to give you a taste of Paine, I'll show you a drawing I've had prepared for my new book where I paraphrase some of his opinions about monarchical rule. I've based my paraphrases on his pamphlet entitled 'Common Sense' ([1776] 1987). (He hands the drawing to E.P., who looks at it.)

Figure 5.3 Paine on Monarchical rule

E.P.: Paine was one *cool* guy!

THOMPSON: (adopting a supercilious tone) I assume you mean that you appreciate that Paine's direct language, colourfuxl rhetoric and forceful argumentation communicated exceptionally well to both literate and illiterate alike? But let's not get too optimistic. By 1800 The London Corresponding Society and Paine's *The Rights of Man* had been banned by the government. As Thompson explained, every time the working classes tried to assert their rights they were repressed, often brutally, by the authorities and their leaders imprisoned. For example, when working people tried to establish unions, a series of Combination Acts prohibited mass meetings.

However, although *The Rights of Man* was banned, it continued to be read and circulated in secret.

E.P.: (again trying to anticipate Thompson) Hmm, I think I now perceive the importance of Thompson's approach to contemporary cultural studies. Doesn't all this suggest that accounts of history as the deeds of monarchs, statesmen, military leaders and politicians can be challenged by other histories? I am now beginning to see much more clearly what it means to see the working classes as active agents of change.

THOMPSON: You're learning! But it's worth remembering that these alternative approaches are not always easy to write: when people and their alternative cultures are repressed or driven underground it is harder for the historian to uncover the details. Part of Thompson's method is to **excavate these dark areas of history**. Despite repression, as Thompson's book demonstrates, working-class consciousness was not extinguished. His book is full of stories of the bravery and resistance of men and women who risked their lives to promote the interests of working-class communities. For this reason alone it makes inspiring reading.

E.P.: (despite himself, starts showing signs of interest) Can't you give me a few examples of working-class bravery and resistance?

THOMPSON: I will with great pleasure. One example can be seen when Thompson quotes a passage from the journal of John Wesley (the man who founded the Methodist Church). Wesley, who was not known for his approval of what he thought were disorderly actions, did sympathize with a 'mob' in James town, Ireland. (Note Thompson isn't entirely limiting his examples to England.) When the price of corn rose exorbitantly, the working-class community took matters into their own hands and (again I quote from memory) Wesley wrote that the 'mob':

> had been in motion all the day; but their business was only with the forestallers [speculators] of the market, who had bought up all the corn far and near, to starve the poor, and load a Dutch ship, which lay at the quay; but the mob brought it all out into the market, and sold it for the owners at the common price. And this they did with all the calmness and composure imaginable, and without striking or hurting anyone. (Thompson, [1963] 1968: 69–70)

THOMPSON: (recommencing) Thompson refers to other situations like (again I quote from my astounding memory):

> In Honiton in 1766 lace-workers seized corn on the premises of the farmers, took it to market themselves, sold it, and returned the money and even the sacks back to the farmers [...]. A Halifax example of 1783 repeats the same pattern of mass intimidation and self-discipline. The crowd was gathered from weaving villages outside the town, and descended upon the market place in some sort of order (formed into 'twos') with an ex-soldier and coiner, Thomas Spencer, at their head. The corn merchants were besieged, and forced to sell oats at 30s. and wheat at 21s. a load

[rather than at what was seen as a ruinous and inordinately high price]. (69–70) (All comments in square brackets are mine.)

THOMPSON: (not letting E.P. get a word in) Thomas Spencer was executed but there was strong military presence at his execution because the authorities feared he might be rescued by the crowd. This suggests that working people were, indeed, organizing themselves and that a class was in the making. Of course, not all resistance was so well organized and peaceful, and riots and violent behaviour were not uncommon; however, you might consider …

E.P.: Oh no, not another practice section from your new book!

THOMPSON: Yes, how did you guess? But here, take a sandwich while you're reading it – I think you deserve it (he hands the practice exercise to E.P., who reads it through while eating the sandwich).

## **practice** EXERCISE 3: Thinking about class, bravery and resistance in the 'Brutish' Isles

To explore some of these ideas with relation to earlier chapters you might like to respond to the following questions:

- You might remember Arnold criticized the 'Englishman's heaven-born privilege of doing as he likes'. In what ways does Thompson's approach to the working class differ from Arnold's?
- In what ways does a knowledge of the political situation at the end of the eighteenth century help you to understand working-class resistance?

As mentioned earlier, the Luddites often destroyed machines that threatened their wages, jobs or way of life. However, the government suppressed all uprisings using the army to protect the mill owners and arrest the attackers – in 1812 there were about 12,000 troops in the disturbed areas (617). Despite repression, working people, through struggle and resistance, gradually forged a sense of class identity:

Thus working men formed a picture of the organization of society, out of their own experience and with the help of their hard-won and erratic education, which was above all a political picture. They learned to see their own lives as part of a general history of conflict between the loosely defined 'industrious classes' on the one hand, and the unreformed House of Commons on the other. From 1830 onwards a more clearly defined class consciousness, in the customary Marxist sense, was maturing, in which working people were aware of continuing both old and new battles on their own. (Thompson, [1963] 1968: 782)

Based on what you now know:

- Can you imagine how this situation helped not only the formation and consolidation of the working class but the dominant classes in England?
- Can you outline why radicalism was so central in Thompson's view to the identity of the working class?
- Can you explain why Thompson refused to define class as a 'structure', or a 'thing'?
- Can you describe why, in Thompson's view, it is so important to have a sense of history with relation to class?
- Can you explain the importance of the idea of 'making' in his title?
- Can you explain why it might be more appropriate to speak not so much of the British Isles but, as I have, of the 'Brutish Isles'?

## **notes** ON PRACTICE: adapting Thompson's ideas

Taking a bird's eye view of Thompson's method, it is possible to extract some very useful ideas for the practice of cultural studies. The technique of tracing key moments of radical conflict, the documentation of demands for social and political rights and the calling attention to the printing and consumption of radical forms of writing etc. can be adapted to the analysis of any marginalized or repressed group. An example of this can be found in Ron Ramdin's *The Making of the Black Working Class in Britain* (Ramdin, 1987). Although this book, like Thompson's, is classified as a work of history, it comfortably fits into the cultural studies idiom because of the way it explores how alternative, popular radical cultures are produced through struggle, political agitation and resistance. This reveals one of the key elements within cultural studies: **resistance and political struggle become legitimate objects of analysis and knowledge**.

One way of practising this kind of cultural studies is to explore the history of your own community to see if there were (or, indeed, are) radical groups or popular movements fighting against the status quo for political or social recognition. You might explore issues like: workers' rights, women's rights, union rights, immigrant workers' rights, gay and lesbian rights, or questions of identity based in and around nationalist movements, green issues, consumer rights etc.

E.P.: (finishing the sandwich) So, what can we conclude from all this?

THOMPSON: Hasn't anyone ever told you it's rude to eat while you're talking? However, a few general conclusions are possible. As suggested earlier, Thompson argued, despite the resistance and repression that united monarchy, landowners, the mill owners and much of the Christian Church, that by the 1830s the working class had finally consolidated itself in such a way that it was a force to be reckoned with. Returning to the question of the *making* of class, Thompson made distinct classes visible through his documentation of the struggles between those who wielded power and those who were subjected to it. As we've seen, Thompson showed that demands for greater liberty were met by laws to restrict collective organization and action; acts of rebellion were met by repression in the shape of the police, the army and the courts – aided by the prisons, and even spies working on behalf of successive governments. All these confrontations helped to consolidate the ruling and working classes. However, in the context of the forging of working-class consciousness, I could say a little more about the role of the radical press ...

E.P.: (interrupting) No! That's enough – I'm starving! That will have to be all for today (and, looking up at the imposing statue of Karl Marx), even old Karl's looking bored.

THOMPSON: But you can't go without knowing how Thompson and Hoggart relate to what's known as 'culturalism' – I think you'll find it useful.

## Culturalism as a method

E.P.: (in a sulky voice) OK, so what is **culturalism**? And hand me another sandwich.

THOMPSON: (proffering another sandwich) It is often used to describe the work of not only Richard Hoggart and E.P. Thompson but also writers like Raymond Williams and the early work of Stuart Hall (who I'll be exploring in the following chapters). Culturalism a particular approach to cultural analysis which is very important from the point of view of method. John Storey, drawing on the work of Richard Johnson, describes the culturalist enterprise in the following way:

> What unites them [Hoggart, Thompson and Williams] is an approach which insists that by analyzing the culture of a society – the textual forms and documented practices of a culture – it is possible **to reconstitute the patterned behaviour and constellations of ideas shared by the men and women who produce and consume the cultural texts and practices of that society.** It is a perspective which stresses 'human agency', the active production of culture, rather than its passive consumption. (Storey, 2001: 37)

As I've emphasized, Thompson made a great effort to show that working people were active *agents* of change, not just pawns being moved around by higher powers. However, the term 'culturalism' is a label that has gained a certain notoriety because of the clash between cultural critics or historians who embraced structuralism, with its tendency to see people as products of cultural systems, and those who tended to put greater emphasis on individual experience and agency. Nevertheless, the culturalists are generally understood to have considerably extended (and democratized) the Arnoldian– Leavisite approach, Storey making the point that from the culturalist point of view popular culture (seen as the lived culture of ordinary people) is now assumed to be worth studying (Storey, 2001: 57) that is, in itself – not only to be shown to be in some way inferior, dangerous and wanting.

## Oversimplification

**W A R N I N G**

Although many historians of cultural studies use the term 'culturalism', it is worth remembering that it is a convenient label to describe some of the writers who have helped to lay down the conceptual and methodological foundations of what is now a recognizable area. That is to say, there *never was* a school of culturalists as such, or even a group that self-consciously worked towards a set of common goals – only writers contributing to what later critics would label 'culturalism'. As Jenks (1993: 154) has stated, it is possible 'to overemphasize the communality of vision' between those defined as culturalists. It is for this reason I deal with them separately. For tips on how to understand structuralism see chapter twelve on feminism and Virginia Woolf.

E.P.: (jumping up from the bench and grabbing another sandwich) Well, it's all been most illuminating – I can now go and write the essay I've been asked to write on Thompson!

THOMPSON: (looking shocked, and hungry) You mean you only invited me because you have an essay to write? And, hey! You've eaten nearly all the sandwiches!

E.P.: Yes, but their sacrifice has all been in a good cause. I've learned quite a lot about E.P. Thompson.

THOMPSON: (grabbing back the last sandwich) Yes, but not enough. Now you'd better go and consume *The Making of the English Working Class* instead of my lunch! (They leave Highgate Cemetery, walking under the huge shadow cast by the statue of Karl Marx).

## *SUMMARY OF KEY POINTS*

This chapter has shown how Thompson defined and traced the formation of the working class in England. It has also emphasized Thompson's commitment to historical writing and Marxism, and his belief that the working class has been an active agent of change. The chapter has given some examples of radicalism both in terms of action and in the expression of ideas. It has also underlined the suffering and repression that were the consequences of political agitation and the fight for rights. The chapter is concluded with some discussion of the importance of culturalism as a method.

Thompson's work can be seen as methodologically significant in the following ways:

- His method is historical and informed by his Marxist beliefs and training, thus class antagonisms, experience and the material relations of production are seen as fundamental to an understanding of history and culture.
- Whereas Adorno emphasized the disempowerment and depoliticization of the working classes, Thompson stresses the growth of radical groups intent on improving their conditions of work and insisting on parliamentary reform.
- Thompson's historical method is one that recounts the multiple stories that coalesce into an identity of dynamic opposition, conflict and resistance in the face of exploitation and repression. His working class and its counter-culture take centre stage, but whereas Hoggart side-stepped radicalism, Thompson makes it an integral part of what it means to be a member of the working class.
- Thompson's method is characterized by an engaged, moving and rigorous historical quest to rescue radicals from historical oblivion.
- Thompson's notion of class as a historical phenomenon that unifies a number of 'disparate and seemingly unconnected events, both in the raw material of experience and in consciousness' (8) means that history is not understood as a seamless narrative.
- *All* classes are understood as complex formations that come about through conflicts of interests. Class is understood as a relation, not a category.
- Class has to be seen historically, it cannot be understood without recognizing its processes of development.
- Thompson's work, while normally classified as history, reveals one of the key elements within cultural studies: resistance and political struggle become legitimate objects of analysis and knowledge.
- Thompson's effort to show that working people were active *agents* of change has led to his work being categorized as a form of culturalism. This approach analyses culture in order to understand the lives, experience, consciousness, values and struggles of particular groups in society.

## References

Hoggart, Richard ([1957] 1958) *The Uses of Literacy*. Harmondsworth: Penguin.
Jenks, Chris (1993) *Culture: Key Ideas*. London: Routledge.
Paine, Thomas ([1776] 1987) *The Thomas Paine Reader*. London: Penguin.
Ramdin, Ron (1987) *The Making of the Black Working Class in Britain*. Aldershot: Wild Wood House.
Storey, John (2001) *Cultural Theory and Popular Culture: An Introduction* (3rd edition). Essex: Pearson Prentice Hall.
Thompson, E.P. ([1963] 1968) *The Making of the English Working Class*. London: Penguin.

## Further reading

Adelman, Paul (1986) *The Rise of the Labour Party, 1880–1945* (2nd edition). London: Longman. This book documents the rise of the Labour Party from the late 1880s and therefore looks at a period of history which Thompson deliberately excluded. Although not a stated aim, this study helps to consolidate and extend Thompson's view of history. The book, like Royle and Fletcher (below), includes useful historical documents.

Harrison, J.F.C. (1984) *The Common People: A History from the Norman Conquest to the Present*. Glasgow: Fontana. A useful and accessible introduction to the history of the 'common' people with relation to their experiences and perceptions. Its historical limits are broader than Thompson's and it touches on many similar themes being, in many ways, indebted to Thompson's work.

Fletcher, Anthony (1983) *Tudor Rebellions*. London: Longman. Read alongside Harrison and Royle, helps to give a sense of the importance of popular uprisings as a threat to social and political order. Fletcher includes contemporary documents and outlines the ideas behind royal supremacy, contemporary attitudes to obedience and the ruthless putting down of rebellion.

Ramdin, Ron (1987, see References above) this book, like J.F.C. Harrison's *The Common People*, is one of many books which have been published in the wake of Thompson's re-writing of British history. Both these books make very few references to Thompson, which is not so much a question of historians kicking over their roots but a reflection of quite how, by the 1980s, Thompson's approach had become absorbed into British social and political history. Ramdin's play on Thompson's title suggests how Thompson's approach can be adapted to other approaches.

*The Thomas Paine Reader* ([1776] 1980, see References above) contains key works like 'Common Sense' and *The Rights of Man* as well as many other essays which take up the cause of libertarian politics and political reform.

Royle, Edward (1986) *Chartism* (2nd edition). London: Longman. Royle's study gives a lucid overview of Chartism and includes very useful period documents.

# Towards a Recognizable Theory of Culture: Raymond Williams

## Introduction

This chapter is the last section of the second part of the book on 'The Transformative Power of Working-class Culture'. After a brief discussion of the importance of Raymond Williams' work, this chapter outlines Williams' lifelong engagement with the task of defining culture and explains how to practise an aspect of Williams' work through the use of keywords. The chapter then moves on to Williams' notion of culture as part of revolutionary processes which would transform British cultural life, his anthropological definition of culture as the theory of culture as a whole way of life, and his idea that culture can be understood through attention to the 'structure of feeling' of a period. The final sections provide an account of how Williams approached the analysis of television through concepts like sequencing and flow, and what effect the idea of dominant, residual and emergent cultures has on the theory and practice of cultural analysis. Each one of these approaches is illustrated with detailed examples.

### *MAIN LEARNING GOALS*

- To appreciate the importance and relevance of Williams' contribution to cultural studies and the breadth of his approaches.
- To see how social and political reforms were fundamental to Williams' conception of culture and to understand the complexity of Williams' various definitions of culture.

- To recognize the centrality and importance of the working classes to his work.
- To become aware of the importance Williams put on social, historical, economic and political contexts to the understanding of cultures.
- To understand a number of Williams' key concepts and see how they can be used in practice, and adapted to further analysis.

## On the vital importance of Raymond Williams

Raymond Williams' contribution to what has now become a cultural studies tradition is of the greatest importance. John Storey has described the range of his work as 'formidable', stressing that he has made important inroads into our understanding of areas from cultural theory and cultural history to television, the press, radio and advertising. Storey finds his contribution 'all the more remarkable when one considers his origins in the Welsh working class (his father was a railway signalman), and that as an academic he was Professor of Drama at Cambridge University' (Storey, 2001: 44).

Williams' activities, however, went beyond his work in the university, for he was also, like Hoggart, involved in adult education and, unlike Hoggart, a novelist. As stated at the end of the chapter on Hoggart, much of Raymond Williams' work focused the experiences and consciousness of the working classes (thus he has been placed in the tradition of 'culturalism'). However, what complicates an introduction to Williams is that his work has not, like that of Hoggart and Thompson, been mainly reduced to one seminal study. You might keep in mind while reading this chapter that Williams was writing for almost 40 years (in the period after the Second World War) evolving as a critic in terms of his use of theory and in his choice of the objects of study. For example, while always a committed and active member of the British Left, he drew much closer to Marxism towards the end of his career, something that makes his inclusion under any simple label questionable.

Indeed, as Terry Eagleton has asserted, given his vast range, it is hard to characterize Williams' work – so much so that conventional labels like 'sociologist, political theorist, social philosopher [and] cultural commentator' do not fit his work either 'exhaustively or exactly' (Eagleton, 1984: 108). Given this breadth I shall outline the areas of Williams' work which I feel are particularly useful for beginners in terms of helping to think about, analyse, theorize and interpret culture.

To introduce Williams' contribution in more detail I'm going to resort to another creative-critical technique, which I hope will be suggestive, interesting and useful from the point of view of how to develop ideas. Let's imagine the following situation. Vidal Tandow is an undergraduate studying cultural studies. He has to sit an exam in a couple of weeks but hasn't revised very well. He hooks up to a private chat line on the Internet to get help from his sister, Ladvi. She is a few years older than him and is now doing postgraduate work at another university.

## Williams and the task of defining culture

VIDAL: Hi! Sorry, but it's the old story, exams are just round the corner and, erm, well, I'm not that well prepared and I missed most of the stuff on Raymond Williams. We've got to have a general idea of Williams' contribution and have some idea about how his theories might work in practice. Is there any way you can help me?

LADVI: It's always the same with you – what would you do without me to bail you out?

VIDAL: Fail! But, come on! If you've got time, can you give me a few hints? Please!

LADVI: OK, but this is the *last* time (although I said that last time). I've got my own work to do. Give me a moment, I'm going to read over a few things and get back to you ... (She returns): Right, I'm back. I haven't got much time so I'll summarize the best I can.

VIDAL: What would I do without you?

LADVI: Fail! Now, let's get down to business. One thing that characterizes Williams' contribution as a whole was his continued effort to offer an adequate **definition of culture**. Let's start by looking at his *Culture and Society* published in 1958. In the foreword he explains that the organizing principle of his study was to be found in the discovery that 'the idea of culture, and the word itself in its general modern uses, came into English thinking in the period which we commonly describe as that of the Industrial Revolution' (Williams, [1958] 1987: iii).

VIDAL: So, is he saying that it is only within this historical framework that the modern sense of the word could be adequately understood?

LADVI: Exactly. Williams is doing something here that characterized just about all his work: he locates the notion of 'culture' in the social and political changes brought about by the Industrial Revolution thereby providing a historical basis for the understanding of it. Williams saw *Culture and Society* as an account and an interpretation of 'responses in thought and feeling to the changes in English society since the late eighteenth century' (iii). One practical consequence of this is that to understand modern culture there is no sense in trying to marginalize popular mass culture and privilege forms of minority or elite culture ...

VIDAL: (interrupting) Cool!

LADVI: (ignoring him) This means that if culture (in its modern sense) was an extension of social and political changes brought about by industrial capitalism (and the gradual struggle for reform) then cultural historians would have to attend to all the historical circumstances that produced the forms of art and life of industrial civilization. In this sense, there are clear affinities with Thompson's approach and echoes of writers from Arnold to the Leavises.

VIDAL: Wow, that's gonna sound great in the exam!

LADVI: Yes, and that's all for now – I've got work to do, and so have you! Have a look at the following practice exercises. Once you've done them, get back to me and I'll see if I can help you a little more.

VIDAL: You mean I have to do these exercises? I thought you were going to explain it all to me!

LADVI: You think I'm going to hand it all to you on a plate! Speak to you later, when you've done what I've suggested. (She gets off line and Vidal, knowing that his sister's help will dry up if he doesn't get down to work, does it. Here are his answers.

## Working with *Culture and Society*

### Ladvi's first question

The history of the idea of culture that Williams develops in *Culture and Society* is a record of what he calls 'our reactions, in thought and feeling, to the changed conditions of our common life' (Williams, [1958] 1987: 295). Briefly explain what this means in practice. Say what you think was the main point of emphasis in *Culture and Society*.

(Vidal's answer does not require you to read *Culture and Society*; however, if you have access to it, you might read the introduction and respond to the question before reading Vidal's reply.)

#### Vidal's answer

What a historical view of culture (as 'our reactions, in thought and feeling, to the changed conditions of our common life') means in practice can be described as follows. It involved an analysis of a whole range of writers from the eighteenth century (Edmund Burke and William Cobbett) to the twentieth century (including, D.H. Lawrence, R.H. Tawney, T.S. Eliot, I.A. Richards, F.R. Leavis and George Orwell) who help to provide a 'map' through which it is possible to observe the 'wider changes in life and thought' that these writers reflect in their works (Williams, [1958] 1987: xiii). The main emphasis in the book is on the social–political, intellectual tradition that has helped to define modern, democratic, industrial society.

## Ladvi's second question

> Look at what Williams has to say about how a number of **keywords** acquired new and important meanings in the last decades of the eighteenth century and in the first half of the nineteenth century and reflect on *what he was doing* in terms of practising a kind of cultural studies. Can you think of ways you might use his ideas and adapt them to new historical contexts?

(Again, Vidal's answer does not require you to read *Culture and Society*; however, if you have access to it, you might read through the introduction and respond to the question before reading Vidal's reply. You'll notice that half way through the answer Vidal offers some notes on practice.)

Figure 6.1 The function of Williams' keywords

## Vidal's second answer

As Williams was aware, his map (mentioned in the answer to question one) was highly selective and focused on five major terms (key words): industry, democracy, class, art and culture. He went on to explain that:

> In the last decades of the eighteenth century, and in the first half of the nineteenth century, a number of words, which are now of capital importance, came for the first time into common English use, or, where they had already been generally used in the language, acquired new and important meanings. (xiii)

In terms of what he was *doing*, Williams' map interrelates his five major terms showing how they developed and were transformed from around the end of the eighteenth century to the 1950s when he was writing his book. These changes of use illustrated transformations in ways of thinking about social, political and economic institutions and also questioned the purposes for which these institutions had been devised. One way of appreciating how Williams was practising a form of cultural studies is to look at how he subjected these keywords to analysis. Here is a summary of some of his main ideas:

**Industry** Before the Industrial Revolution this word referred to things like skill or hard work but it was extended to include the general activities of manufacturing and productive institutions by writers like Adam Smith, who wrote *The Wealth of Nations* ([1776] 1982). The increased use of this word reflects the fact that modes of production in Britain were taking on their industrial character and would bring about not only technological innovations but important social, political and cultural changes, which Williams illustrated with reference to the other key terms.

**Democracy** At the end of the eighteenth century and the beginning of the nineteenth democrats were commonly seen as 'dangerous and subversive mob agitators' (Williams, [1958] 1987: xiv). However, the introduction of words like democracy and democrat into ordinary speech recognize the importance of the French and American Revolutions and mark a decisive phase in the struggle for democratic representation in Britain. Industrialization, then, was linked to reform movements which would help to transform politics and social thinking.

**Class** Towards the end of the eighteenth century the word class is extended (from its meaning as division or group of people or things) to refer to the lower, middle and higher classes as social groups. The rising importance of the capitalist and working classes would help to transform not only the means of production but politics and all aspects of society.

**Art** During the same period, this term, once referring to skills, began to refer to the 'imaginative' or 'creative' arts (literature, music, painting, sculpture and theatre). The artist was now no longer an artisan but the producer of 'art' with its forms of 'imaginative truth' (xv–xvi) and the word 'aesthetics' was adopted to be able to discuss and judge artistic productions. Art is a particularly important term because it registers reactions to the changed conditions of life.

*(Continued)*

*(Continued)*

**Culture** This term once referred to cultivating plants or animals but, by the nineteenth century, it had become associated with ideas of intellectual perfection, 'the general body of the arts' and 'a whole way of life, material, intellectual and spiritual' (xvi). For Williams, this term was of particular importance because the questions 'now concentrated in the meanings of the word *culture* are questions directly raised by the great historical changes which the changes in *industry*, *democracy* and *class*, in their own way represent, and to which the changes in *art* are a closely related response' (xvi).

What Williams was *doing* here was describing the historical formation of these and other words. Actually, you hinted at his method earlier because he locates all these ideas in the social and political changes brought about by industrial society, thereby providing a historical basis for the understanding of these terms. By the way, Williams published a book in 1976 entitled *Keywords: A Vocabulary of Culture and Society* (revised edition, Williams, 1983) which is a very useful cultural studies dictionary of important terms. This is an extension of the kind of work he was doing in *Culture and Society*.

## **notes** ON PRACTICE: adapting keywords to new contexts

Reflecting on how his ideas may be adapted to new historical contexts, I think a lot could be done with this simple procedure. However, although the basic approach is simple, I think the practice might prove to be rather difficult. Here are a few ideas that occur to me:

1. We could look at the words Williams mentioned (these include ideology, humanitarian, utilitarian, atomistic, highbrow, collectivism, communism, solidarity, strike, and many more) and see how they have evolved to the present day, or are less important or have begun to disappear.
2. We could, like Williams, try to trace the history of words which have become dominant in recent times. For example, we could explore the contemporary importance of terms like: micro chip, aerobics, *virtual reality, the green house effect, *environment/ecology, famine relief, artificial intelligence, *information technology, digitalization, the World Wide Web, robotics, intelligent missiles, cybernetics, *globalization, tele-surveillance, *celebrity, cloning, biopolitics, real time, sampling, AIDS, abortion, euthanasia, asylum seekers, hostages, new world order, international terrorism, reality TV, sex workers, the metrosexual, solidarity, the *postmodern, *postcolonianism, *deconstruction, waste etc. Those terms marked with an asterisk are included in the latest updated version of Williams' *Keywords* entitled *New Keywords* (Bennett et al., 2005). It's possible for students to make a list of terms they feel are particularly relevant to their own circumstances and culture.

3. We can look at when the words we have chosen entered common usage and explore how they may help to define the kinds of social, political, technological and economic changes that have occurred, or are still in process. We might also analyse how they relate to and are reflected in the arts, media and entertainment and how they may be used to mirror differing values, beliefs and conflicts.
4. A study focused on contemporary uses of the term *culture* might still serve as a particularly useful key term. All this would help us to map and record changes in our particular social, economic and political life. It would also be interesting to explore how the other terms like industry, democracy, class and art have evolved.
5. Williams chose to look at the way the terms he chose were used by writers to give meaning to their experience (Williams, [1958] 1987: xix) and I think we could do something very similar. However, I think we could go beyond Williams' sources and look at all kinds of media by drawing not only on the printed word but TV, films and the internet etc.
6. We could consider our own time as if we were viewing it from the future, trying to understand it by looking at how dominant keywords were discussed or represented in various kinds of **media**. For example, if we wanted to understand **mobile phone culture** we would not only need to know about the technological **infrastructure** necessary for its existence and how it was used (for calls, **text messaging**, taking **photos**, hooking up to the **Internet** etc.) but how contemporaries represented and reacted to it – as a positive amalgam of technologies, as a form of **pollution** (**noise** and **radiation**), as a negative effect on **literacy** (some critics blaming the elliptical style of short text messages for decreasing **standards** in writing), fears that phones may be used for the purposes of **surveillance** and **social control** etc. Each word written in bold could be explored separately and with relation to the others to interpret contemporary life through its dominant and less dominant vocabularies. Of course, the specific characteristics of each cultural context have to be considered: my comments here tend to reflect *my* situation and ways of seeing. It's also worth considering how relevant these terms are *across* cultures. If someone moves between cultures (if you were born to mixed parents, if you were born in one country but now live or study in another etc.), this may give you special insights into how keywords function in, or pertain to, different geographical, cultural spaces.
7. Finally, we could adapt this approach by putting the emphasis on colloquial languages associated with different generations, rather than on words drawn from the intellectual world. In Britain all kinds of terms like, 'wicked', 'big yourself up', 'pants' etc. have been adopted by younger people. Much of this language may be transitory and already changing (although exclamations like 'cool!' have a longer history of usage behind them) but questions about the cultural origins of the terms and who uses these alternative vocabularies may give us insights into different kinds of cultural history. To do justice to the terms and understand *how* they are transmitted and perpetuated it may be necessary to explore cultural forms as distinct as North-American hippy culture, cartoon series, popular TV, film, songs, poetry, drama and novels etc.

## Culture and *The Long Revolution*

Ladvi has read Vidal's answers and they are now back online:

LADVI: Hey, that's not at all bad! Almost as good as I could do!

VIDAL: OK, so is there anything else I should know about Williams?

LADVI: Anything else! We've only explored the tip of the iceberg! But since I can't review every aspect of Williams' contribution, I'll try to give you a few more useful ideas that can be used in practice. One general point you might take into account is that for Williams culture was no longer a fixed category: he saw it as a process, not a conclusion (Williams, [1958] 1987: 295). As mentioned earlier, that means it was (and still is) subject to historical forces and change.

VIDAL: So, Williams' approach to culture was a little like Thompson's approach to class – *dynamic?*

LADVI: Yes, I'd say that's a good way to put it and this brings me to another aspect of Williams' work which links into some of the themes we found in Thompson: the idea of **culture as a product of struggles for social and political change**. This approach is reflected in *Culture and Society* but it is a view more closely associated with Williams' book *The Long Revolution* published in 1961. In this study the Industrial Revolution, while bringing its own forms of exploitation, subordination, hardships and injustices, is not dismissed as the progenitor of degenerate or unhealthy cultural forms but a *vital force* that would, through great struggle, bring about the reforms associated with **modern democracy**. However, modern democracy was in no way complete in Williams' mind, it being part of long revolutionary processes that could, and should, be extended. It had brought reforms in voting rights, working conditions, improvements in educational and health care (dependent on changing conceptions of both individuals and society) and more enlightened social thinking. And *these* aspects were every bit as much a part of developing cultural life as contributions in the sphere of the arts. Actually, Williams wrote of three interrelated revolutionary processes in this book: the democratic, industrial and cultural ([1961] 1992: x–xi).

VIDAL: Williams' view of culture, then, was linked to a belief in the importance of a continuing political project to transform society. So, fundamental to Williams' view of culture was political change linked to working-class struggles for a better life.

LADVI: Yes, if you add class consciousness, change through activism, and the creation of institutions within the context of industrial civilization you get democracy. These are all part of **the long revolution** that Williams describes in this book. Looking at both Thompson's and Williams' contributions you can get an idea of a key component of much work in cultural studies: **the importance of politically engaged readings of culture which recognize the value of working-class activism**.

VIDAL: I'd never thought of defining culture in terms of social and political reform. In terms of method, then, I can see that the cultural critic has to be constantly aware of the implications of how cultural forms are related to these revolutionary processes. Are there any other lessons to be learnt from this book?

LADVI: Yes, many and the whole book deserves careful reading. One of the most important chapters of *The Long Revolution* is called 'The Analysis of Culture', which has become crucial reading on many courses dedicated to cultural studies. In this chapter Williams offered three general categories which have often served as starting points for the definition of culture. Here, why don't you look at them for yourself and answer the following question?

VIDAL: Not another question!

LADVI: I'm afraid so!

## Ladvi's question

Read the first part of 'The Analysis of Culture' and give a brief outline of the three categories that Williams uses to define culture and describe the value of each approach.

(Vidal's answer does not require you to read 'The Analysis of Culture'; however, if you have access to it, you might read it through and respond to the question before reading Vidal's reply.)

### Vidal's reply: Williams' definition of culture as the ideal, documentary and social

Williams divided culture into the **ideal**, the **documentary** and the **social**. The *ideal* he described as 'a state or process of human perfection, in terms of certain absolute or universal values'. The analysis of culture, from this point of view, is the 'discovery and description', whether in lives or works, of the kind of values which are seen as composing 'a timeless order, or to have permanent reference to the universal human condition' (1961: 41).

Williams' second category is the *documentary* which he describes as 'the body of intellectual and imaginative work, in which, in a detailed way, human thought and experience are variously recorded'. From this point of view, the analysis of culture would be a form of criticism where 'the nature of the thought and experience, the details of the language, form and convention in which these are active, are described and valued'. This approach includes the *ideal* category (the Arnoldian task of discovering 'the best that has been thought and written in the world'), where exemplary works are analysed in order to clarify and value them but also embraces 'a kind of historical criticism which, after analysis of particular works, seeks to relate them to the particular traditions and societies in which they appeared' (41–2). Actually (and surprisingly), despite being 'documentary', Williams included things like architecture and dress fashions in this category (49).

Thirdly, there is the *social* category 'in which culture is a description of a particular way of life, which expresses certain meanings and values not only in art and learning but

*(Continued)*

*(Continued)*

also in institutions and ordinary behaviour'. What this definition involves in terms of practice is an effort to clarify the meanings and values (whether implicit or explicit) in a particular way of life. This kind of analysis would include the *documentary* approach but would also include analyses that to the defenders of the other approaches would not be 'culture' at all: 'the organization of production, the structure of the family, the structure of institutions which express or govern social relationships, the characteristic forms through which members of the society communicate' (42).

Finally, Williams argued that it is necessary to distinguish between '**lived culture**', which was only fully accessible to those living at a particular place and time, the '**recorded culture**' (of all kinds) and the culture of the '**selective tradition**' – those elements of culture which are chosen as being in some way exemplary or illustrative (to some extent this takes place within the period itself) (49–50). The value of these approaches is to be found in considering them of equal importance because each one helps the critic to appreciate the complexity of a culture in different way.

## The theory of culture as a whole way of life

LADVI: (back online) Good, taking these categories into account it is now possible to understand more fully Williams'theory of culture which he described as '**as a theory of relationships between elements in a whole way of life**' (46) – actually, if you look at his foreword to *Culture and Society* [1958] 1987: ii) you'll see that he had already anticipated this anthropological definition. Getting back to *The Long Revolution*, Williams warned that it was a 'fatally wrong approach' to assume 'that political institutions and conventions are of a different and separate order from artistic institutions and conventions'. For him, absolutes like politics, art, science, religion and family life 'belong in a whole world of active and interacting relationships, which is our common associative life' ([1961] 1992: 39).

VIDAL: So, if you're going to look at sex and drugs, you'd better not forget the rock'n'roll!

LADVI: Well, that's one way of putting it! But all this has profound implications for a theory of culture and practice: if the end of cultural analysis is to understand the significance of objects with relation to history, and how they relate to society, classes, groups and cultural institutions and forms etc., it is just as important to analyse things like gender relations and reality TV as literary texts or the Western tradition of classical music or fine art. Williams put it like this: 'a good living culture is various and changing, [and] the need for sport and entertainment is as real as the need for art' (337).

VIDAL: Hey! That means I could legitimately study, Grunge, video games, the *Simpsons* or the World Superbike Championship!

LADVI: Yes, and I, from this point of view, could offer a cultural analysis of popular magazines or martial arts. Thinking about it, you might consider how the use of an idea like this would have changed Hoggart's attitude towards the Teddy Boy culture of the 1950s (you remember me recommending you read his *The Uses of Literacy*?).

VIDAL: Yes, I did read ... some of it, but I can see that Williams wouldn't have read post-1930s mass culture in such a biased way and he would have related rock'n'roll to wider social, economic, political and cultural tendencies.

LADVI: In this respect Williams' work has been fundamental in terms of a transition from analyses which tend to write-off popular cultural forms to analyses which take them more seriously by putting aside simple value judgements. This does not mean that he had entirely moved beyond judgemental comments (the terms 'good' and 'bad' are not abandoned) but that he does not dismiss popular forms of culture (or mass commercial culture). If Williams analysed and took seriously the novel and drama (he wrote important books on both), he was also prepared to consider the importance of other things like advertising, the popular press, film, television, language and all systems of communication, exploring how these were vitally linked (and contributed) to economic, social, political and cultural change.

VIDAL: How did he manage all this?!

LADVI: In very general terms, what Williams urged those studying culture to do was to search for **meaningful patterns** and then look for the relationships between these patterns. It was Williams' insistence that cultural forms should be understood with relation to **the material circumstances** in which they are produced (taking account of processes of production and the social relations that these imply) that has helped to underline the significance of his work. In fact, by the 1980s critics like Alan Sinfield and Jonathan Dollimore had helped to establish a critical method which became known, following Williams (1980:243), as '**cultural materialism**', a hybrid form which unites literary and cultural studies. Well, I reckon that's enough for now.

VIDAL: Great, so we've finished with Williams?

LADVI: By no means! It just means I've got another exercise for you! I'll get back to you when you've completed it.

## Ladvi's question

Read through 'The Analysis of Culture' and have a look at the way Williams practised his own method of analysis. Concentrate on the *way* he conducts his analysis rather than the content. See if you can suggest ways that this method might be adapted to the world you live in.

(Again, it is not necessary for you to read 'The Analysis of Culture' but again, if you have access to it, you might read it through and respond to the question before reading Vidal's reply. As Vidal's reply relates to practice, it will be presented as such.)

## **notes** ON PRACTICE: Williams and method – Vidal's reply

Williams illustrates his theories and concepts with relation to a discussion of the culture of the 1840s in England. He starts out by looking at the selective tradition with reference to newspapers and literature, which gives us an insight into reading habits and taste. This immediately leads Williams to a consideration of social history where he finds important changes in cultural institutions like the rise of the Sunday press, new journals, the printing of cheap fiction, and the development of minor theatres and the rise of the music halls.

He shows how these institutional contexts imply technological changes associated with new productive forms: for example, machinery which facilitated printing and the railway boom (which created new locations for reading, sales and distribution). These factors are connected to business speculation, commercial organization and efforts to influence public opinion (through the press). Alongside these developments Williams sees other phenomena like the appearance of public museums, libraries and parks, which show how the decade 'brought crucial developments in the commercial exploitation of culture, in its valuable popular expansion, and in enlightened public provision' ([1961] 1992: 56–7). Williams also outlines important trends in political and social history, including the importance of class relations, arguing that the political and social history of the 1840s was reflected in contemporary literature.

For analytical purposes Williams draws two conclusions from this. The first is that none of these things should be considered in isolation; the second is that 'each is subject to highly selective interpretation, according to subsequent directions and commitments' (58). What he means by this second point is that, in hindsight, we do not necessarily understand trends in the 1840s (or any period) in the same way as contemporaries understood them. This illustrates an earlier point he made which was that there is a tendency to underrate the 'extent to which the cultural tradition is not only a selection but also an interpretation' (53). It seems to me that the general point here is a valuable one: **what we understand as culture is not only the product of how contemporaries saw and interpreted themselves** (which is of great interest to cultural criticism) **but also how successive generations see and interpret the past**.

Williams then goes on to examine what he calls the '**social character**' of the period. The dominant social character is associated with things like the belief in marriage, fidelity, the family, self-help, thrift, sobriety and piety, hard work, individual effort, suffering as ennobling, and a belief that the poor are 'victims of their own failure'. All these can be detected in cultural forms and reflect the morality of the dominant group: that is, the industrial and commercial middle classes (61). To be more accurate, Williams argues that there were social *characters*, in the plural because alongside the dominant middle-class values were those of the aristocracy and the working class. It is by studying the relations between these that 'we enter the reality of the whole way of life' (63), although this is complicated by the fact that the social character is in a constant process of change.

After this Williams asserts the importance of understanding the '**structure of feeling**' of a period which, like the social character, is not 'uniform throughout society' but is

*(Continued)*

*(Continued)*

primarily evident in the dominant social group' (63). Through the idea of the structure of feeling Williams tried to describe what he called the lived culture of a period (an idea I mentioned at the end of my answer to 'Question 1'). An analysis of art (especially the novel) is given particular importance here because it is able to give valuable insights into what it meant to live during the 1840s. However, as Williams' final comments make clear, the creative activities of the period are to be found not only in art but in industry, engineering and new kinds of social institution.

His general conclusion, that re-emphasizes the idea of understanding culture as a whole way of life, is that it is not possible to understand 'the creative part of culture' without reference to other social factors 'which are as strong and as valuable an expression of direct human feeling as the major art and thought' (70–1). I think Williams gives a good example of the importance of seeing culture as a whole way of life when discussing the rise of the popular press in England. In the following heuristic I've tried to show how Williams goes about exploring different contexts in order to understand its emergence as a social phenomenon:

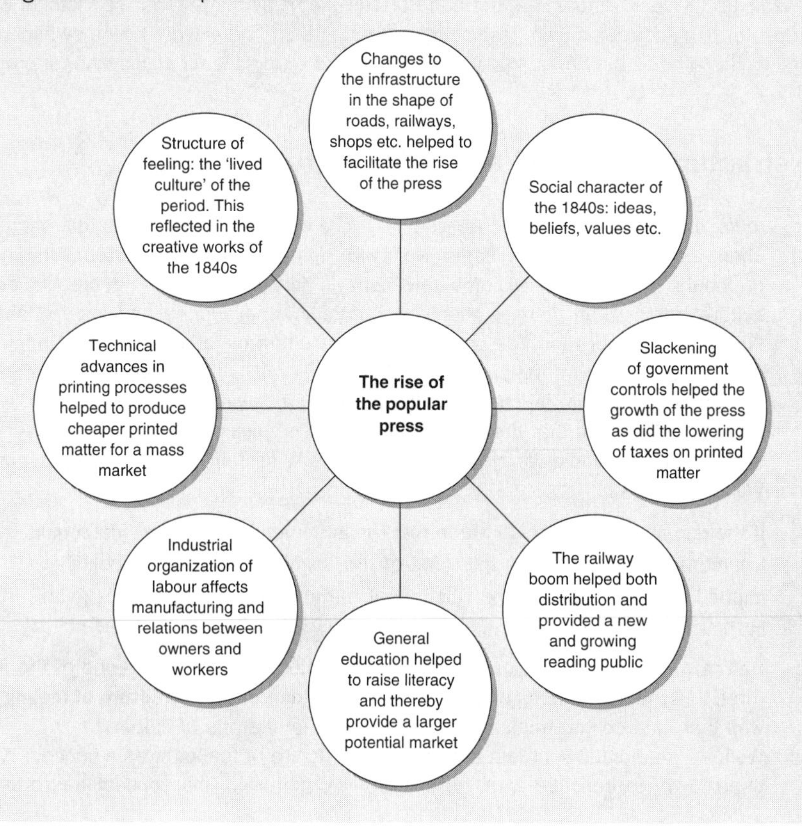

This doesn't exhaust the possibilities that Williams suggested but I think it gives a general idea of his approach. In all this Williams is trying to find meaningful patterns which can give an insight into the 1840s.

**Adapting Williams' theories**

In terms of the way Williams' ideas might be adapted to the world today, it is possible to use the above heuristic and replace the central term with another cultural form. Then we could look at the technological, scientific, educational, ideological contexts in which the form is produced and consumed, as well as things like the organization of labour and the social–political circumstances that surround it, and what kind of infrastructure is needed to sustain it. Some things which come to mind which might help to characterize the contemporary world are: the world wide web, e-mails, mobile phones, text messaging, nuclear power, video games, celebrity culture, DVDs, the consumption of brand names etc. (my list of keywords in my second answer – 'adapting keywords to new contexts' – would be very helpful here). Another approach would be to pick a decade like the 1960s, choose a cultural phenomenon (like space exploration, black rights, civil rights, feminism, independence movements, nuclear armaments, the Iron Curtain, the hippy movement, the Vietnam war, the rise of pop and rock music, fashion, globalization etc.) and explore how they might be used to characterize the period in more general terms by looking for significant patterns.

## The 'structure of feeling' and doing cultural studies

LADVI: (back on line) Good, now we're ready to move on a bit further. Let's talk a little more about the importance of Williams' work with relation to popular culture. Take the case of popular newspapers. Williams saw them as part of an expanding, creative and vital culture, rather than dismiss them as culturally impoverished and impoverishing. As Williams emphasized in *The Long Revolution*, culture (whether novel or Sunday paper) is a 'creative activity' or process ([1961] 1992: 40). Here he was challenging the clichéd idea that cultural forms like the popular press were a result of 'vulgar' working-class taste, arguing that they were products of complex cultural processes, very much dependent on middle- and upper-class taste. A certain irony is brought out when Williams writes:

> If the rich and the well-to-do are in fact (as is sometimes claimed) defending traditional culture, and the interests of the 'highly educated and politically-minded minority', against the vulgarity of the intruding masses, they seem, in their buying of newspapers, to be doing it in a very odd way. (213)

VIDAL: Before we move on, I'd like to ask you a question. I remember in one of the few lectures I attended, Williams was criticized for his idea of the '**structure of feeling**' – why was that, and do you think it's still useful for the analysis of culture?

LADVI: Well, as you said in your last answer, the 'structure of feeling' was a concept Williams used to try to describe what he called 'lived culture'. This concept has often been criticized because it seems too vague. However, I would argue that it *is* useful from the point of view of practice. Let's try to clarify the idea a little further – the structure of feeling is related to 'the meanings and values which are lived in works and relationships' (293). It is used to describe:

> a particular sense of life, a particular community of experience hardly needing expression, through which the characteristics of our way of life that an external analyst could describe are in some way passed, giving them a particular and characteristic colour. (48)

Williams argued that searching for cultural patterns resulted from abstracting from social activities, but getting to the 'structure of feeling' is a question of getting close to shared values and experience: the 'actual life' as it was lived by particular groups in society. What I'll do here is to show you how the concept worked in practice, then discuss some of its shortcomings.

VIDAL: At last, I can have a rest!

LADVI: But not for long!

As Ladvi's advice relates to practice it will be presented as such.

## **notes** ON PRACTICE: advice on practising cultural analysis with the structure of feeling

One example of 'structure of feeling' can be seen in the popular fiction in the 1840s. If you read the novels of this period you'll see that there are what Williams calls '**magic formulas**'. These are often used to resolve plots that would otherwise be in conflict with the dominant values governing marriage and divorce. Analysing magic formulas is a way of using the art and thought of a period to reveal structures of feeling and this technique helps the critic to discern meaningful patterns that can help analysis and understanding.

Now, let's take the case of a hero or heroine in a novel of the 1840s trapped in an unhappy marriage. One fine day, the protagonist meets his or her romantic ideal at a party. It's love at first sight! But the prevailing values of the period demand that marriage is a question of 'till death do us part'. The question is, how did novelists adapt plots to resolve the unhappy marriage without offending predominant moral attitudes? Firstly, the unloved partner is often described as cruel, violent, unfaithful, a gambler, a drunkard, or even mad. Now, what's the magic solution to the problem, where dominant social values mean that you can't just leave your cruel wife or husband? Illnesses! Accidents! Even murder! Yes, DEATH, of course! Anything, rather than divorce! (Williams, [1961] 1992: 65f.). Williams puts it like this: 'at a given point, and after the required amount of resigned suffering, there is a convenient, often spectacular death, in which the unloving partner shows great qualities of care, duty, and piety; and then, of course, the real love can be consummated' (66).

Another dominant 'magic formula' was associated with the problem of instability and debt. Many novels are structured around the very real problem of the loss of fortune. The dominant social codes demanded that once ruined, the impoverished protagonist had to be exiled. How could a protagonist be conveniently restored to society? The answer is through the use of two main devices. One is the time-worn unexpected legacy which could always, like appearance of the cavalry in Western films, save a hero in an impossible situation. The other device is in having the ruined hero take advantage of the economic possibilities offered by the British Empire by disappearing for a few years to some distant land and returning with a vast fortune (66). In fact the Empire could be used to reward or punish – all undesirables could be conveniently deported to the new lands.

These magic formulas were seen by Williams as a form of 'cheating' where the social character was in conflict with the structure of feeling. That is to say, if there was 'no general solution to the social problems of the time' individual solutions could be found to resolve situations that otherwise might have contradicted dominant beliefs. To give a quick example that Williams discusses, the British novelist and politician, Benjamin Disraeli, dramatized the social problems of the time in his novel *Sybil, or The Two Nations* ([1845] 1980) where an aristocrat falls in love with a Chartist girl. Disraeli solved the problem of the 'two nations' of rich and poor not through finding a viable political solution but by having his Chartist heroine, Sybil, discover that she is actually a member of a family of dispossessed aristocrats!

Williams further argues, and here his theory gets more interesting, while these magic formulas conveniently solved difficult social problems they existed in works which, at the same time, expressed these unresolved problems. The cruel realities of the lives of vulnerable members of the community (like the exposed child, the orphan or the girl from a poor family) could be expressed with great intensity, especially by a skilled novelist. So, within these neat magical formulas there was also the expression of '**a radical human dissent**' (68), a recognition of how society fails. This also reveals important elements of the dominant structure of feeling, or what we might call the 'sensibility' of a particular social group.

It is also possible to discern structures of feeling which are in conflict with one another within the same form. For example, Williams discussed Elizabeth Gaskell's novel *Mary Barton* ([1848] 1997) seeing in it both deep sympathy for the industrial poor but, at the same time, fear of working-class violence which is reflected in the novel's plot (91).

To see how this concept might be practised today you might extend Williams' range of reference to include not only novels (popular and literary) and magazines but other forms like drama, films, TV programmes and even video games. We might ask a series of questions like:

- How are plot lines resolved? Can you discern dominant values behind different kinds of resolution?
- Do resolutions imply some kind of common system of values (and is it in conflict with these dominant values)? You might think about popular heroes and heroines from films like *Batman, Superman, James Bond, Rambo, Dirty Harry, Robocop, Taxi Driver, Lara Croft, Matrix, Harry Potter, Cat Woman, Resident Evil* and *Kill Bill* and see how far they manage to solve different kinds of problems within the established laws and values of the cultures in which they are produced and circulated.

- How far do contemporary forms still rely on 'magic formulas'? Do these reveal significant patterns that suggest anything about dominant values and the inability of contemporary societies to solve conflicts at an official level?
- Another activity you might try is to see how well contemporary forms of culture both conveniently solve difficult social problems but also express these unresolved problems. Works often described as 'social realism' generally explore the harsh realities of the lives of vulnerable members of the community with great intensity and express 'radical human dissent'.
- Do you discern contradictory forms of the structure of feeling in single a single work?
- Finally, you might consider how 'magic formulas' transform over given periods of time and the significance of these changes, or their disappearance.

Much popular culture still works with highly conventionalized magic formulas, like the effect mentioned earlier of the cavalry riding in at the climax of a Western. Just to take a couple of dominant conventions, contemporary film is full of unhappy protagonists who ultimately find happiness and the promise of fulfilment in the arms of an attractive partner (most romantic comedies draw on this convention from early Hollywood classics to *Notting Hill* (1999)). Alternatively, social, political or military problems are often solved by the actions of extraordinary individuals. Look at the list of films above – most of them are dominated by the existence of this type of hero or heroine.

This mythology, drawing on other cultural forms like comics, reflects the importance of values like individualism but also the fascination with violent action, speed, spectacle, the erotic, magic, deception, the criminal underworld, the mystical and horror etc. If you think about it, the reason why the 'ordinary' people behind the super hero/heroine (of the Batman/Batwoman variety), can't be fully adjusted to conventional life is that these extraordinary individuals are forever trapped by the problems they wish to eradicate – because their implausible feats tend to work on the effects rather than tackle the deep social causes. It could be argued that this genre implicitly recognizes social failure at the heart of crime because the only way to deal with it is through an outrageous form of the magical formula.

You can go a long way with this idea but it's best not to oversimplify because much popular culture *may not* be characterized by such simplistic magic formulas. However, it is still possible to ask questions about whether or not there are dominant patterns and try to link them to the societies in which they are produced and/or consumed, and look into how different works deal with the lives of the vulnerable, and the social systems in which they live.

Coming back to criticisms of Williams' the 'structure of feeling', there are possible weaknesses in the way his theory hangs together. Although Williams stresses the importance of 'lived culture', his idea tends to remind readers that cultural criticism can never *fully* capture what it means to live a culture. Williams admits that looking for larger patterns in documentary culture and abstracting from them does not reproduce the uniqueness of personal experience. We can imagine someone in 200 years trying to understand what it's like living in the first part of the twenty-first century by looking at things like film, newspapers, magazines, novels, TV programmes, sports, video games, the internet, mobile phones etc. However, Williams says that although you could try to look for patterns in a past historical era you'd never really *know* what it felt like to live in a period that was not your own.

And all this is complicated further because, even if we have direct experience of a particular culture at a particular time, there's no guarantee that we'd be able to understand the 'structure of feeling' that could be said to characterize a particular period:

> At the same time, if we reflect on the nature of a structure of feeling and see how it can fail to be fully understood even by living people in close contact with it, with ample material at their disposal, including the contemporary arts, we shall not suppose that we can ever do more than make an approach, an approximation, using any channels. (Williams, [1961] 1992: 49)

This seems to be rather limiting and the 'structure of feeling' (as actual lived experience) seems to be an absent ideal, rather than something that can be revealed through cultural criticism. We live at a certain time but cannot be trusted to fully understand the structure of feeling that governs our lives; we die, and leave documentary culture behind us. The future critic has to navigate paths through it. We might ask Williams:

- How many structures of feeling are there?
- Should some be privileged?
- Are some more relevant than others?
- Is there such a thing as a false or misguided structure of feeling?
- In what ways might structure of feeling be complicated by questions of class, gender, race or sexuality?

Nevertheless, despite weaknesses in the notion of the structure of feeling, I hope I have demonstrated that it *does* provide a way of analysing and understanding culture and may have considerable explanatory power. Also, I think it's a credit to Williams that he recognizes a number of shortcomings, rather than brush the theoretical and practical difficulties under the carpet. Finally, we might use some of the questions posed above to open out the notion in interesting and revealing ways.

VIDAL: Hey, thanks. That is going to be really useful! So, is that the extent of Williams' contribution?

LADVI: Well, no, not by any means! But this should give you some idea of the extent of his work. To finish I'll just mention a few more concepts that can easily be put into practice: **sequencing** and **flow** in television and **emergent**, **dominant** and **residual cultures**. One other thing, Williams' relevance has also been maintained by his willingness to adapt the ideas of important Marxist theorists like Althusser and Gramsci and I'm sure you'll be hearing about these before too long.

AUTHOR: (intervening for a moment) Yes, see chapters ten and eleven.

LADVI: (directing herself to the author) Hey, do you mind? This is not *your* conversation (the author disappears).

## Williams and television: sequencing and flow, and dominant, residual and emergent cultures

VIDAL: So, what's this television flow, and does it give me a good excuse to watch TV?

LADVI: Actually, it does but not, perhaps, in the way you're used to. In 1974 Williams published his *Television: Technology and Cultural Form* in which he developed a series of strategies in order to analyse technological structures and their characteristic forms (reflecting his general interest in communications, see Williams, 1962). This is a complex book which covers a lot of ground but a number of ideas have been of particular use to those interested in visual media. One aspect that has been of interest is Williams' attack on an approach associated with Marshall McLuhan: that 'the medium is the message' or, in an even more playful form, 'the medium is the massage' (McLuhan and Fiore, 1967).

VIDAL: What on earth does McLuhan mean by that?

LADVI: To simplify, the main idea here is that technologies (whether we are talking of printing machines, transport, television or computers) determine cultural change and the way human beings perceive and understand reality. In this way McLuhan tended to privilege the medium over the message. Williams reacted strongly against this way of seeing, criticizing what he saw as McLuhan's simplistic determinism (his tendency to describe history with relation to cause and effect). To give an example, McLuhan claims that 'Print technology created the public. Electric technology created the mass' (McLuhan and Fiore, 1967: 68). One technology replaces another transforming society and perception as it goes.

VIDAL: Hey! I like it!

LADVI: It's suggestive, I agree (and I think there's a lot that's of interest in McLuhan's work), but Williams argued that technologies don't cause change in themselves, neither do they exist autonomously outside social, political or military needs. They are responses to the need to solve human problems. Radio, for example, was first used by the Navy as a technological response to the need for communications between ship and shore. We could extend this to the use of the World Wide Web: its origins were military not commercial. Putting too much emphasis on the medium underplays the role of active human transformation and change.

VIDAL: Sounds like we're back with the idea of human agency!

LADVI: Yes, you've noticed that this is never far away from Williams' conception of cultural forms – hence his relation to culturalist approaches.

VIDAL: (interrupting) But what's all this got to do with sequencing and flow?

LADVI: Well, all this is part of the context in which these ideas are developed. In a famous passage in *Television: Technology and Cultural Form* we find Williams in Miami watching a film. Used to British broadcasting (including the non-commercial BBC) he expects all interruptions of the film, for TV advertisements, trailers etc., to be 'marked', that is, neatly separated from the film – but this is not the case. He is surprised by the sheer number of advertisements and he registers a certain disorientation when the crime film he was watching, set in San Francisco, is disrupted by trailers featuring a romance in Paris and a prehistoric monster laying waste to New York. In Britain, Williams expected trailers *between* programmes and commercial breaks to be announced (something which would change very quickly). The tendency in North American TV was to insert ads and trailers with no warning whatsoever (Williams, 1974: 92). This experience led Williams to the idea of analysing TV from the point of view of sequence and flow. That is, he studied how sequences, including all the interruptions, are organized and incorporated into a channel's general programming. The important point about all this is that by being aware of these conventions it is possible not only to describe the experience of watching TV but analyse how TV companies try to keep audiences watching the same channel.

VIDAL: By constantly giving previews of what's to come?

LADVI: Yes, that's part of it. But as we saw earlier, Williams went beyond this, when he observed that programmes and advertisements were not neatly divided from one another. If you think about it, if advertisements are featured at the beginning and/or at the end of a programme it is easier to switch to another channel to avoid them. Thus, commercial stations slip the ads into the flow of the programmes. Methodologically, this way of looking is very characteristic of Williams' general approach to understanding cultural forms. His subject is television, but his analysis, instead of trying to describe particular programmes and what they mean, looks at *how* broadcasters use the available technology to organize TV schedules etc.

VIDAL: So, in order to understand television its not enough to watch the programmes but study what happens around them.

LADVI: Yes, that's it. You'll get an idea of the scope of the book by reading what Graeme Turner has written about it. He summarized the book's general importance by stating that concepts like sequence and flow help to describe the experience of television through the 'complex articulation of production practices, technological and economic determinants, and the social function of television within the home, as well as the formal structures of individual television genres' (Turner, 1996: 58). These ideas have been very suggestive for cultural critics interested in modern communications, or what Rushkoff has called 'screenagers 1997: 3). As far as practice is concerned we might look at how television today has changed in terms of sequencing and flow.

Figure 6.1 Williams relaxes in front of the television

VIDAL: Well, I can see that television flow is much more complicated now because, apart from advertisements, trailers and announcements, the flow includes all kinds of other messages simultaneous with the programmes being shown – we're often bombarded with information appearing at the bottom of the screen.

LADVI: Also, I think that TV companies are not only trying to keep us watching the same channel but encouraging us to spend money on other related media like sending mobile phone text messages (to vote, give opinions etc.). But there's much more in *Television: Technology and Cultural Form* than I've had time to go into here. I'd advise you to look at it for yourself.

VIDAL: OK. Is that it? I'm tired. This has been a long chapter.

LADVI: Don't worry, we're nearly finished. To conclude, let's look at some categories Williams put forward in his 1981 study that he called, very simply, *Culture*. In that book he wrote about **dominant**, **residual** and **emergent** cultures. The idea here is that the dominant forms of culture at any given moment coexist with older forms (which may or may not be in decline) and new possibilities which may challenge or replace, challenge or modify the dominant forms. For example, although it isn't always easy to state with certainty what is emergent or in decline, it is possible to see how older forms of culture coexist with dominant contemporary forms (Williams, 1981: 204–5).

VIDAL: Can you give me examples?

## **notes** ON PRACTICE: dominant, residual and emergent cultures

LADVI: For example, alongside the consumer culture that is lived in capitalist democracies there are remnants of ways of life, like those associated with rural life or organized religious groups, that look back, but are incorporated into, the dominant culture (Williams, 1977: 122f.). Or take the example of the rise of the working class in Britain. As an emergent culture it brought with it particular ways of seeing the world (often in conflict with the dominant order), distinct values, beliefs, institutions and leisure time activities (which may or may not be extensions of, and in opposition to, existing forms) etc. Just as the landed classes in Britain in the nineteenth century had to incorporate middle-class ways of thinking and values etc. into the dominant culture (especially after the political reforms), so these classes had to do the same with relation to the working classes later in the century. It's also possible, then, to analyse if a cultural form or practice is merely 'alternative' or 'oppositional' (Williams, 1980: 41). You might think of astrology on the one hand and radical political movements on the other. But, wait, why am I doing all the thinking here? Why don't you give *me* a few examples?

VIDAL: (groaning) Well, I suppose we might extend these ideas in a more general way to popular music: 1950s rock'n'roll has given way to, but coexists with, later pop and rock styles. In hindsight, it is easier to see how mobile phones and the World Wide Web were emergent in many cultures and are now dominant. And, er, well ...

Figure 6.3 Dominant, residual and emergent cultures

LADVI: OK, I can see you've had enough for one day! I hope you can see that this way of looking at culture challenges simplistic notions of it as static and introduces the idea of culture as a series of processes which link past, present and emergent future. In practice you can use this idea to explore different moments of cultural history by choosing a historical period and exploring the relations between different forms of culture. The image of culture that emerges here is one of dominant forms perpetually in potential conflict with historical residues and gradually emerging potentialities. Here, as in much of Williams' work, culture is seen as a dynamic, vital, complex process in constant evolution, rather than as something fixed, uncomplicated and universal. This idea is always worth keeping in mind, but that's all I have time for. Hope this has been of some help – and good luck with the exam ...

## SUMMARY OF KEY POINTS

This chapter has emphasized Williams' importance to cultural analysis and outlined his efforts to offer adequate working definitions of culture that would aid critical practice. We have seen that Williams' conception of culture as a whole way of life or as a long revolution have helped to provide valuable starting points for practice. This chapter has also explained and illustrated his use of keywords and explored his suggestion that culture can be understood through the 'structure of feeling' of a period. The final sections provide an account of how Williams approached the analysis of television through concepts like sequencing and flow, and what effect the idea of dominant, residual and emergent cultures has on the theory and practice of cultural analysis. Williams' importance in methodological terms can be summed up in the following ways:

- Important to Williams' approach is the recognition that if culture, in its modern sense, is an extension of social and political changes brought about by industrial capitalism then cultural historians would have to attend to the historical circumstances that produced the forms of art and life of industrial civilization. This provides a historical (materialist) basis for the understanding of culture which also emphasizes class relations. In this sense, there are clear affinities with Thompson's (Marxist) approach and echoes of other writers like Arnold, Adorno, Hoggart and the Leavises.
- One practical consequence of Williams' division of culture into the *ideal*, the *documentary* and the *social* is that to understand it there is no sense in trying to marginalize popular mass culture and privilege forms of minority or elite culture.
- Williams shows how the analysis of keywords can give valuable insights into cultural formations. An exploration of changes of use of these keywords helps to reveal transformations in ways of thinking about social, political and economic institutions.
- At a general level, Williams' method shows how important writers reacted to key issues like industry, democracy, art, culture and class. This is significant from the point of view of practice because it shows how it is possible to understand culture through explanatory

maps by which it is possible to observe the 'wider changes in life and thought' that writers reflect in their works.

- Williams' conception of culture 'as a theory of relationships between elements in a whole way of life' has profound implications for theory and practice: it is just as important to analyse things like sport, gender relations and TV as literary texts or the Western tradition of classical music or fine art. No aspect of culture should be left off the analytical map. In this way Williams helped to reinforce an anthropological view of cultural analysis.
- Williams' chapter 'The Analysis of Culture' offers a practical example of how the cultural critic might go about practising cultural analysis. We saw how a study of the popular press illustrates the importance of the multiple contexts that Williams argued were important for an adequate understanding of culture.
- Important to Williams' method was the idea of getting close to shared values and experience, the 'actual life' as it was lived by particular groups in society. For this he coined the term the 'structure of feeling'. Despite weaknesses in this idea, it has been presented as methodologically useful.
- One way of revealing the 'structure of feeling' is to focus on 'magic formulas'. This critical strategy uses the art and thought of a period to discern meaningful patterns that can help to appreciate the dominant values, unresolved problems and sensibility of a particular social group. They can also give insights into forms of 'radical human dissent' providing criticisms of social systems.
- As far as analysing television is concerned, Williams' attention to sequencing and flow can help us to understand not so much the content of programmes but the *way* programming is organized to expose audiences to advertising and entice viewers to continue watching the same channel.
- Finally, the idea of dominant, residual and emergent cultures is methodologically significant because it can help to show that culture is a dynamic, vital and complex process, rather than something fixed, uncomplicated and universal.

## References

Bennett, Tony, Grossberg, Lawrence and Morris, Meaghan (eds) (2005) *New Keywords*. Oxford: Blackwell.

Disraeli, Benjamin ([1845] 1979) *Sybil, or The Two Nations*. London: Penguin.

Eagleton, Terry (1984) *The Function of Criticism: From the Spectator to Post-Structuralism*. London: Verso.

Gaskell, Elizabeth Cleghorn ([1848] 1896) *Mary Barton*. London: Penguin.

McLuhan, Marshall and Fiore, Quentin (1967) *The Medium is the Massage: An Inventory of Effects*. New York: Bantam Books.

Rushkoff, Douglas (1997) *Children of Chaos: Surviving the End of the World as We Know It.* London: Flamingo.

Smith, Adam ([1776] 1982) *The Wealth of Nations, Books 1–3.* London: Penguin.

Storey, John (2001) *Cultural Theory and Popular Culture: An Introduction* (3rd edition) Essex: Pearson Prentice Hall.

Turner, Graeme (1996) *British Cultural Studies: An Introduction* (2nd edition). London: Routledge.

Williams, Raymond ([1958] 1987) *Culture and Society: Coleridge to Orwell.* London: Hogarth.

Williams, Raymond ([1961] 1992) *The Long Revolution.* London: Hogarth.

Williams, Raymond (1962) *Communications.* Harmondsworth: Penguin.

Williams, Raymond (1974) *Television: Technology and Cultural Form.* London: Fontana.

Williams, Raymond (1977) *Marxism and Literature.* Oxford: Oxford University Press.

Williams, Raymond (1980) *Problems in Materialism and Culture.* London: Verso.

Williams, Raymond (1981) *Culture.* London: Fontana.

Williams, Raymond (1983) (Revised edn) *Keywords: A Vocabulary of Culture and Society.* London: Flamingo.

## Further reading

Most introductions to cultural studies offer overviews of Williams' work and most readers include at least passages from 'The Analysis of Culture' (Storey, 1998, below). Bennett et al. (see References above) includes a very useful introductory essay on Williams' use of keywords.

Dollimore, Jonathan and Alan Sinfield (eds) (1992) *Political Shakespeare: New Essays in Cultural Materialism.* This book gives an idea of the way Williams' approaches relate to cultural materialism (see the chapters by the editors).

Eagleton, Terry (1976) *Criticism and Ideology.* London: New Left Books. Along with the title mentioned above (Eagleton, 1984), this book offers a much more theoretically complex view of Williams' work than I do here.

McLuhan, Marshall (1964) *Understanding Media.* New York: McGraw. In this book McLuhan sets out his basic ideas. However, the book mentioned above, *The Medium is the Massage*, is brief, accessible and full of images to help readers appreciate the points being made and is, therefore, a good introduction.

Middleton, Peter (1989) 'Why structure feeling?' *News from Nowhere*, 6. This looks at the structure of feeling in a sympathetic way.

Milner, Andrew (2002) *Re-Imagining Cultural Studies: The Promise of Cultural Materialism.* London: Sage. Having explored some of the ways Williams might aid practice in my introduction you might now move on to look at this study which offers a much fuller exploration of Williams' work within the context of materialist conceptions of culture. Milner's wide-ranging book repeatedly emphasizes the relevance of Williams' ideas for contemporary cultural analysis and would make a good starting point for anyone interested materialist approaches to research.

Storey, John (1998) (ed.) *Cultural Theory and Popular Culture: A Reader* (2nd edition). Essex: Pearson Prentice Hall. If you do not have access to a copy of *The Long Revolution*, this reader offers the first part of Williams' chapter where he outlines his theory. As mentioned above, most readers feature a section from Williams' landmark study.

Tudor, Andrew (1999) *Decoding Culture: Theory and Method in Cultural Studies*. London: Sage. Chapter two of this book offers some useful criticisms of Williams.

Turner (1996, see references above) Turner, apart from offering a an accessible and broad-ranging overview, also discusses some of the possible weaknesses in Williams work.

Williams, Raymond (1983) *Writing in Society*. London: Verso. Although I would recommend reading *Culture and Society* or *The Long Revolution* to begin an exploration of Williams' work, this title will give you an idea of the incredible range of Williams' thought. He moves with ease from essays on drama and English prose to fiction, English Studies, even writes a poem (a piece of creative criticism!) and finishes the book with an essay on the history of the imagination. If you consider that I've not referred to all of Williams' work (I've tended to downplay his literary criticism) and only mentioned his novels in passing, you may get an inkling of the breadth of his interests and erudition.

# PART III

## Consolidating Cultural Studies: Subcultures, the Popular, Ideology and Hegemony

# Introducing Stuart Hall: The Importance and Re-evaluation of Popular Mass Culture

## Introduction

This chapter is the first of five chapters dedicated to 'Consolidating Cultural Studies: Subcultures, the Popular, Ideology and Hegemony'. As the section title suggests, in these chapters you'll be introduced to things like popular cultural forms and the study subcultures: areas which have become fundamental to cultural studies. This chapter, and the two following it (chapters eight and nine) are intimately related in the way that they focus on subcultures (mainly youth subcultures). For this reason I have included all the further reading for these chapters at the end of chapter nine. In the final two chapters to this section (chapters ten and eleven) you'll see how cultural studies consolidated itself (and is still consolidating itself) through engaging in very productive ways with various aspects of Marxist thought. The common theme that runs through the five chapters of this part of the book is the idea of the 'popular'.

In this chapter I will begin by outlining the importance of Stuart Hall's contribution to cultural studies and discuss the institutional consolidation of the area. I shall then offer a dialogue which is intended to summarize and contextualize the approaches introduced in earlier chapters while introducing a series of ideas focused on youth culture. This will give an idea of some of the important developments within British cultural studies in the 1970s, while providing further concepts which can be experimented with in practice. Let's begin, then, with the first of the three chapters dedicated to the exploration of subcultures.

## MAIN LEARNING GOALS

- To appreciate Stuart Hall's contribution to cultural studies.
- To see how the book *The Popular Arts* extends the understanding of popular culture introduced in earlier chapters.
- To appreciate how popular cultural forms might be evaluated on their own terms.
- To recognize how youth cultures help young people to distinguish themselves from the adult community.
- To understand how the concepts introduced may be put into practice.

## Stuart Hall and the institutionalization of cultural studies

In a book which emphasizes relatively easy ways of beginning to practise cultural studies it would be unrealistic to offer a very detailed view of Stuart Hall's contribution, partly because of its extent and partly because Hall helped to open up a range of complex questions which would be out of place in a basic introduction. However, in the following three chapters Hall will feature prominently, and I hope to give an idea of some important ways in which Hall and his collaborators have influenced cultural studies.

In the chapter on Richard Hoggart I mentioned that in 1964 he became the founding director of the Centre for Contemporary Cultural Studies at Birmingham University. In 1969 Stuart Hall replaced Hoggart as director, a post he held right through the 1970s – a crucial period for the rise and consolidation of cultural studies (Turner, 1996: 67). As Roger Bromley has pointed out, leaving aside Raymond Williams, Stuart Hall 'has been the most influential figure in British cultural studies' and, even outside Britain, his work 'has probably been more responsible than any other for the spread of the field' (Munns and Rajan, 1995: 194).

It ought to be stressed here that the Birmingham Centre was by no means the only institution in which cultural analysis was being developed and carried out, even if it was to become one of the most important centres, not only in Britain but in the world. For the sake of concision I shall be using the Birmingham Centre as a microcosm of some of the important changes and shifts in focus within British cultural studies. When reading about Stuart Hall in introductions to cultural studies there is usually the sense that an area has been established, that there is no longer a sense of isolated writers developing ideas that would one day be gathered together under a new label. However, while Hall quite rightly insisted that work in the Birmingham Centre was a collaborative effort, his enormous contribution to cultural studies has rarely been questioned.

Coming back to Bromley, Hall's significance can be said to have manifested itself in 'an astonishing range of articles and co-authored books, many of which have a definitive place in the literature of the field' (194). This is true but the 'co-authored' characteristic of his output should alert you to the danger of confusing the Birmingham Centre with Stuart Hall – without, that is, undermining his personal contribution or his enormous importance as director, figurehead, inspiration and guide.

As I did with Williams, I shall begin my exploration of Hall by referring to an early work, *The Popular Arts* (1964), which was written in collaboration with Paddy Whannel – and which actually preceded Hall's work as director of the Birmingham Centre. The reason for starting with this work is that it not only focuses on popular music, and thereby extends some of the ideas already looked at with relation to earlier critics, but also introduces a number of approaches that would become important to the development of cultural studies (both inside and outside Britain).

## Hall, Whannel and *The Popular Arts*

In *The Popular Arts*, Hall and Whannel acknowledge their debts to Hoggart, Thompson and Williams and, although critical of the Leavisite tradition, recognize its importance. In this sense, the book acknowledges an important twentieth-century tradition of cultural studies; it might even be said that the book helps to create a sense of a recognizable cultural studies identity in Britain (which would be consolidated by the 1970s). *The Popular Arts* continues and revises arguments we have already reviewed in earlier chapters to do with cultural value. Put very simply, what Hall and Whannel set out to do is develop a critical method that could serve to analyse '**problems of value and evaluation**' with relation to popular cultural forms (Hall and Whannel, 1964: 15).

In order to explore this, let's imagine a small group of postgraduate students at a party somewhere in Britain. The year is 1965 – a year after the publication of *The Popular Arts*. Pat and Paddy Hall represent Whannel and Hall and, apart from Rod, each one of the speakers represents a view that has already been outlined in earlier chapters. By now you should be able to recognize the different stances and write the name of the critic by the side of the idea (if not, *just look at the surnames carefully*). This dialogue is designed to revise, summarize and contrast the different views introduced up to now and introduce some new ideas from *The Popular Arts*. By some odd coincidence, our speakers use many phrases from that book (which all appear between quotation marks and include page references).

## Judging popular culture on its own terms

A Rolling Stones' album is playing and Rod Richards enters the room strutting over to a group of people. He wears his hair long (for the time) and has a look based on his idol, Mick Jagger.

ROD: (approaching Pat) Hi, Pat, why aren't you moving to the music?

PAT: Well, right now we're talking.

ROD: Talking! What, don't you like the Stones?

PAT: It's not that ...

FRANK SILVEA: (looking down his nose) It's bad enough having to listen to this debased nonsense without having to have to dance to it. To be honest, I'd rather be listening to Beethoven or reading a decent novel. There really isn't anything for the intelligent person in all this noisy twaddle.

RICK GARTHOG: Well, we don't necessarily have to resort to Beethoven to experience meaningful music. I mean the working class has often produced meritorious forms of entertainment but now, I fear, these days are passing, especially with the arrival of this ...

ROD: (interrupting) I don't believe it! Conformists! This music is where it's happening. You lot had better crawl back to the Jurassic Age where you belong!

DORIS NORADO: (turning round and looking at him ironically) So, I suppose you think you're something of a rebel? Don't you see, you're just victim of the culture industry. While you're buying your Rolling Stones records you're just indulging in anti-social fantasies – and paying for them, thus enriching a few musicians and a lot of capitalists. And you call that non-conformity!

ROD: This music is more relevant to me than all that classical stuff you're always going on about. You're just an elitist. Times are changing and we have to change with them. I don't want to be like my parents, my grandparents, or you!

DORIS: OK, Rod, but don't you see that you're not going to change the world by identifying with the Stones or any other product of mass culture. The only real change will come from fighting the inequalities of the present economic and political conditions. Why don't you get into things which really challenge your intellect? Mass culture only works to dumb people down, pacify the audience, keep them where they are and leave them weak and depoliticized.

| | |
|---|---|
| ROD: | This is boring! I didn't come here to be turned into a revolutionary Marxist! |
| RAY WIMISALL: | (who has been listening patiently) Listen, Doris and Frank, while I don't think we need to discount the value of art, we should be able to admit the social importance of things like entertainment and sport. |
| PADDY: | (cutting in) I agree. There are *other* ways of looking. Pat and I have just read this book called *The Popular Arts* which I think can help us to understand your position, Rod, while taking up a critical attitude towards what we listen to. |
| PAT: | Exactly, the authors of this book, Hall and Whannel, reckon that it's possible to distinguish *between* the products of mass culture aimed at the young, and thereby value outstanding examples of all kinds of culture. In this way a more demanding audience might be trained rather than just repeat the 'misleading generalizations' that simply reject mass culture because it is, well, mass culture! (Hall and Whannel, 1964: 35). |
| DORIS: | You're not trying to persuade us that there is some value in listening to popular styles of music? |
| PADDY: | Yes, there's both value and meaning. Part of what we're saying is that it's important to be able to discriminate between different kinds of popular culture. |
| FRANK: | Now you're talking, I'm all for teaching people to distinguish between superior and inferior forms of culture and *why* mass culture is inferior. |
| PADDY: | OK Frank, I can see what you're saying but there's one crucial difference between what you're putting forward and the position we're representing here. What we're arguing is that **fine distinctions could be made *within* popular, mass culture** itself, rather than between it and forms of 'high' culture. |
| FRANK: | I can hardly believe that you are going to waste time making fine distinctions between Romance novels, Westerns and rock'n'roll! |
| PAT: | Look, we're not saying everything is of the same value but listening to some of the more innovative jazz music isn't the same as listening to some popular style with hardly any originality. Not all cinema is as predictable as the Hollywood blockbuster. |
| DORIS: | OK but jazz is not Schoenberg, Kafka or Proust! |
| ROD: | Or the Stones! |
| RICK: | So how do you propose to make these distinctions between popular forms of culture? |
| PADDY: | Through **informed choices**. According to *The Popular Arts* we have to ask ourselves if an example of popular culture is dependent on **pre-digested formulas** that generate **predictable products and responses** and if it **challenges** the audience in any way. If it's emotionally unrewarding or doesn't live up to the above criteria, then it's inferior. |
| DORIS: | I agree with your *way* of evaluating different works but popular forms may display some originality when they first appear but they always get snapped up by the culture industry and churned out as saleable formulas – (looking at Rod) in a couple of years there'll be dozens of Stones sound-alikes. |
| PADDY: | True, but popular culture has to be **judged on its own terms**, according to its own rules. |

ROD: I'm all for that.

PADDY: We would recommend this method because it is both flexible and practical: it can be used to judge all forms of culture, regardless of whether they are considered high art or commercial mass forms.

PAT: We'd also want to emphasize that it's not much use saying that Cole Porter's music is inferior to that of Beethoven's. They may not be of equal value, but Cole Porter wasn't trying to make an unsuccessful attempt to create music comparable to Beethoven's (39).

ROD: Who the hell's Cole Porter?!

PAT: You mean you've never heard a Porter classic like 'Love for Sale'!

DORIS: Ignore him, Pat, of course he has.

FRANK: Hold on a moment, I need a bit more clarification here. As I understand it, your authors are related to earlier forms of criticism in so far that they feel the need to alert teenagers to the severe limitations and ephemeral quality of pop music which is, more often than not, dominated by formulas and governed by the standards set by the commercial market. Now, most of us here agree that the 'high' arts are privileged forms generally beyond question and that culture based on predictable formulas is debased. However, I'd argue that traditional folk art or culture is also to be valued. How do your authors stand with respect to that?

PADDY: Well, in *The Popular Arts* traditional folk arts (those forms made for the community by the community) are seen to create a special **rapport** between performer and audience so these are highly valued. However, the products of industrial, mass culture are understood to lose this rapport and depend more on a performer's skills and the force of 'a personal style' to express and interpret community values and experiences (66).

RICK: Now you're beginning to make sense!

ROD: So, the Stones have got to become a folk band to win approval!

PAT: Not necessarily. What our authors call the 'popular arts' (the best of commercial culture) can actually reclaim the vital relation (the rapport found in folk forms) lost between audience and performer in forms which are, nevertheless, products of industrial capitalism. Our authors, however, weren't thinking of the Stones but more, as I hinted earlier, of things like independent film and innovative jazz – but you could always make a case for the Stones!

ROD: Oh, thanks a lot!

FRANK: But you'd be wasting your time.

## Cultural studies and youth culture

RAY: These ideas seem to me to be very interesting but I think youth culture has to be seen in terms of a whole way of life (looking at Pat and Paddy). I think the Stones' music has to be understood with relation to not only the fans but the wider society.

PADDY: Actually the authors we're representing do see the necessity of taking into account multiple contexts. They emphasize not only the music, the lyrics, 'the vocal texture' of the voice and the 'feelings which are caught up and transposed by the beat' but also the **relationships between the performers and the audience** and the **importance of the role the music industry** has in promoting its singers and bands (269).

RAY: I think your writers are wise to take account of the institutional contexts in which the music is produced, performed and promoted.

PAT: Yes, they recognize that the music is more than just listening to performers but is bound up with all kinds of other paraphernalia like recordings, magazines, concerts, TV performances and interviews with pop stars. They also stress the importance of other contexts like **work, politics, family relations, social and moral beliefs** (269). Then there are the dance styles, fashion, the slang words that help to distinguish **youth cultures** from what they're reacting against.

ROD: Look, listening to bands like the Stones is ... well, it's a way of life – it's like young people identifying with one another through their own culture. I didn't expect you lot to understand – you sound like a lot of squares – just the kind of people I'm reacting against.

DORIS: You just want to be a romantic, misunderstood, teen rebel and revel in adolescent nonconformity! You're addicted to the *idea* of rebellion, but you'll never change anything.

PADDY: Well, from the point of view we're arguing here we shouldn't just mock popular culture because it's important to understand how youth culture functions in helping young people to distinguish themselves from the adult world in terms of things like **rebelliousness and nonconformity**. Also, we can see that the consumers of youth culture are not necessarily as controlled and exploited as some people believe. Pop music helps young people to establish **a sense of identity**.

PAT: We agree with you, Doris, mass commercial culture is what our authors call '**a lush grazing pasture for the commercial providers**' but we should also recognize that it reflects the attitudes and sentiments of the audience in providing an **expressive field** and 'a set of symbols through which these attitudes can be projected'. In this way teen culture is a 'contradictory mixture of the authentic and manufactured' (276).

PADDY: According to *The Popular Arts*, pop songs also reflect the difficulties of adolescence helping young people cope with emotional and sexual problems. They reflect the need to experience life directly and intensely and express 'the drive for security in an uncertain and changeable emotional world' (280), while dealing with romantic love and sexual urges.

RICK: Hmm, I'd never thought of looking at adolescent culture in quite in this way – I thought it was all too trivial to dedicate much time to looking at it from the inside.

DORIS: So, these authors not only deal with questions of value and the commercial context but consider **the social, emotional and psychological role of teenage culture**?

ROD: And it sounds like, at last, someone recognizes that the songs do 'dramatize authentic feelings' (280) and that young people are actively creating forms of culture through what you called an 'expressive field'?

PAT: Yes and yes!

Figure 7.1 Understanding youth subcultures

ROD: But music is more than all this! You've got to hear the insistent beat, the roar of the bass, the gritty sound of the guitars, the inflection of the voice. Then there's how you might express yourself, distinguish yourself, through your look, through dress styles – it's not all in the lyrics!

PAT: Yes, you're right, without a consideration of the **non-verbal aspects** you wouldn't get much of an understanding of youth culture and that's why our authors do touch on the aspects you've mentioned.

DORIS: Oh, yea, the look, just like the music, is 'off the peg' – the product of marketing strategies. I've been reading some magazines aimed at teenage girls where you can learn to be different – through fashion, cosmetics and listening to pop bands. But it's all wonderfully contradictory! Let's all reject the authority of our parents, convention and conformity – by *buying* our way out of it! Let's all be anti-social by conforming to the authority of the market!

PADDY: You're echoing here a number of preoccupations and contradictions that our authors share. They see that the rebellious teenager is a media construction but they also see that the pop phenomenon can't be reduced only to market forces. They are also aware that much criticism of popular styles comes from prejudice and that some adult critics quite wrongly associate teen culture with delinquency (310f.).

FRANK: Well, you won't convince me to listen to any more of this caterwauling, rattling and blaring blather. I'm off! I'm sick of having my ears exposed to the same old clichéd drivel: 'Oh, I'm in love and I've never felt like this before!' 'Oh, ba-by, be mine – if only you knew I existed!' 'I'm a loner, I'm free and I'm gonna conquer the world.' 'Whoa, my ba-a-aby's left me! Get out of my life – I don't love you any more! Bah!' (He leaves.)

DORIS: I'm off, too, but not with Frank – he thinks he can improve the world just by teaching people discrimination and returning to a golden pre-industrial age, but without considering that only through radical politics can we really expect to bring about a better and more just world. I'm off to a political meeting. (She leaves.)

RICK: Give me pre-1930s working-class culture any day! However, you've raised some interesting points that aren't that far from my way of thinking. I'm off to my local Working Men's Club. Catch you later. (He leaves.)

Pat, Paddy, Rod and Ray remain listening and observing. Ray, with a glint in his eye, is about to treat his friends to a few ideas about whether or not it is possible to see significant patterns in all this and whether it is possible to arrive at a few conclusions about the structure of feeling in the early 1960s … But let's leave the speakers and consider how you might use some of these ideas in practice.

## **practice** EXERCISE: Interpreting with *The Popular Arts*

To understand a product of youth culture like music you need to take into account many interrelating factors. To prepare an essay or project based on Hall and Whannel's ideas on a particular style of music you might try using the heuristic presented on the following page.

To explore the value of the categories presented in the heuristic for cultural criticism you might take a style of music you particularly like or find interesting and respond to the two groups of questions. The first group should help you to analyse a particular kind of music; the second set of questions is designed to get you to think about and evaluate some of the theories in more general terms. If you did the practice exercises in chapter three (on hip-hop or another kind of music) you may find some of that information helpful for answering the following questions:

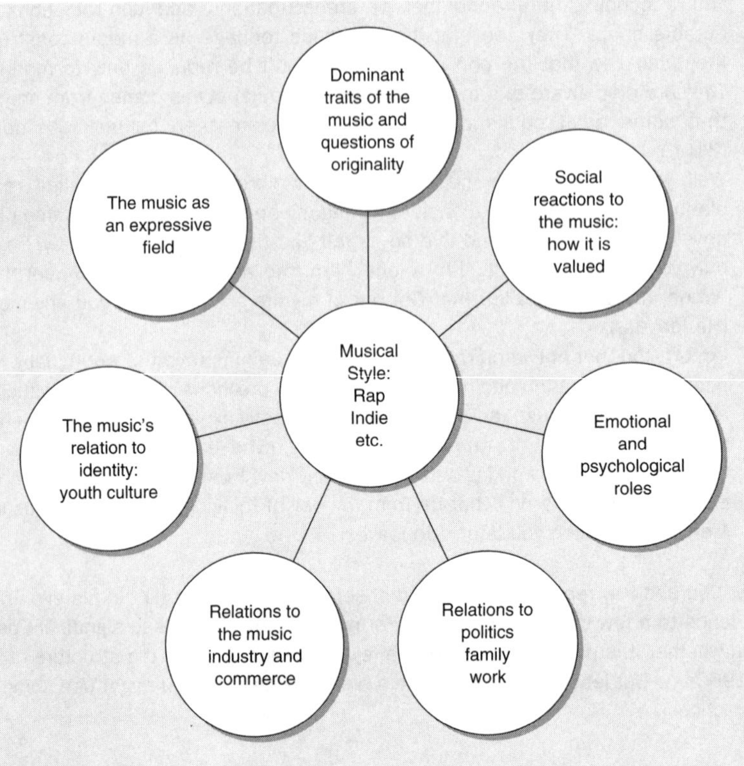


*Group One*

- What attitudes are expressed toward things like the family, politics, moral beliefs and work?
- Do many of these features reinforce a sense of identity and difference from the adult world or dominant culture?
- How important are rebelliousness and nonconformity? If they are important, in what ways do you think they are constructed and manifested? Do you discern resistance to dominant values? If so, how are they mobilized?
- In what ways might the style be said to be an 'expressive field', and what kinds of things are being expressed?
- Looking at the lyrics, how far do the songs reflect the difficulties of being young, and how far do they help young people cope with change, emotions, romantic love and sex?
- Would you say that the style and lyrics reflect the need to experience life directly and intensely and express 'the drive for security in an uncertain and changeable emotional world'?

- Can all the features explored so far help to define a particular youth culture? Would you say that the musical style you have chosen only appeals to youth?
- How far can the musical style be said to be 'a lush grazing pasture for the commercial providers'? How far do you think the audience is manipulated and exploited by the record companies, and how far does it construct or reflect the attitudes and sentiments of its audience?
- Drawing on your answers to the above questions, would you agree that teen culture is a 'contradictory mixture of the authentic and manufactured'?
- Looking at common reactions, would you say that the music has been the victim of prejudicial adult opinion and that it has been wrongly associated with delinquency?

*Group two*

Considering the answers you've given to the above set of questions:

- How useful do you think it is to make fine distinctions *within* popular, mass culture itself, rather than judge it with relation to forms of 'high' culture?
- Are you convinced that popular cultural forms should be judged on their own terms and with relation to informed choices?
- Do you think judging youth culture (or any form of popular mass commercial culture) to see if it is characterized by pre-digested formulas that generate predictable products and responses is a useful tool for distinguishing between different kinds of culture?
- Do you think that cultural forms have to challenge the audience in some way to be considered superior? In what ways might popular culture challenge?
- Do you think that the idea of establishing rapport between performer and audience is fundamental to evaluating the success and worth of the musical style you have studied? Do you think that music, or any other popular form, is likely to lose rapport because it is mass produced?
- Taking into consideration your answers so far, do you think Hall and Whannel could have considered other factors not mentioned in this introduction?
- John Storey has claimed that Hall and Whannel 'adopt uncritically the standard criticism made of mass culture' and 'rather than confront the mass culture critique, they instead seek to privilege and thus to remove certain of the texts and practices of popular culture from the condemnation of the critics of mass culture' (Storey, 2001: 54). How far do you agree with these claims?

If you consider these questions carefully you will be especially well prepared to move on to chapter eight, which deals with youth subcultures and the notion of resistance.

## SUMMARY OF KEY POINTS

In this short chapter I have emphasized the importance of Stuart Hall and the Birmingham Centre, and shown how Hall and Whannel's *The Popular Arts* helped to re-evaluate popular culture by getting readers to judge popular forms on their own terms. This chapter has also contextualized Hall and Whannel's work by summarizing earlier approaches and suggested how concepts from *The Popular Arts* might be broken down into heuristic form. Hall and Whannel's book can be seen as methodologically relevant in the following ways:

- The authors argue that fine distinctions could be made *within* popular mass culture.
- Their account of popular music takes into account the *circumstances* in which the music is produced.
- Their account of music also recognizes the role of youth cultures which help young people to distinguish themselves from the adult community through difference, rebelliousness and nonconformity.
- They show how music, however banal it may seem on the outside and however implicated it is in what Adorno called the 'culture industry', provides an expressive field which helps young people to cope with adolescence.
- We might say that one of the strengths of the strategy is that it attempts to empathize with youth culture but, at the same time, maintains a critical distance from it.

## References

Munns, Jessica and Rajan, Gita (eds) (1995) *A Cultural Studies Reader: History, Theory, Practice*. London: Longman.

Hall, Stuart and Whannel, Paddy (1964) *The Popular Arts*. London: Hutchinson.

Storey, John (2001) *Cultural Theory and Popular Culture: An Introduction* (3rd edition). Essex: Pearson Prentice Hall.

Turner, Graeme (1996) *British Cultural Studies: An Introduction* (2nd edition). London: Routledge.

## Further reading

(see the end of chapter nine)

# Youth Subcultures and Resistance: a Dialogue with *Quadrophenia*

## Introduction

This chapter is the second of those dedicated to 'Consolidating Cultural Studies: Subcultures, the Popular, Ideology and Hegemony'. My intention in it is to give a detailed account of a book entitled *Resistance through Rituals* (Hall and Jefferson, 1976). I shall use it to give a general introduction to some of the approaches associated with the Birmingham Centre in the 1970s believing, like Morag Shiach, that it 'embodies many of the most important theoretical models and methodologies developed at the Centre' (Shiach in Storey, 1998: 337). Another important aim is to outline some of the concepts which can be easily adapted to the analysis of subcultures or subgroups in general. That is, while the ideas in *Resistance through Rituals* pertain to *youth* subcultures I shall, in the practice sections, recommend that they be used to analyse and interpret subcultures which may include but transcend youth. To show how these ideas may be practiced I offer multiple readings of the film *Quadrophenia*.

### MAIN LEARNING GOALS

- To appreciate how the Birmingham Centre approached the analysis of youth subcultures and broadened its approaches and concepts.
- To understand a series of key ideas and see how they can be applied to the film *Quadrophenia* in order to develop practical skills.
- To see how an analysis of subcultures relates to questions of class, gender, race and ethnicity.

## The investigation of practices of resistance within youth subcultures

As can be seen from the last chapter, Hall and Whannel helped to challenge simplistic assumptions about the production and reception of mass popular culture – a form of questioning which would lead to studies that attempted to take much more account of variations and difficulties in audience response. *The Popular Art*'s focus on teenage culture helped to establish the idea of **subculture** as an important area of study.

One of the books that came out of the Birmingham Centre was *Resistance Through Rituals: Youth Subcultures in Post-war Britain* (1976) (hereafter *Resistance*) – a collaborative effort co-edited by Stuart Hall and Tony Jefferson. The book, while offering further insights into how different youth cultures developed styles which become symbolic forms of resistance, also helped to sum up work already done and give further impetus to a British tradition of analysis of youth subcultures. It has become a classic study within British cultural studies.

## Reading Mod subculture through *Quadrophenia*

In the following sections, rather than present ideas in dialogues, I'm going to suggest ways in which practice might be done by setting up a dialogue with the film *Quadrophenia* (1979). This film focused on the Mods – a British youth culture of the earlier 1960s, which was of considerable interest to the authors of *Resistance*. This chapter will show how a whole series of concepts explored in this book may relate to the film. This will prepare you for the last of the three chapters on subcultures, where I shall suggest ways in which these concepts may be further adapted.

Let's start, then, with a few preliminary points to prepare us for practice. *Quadrophenia* is what was referred to on the original video cover as 'Modstalgia' – a film which invokes the Mod culture of 1964. The film is set in London, which was an important centre of Mod culture (but not the only one), and is focused on the last few days of a young Mod, Jimmy Cooper. Rather than discuss the plot here, I'll gradually reveal it throughout the chapter.

## Think historically! Changes in post-war Britain

One general point made in *Resistance* that relates to method is that any effective analysis of subculture has to take into account the **particular historical**

**moment** in which a subculture appears. As the authors of the book insist, '[i]t is vital, in any analysis of contemporary phenomena, to think historically' (Hall and Jefferson, 1976: 17). If you look at the subtitle of the book you'll see that it is *Youth Subcultures in Post-war Britain*. Thus, a number of interrelated changes in the years following the end of the Second World War (which ended in 1945) may be seen as important to the rise of youth subcultures and **generational consciousness**. The following list by no means exhausts the possibilities but it will give an idea of the kinds of contexts that might be taken into account (other contexts will be explored in later sections):

1. **Affluence** The 'increased importance of the market and consumption' helped the rise of the 'teenage consumer' through the leisure industries which were able to focus on the young adult population as consumers (18). The basic point here is that subcultures depend on consumption. This economic explanation was linked to sociological theories about whether the working classes were disappearing or resembling the middle classes (in Sociology a process known as 'embourgeoisement') and whether or not old class conflicts were being replaced by a widespread sense of consensus (the authors of *Resistance* question both these assertions (21f.)).
2. **The rise of mass culture** The growth of the press, radio, mass publishing and, particularly, TV are seen as playing a key role. Mass culture created the possibility for widespread imitation of new styles by the young and the manipulation of young consumers by the commercial providers. Also, in line with Hoggart's thinking, mass culture was seen as breaking down more traditional working-class values, in favour of cultures of mass consumption.
3. **The disruptive effects of the Second World War** Disruptions of family life owing to the Second World War (absent or dead fathers, communities being uprooted from bomb-hit areas) were read by some sociologists as being responsible for the juvenile delinquency that was associated with the more violent sides of youth subcultures (19).
4. **Education** Changes in education meant that from age eleven onwards more young people were studying in 'age-specific' schools (before the War many students over eleven were still studying in all-age elementary schools). This was seen as creating the possibilities for the emergence of an 'adolescent society' where pupils of the same age interact in relatively restricted social groups. Added to this was the considerable growth of higher education in post-war Britain which helped to consolidate a sense of belonging to a specific generation with its own styles and tastes (20).
5. **The historical organization, development and significance of leisure** The idea here is that ideal contemporary images of youth and adolescence in Britain had their roots in the Victorian middle-classes' efforts to train adolescents to become healthy, law-abiding citizens. These efforts extended to the working classes in the shape of movements like the Boys' Brigade and the Boy Scouts (193) which organized working-class youth in accordance with patriotic imperial aims. However, by around the mid-twentieth century, the generational consciousness of youth could be seen to be related, not only to institutions like schools and the Boy Scouts, but to the entertainment industry and

a 'society of leisure' (197–9). Leisure time in the post-war period was increasingly serving as a space where the young forged a generational sense of self.

## **notes** ON PRACTICE: *Quadrophenia* and historical contexts

Let's see how you might discuss some of these historical contexts. As far as **affluence** is concerned, if you watch *Quadrophenia* (while accepting its limitations as a *film*) you'll see that Jimmy and his immediate group of friends, while being members of a working-class community in West London have, more or less, enough money to go to cafés and clubs and consume things like stylish clothes, motor scooters and drugs (even if they resort, at one moment, to stealing amphetamines from a chemist). However, the film tends to support the idea that the working classes were not undergoing 'embourgeoisement' because both Mods and their parents (where they appear or are mentioned) still retain their *relative* economic and cultural distance from the middle classes. Jimmy and his friends all have either manual jobs or menial office jobs and class differences are constantly emphasized through things like language, work and environment.

Signs of **mass culture** abound in the film from music, clothes, radio, TV, and the press. Jimmy's bedroom wall is covered with press cuttings featuring Mod incidents, Mod style, musicians and pin-ups. The Mod band, The Who, feature widely in terms of mass pop culture. There are photos and cuttings of them on Jimmy's bedroom wall and they appear on the popular TV programme 'Ready, Steady Go!' (a must for most 1960s teenagers interested in the latest sounds). Much of the film's soundtrack features Who songs – hardly surprising given that the film was the brainchild of The Who's Pete Townsend and based on the band's album *Quadrophenia*. The film reflects how a set of styles in music, dress and transport etc. were imitated, reproduced and commercialized. Jimmy spends a significant part of his time as a consumer of products associated with mass culture.

**Delinquent behaviour** is expressed in *Quadrophenia* through street violence (gang fights), drug taking, theft and vandalism and, as the authors of the introduction to *Resistance* stress, delinquency was one of the preoccupations of politicians and social commentators during the post-war years. However, in the film the broken home and the absent father as a result of the war are not explored, although family life is often represented as dysfunctional. For example, Jimmy is eventually thrown out of home and his friends, in conversation, make it clear that relations with their parents are conflictual. The source of conflict is represented as generational (Mod styles, values, tastes and behaviour as unacceptable, ugly or misunderstood by parents).

**Education** is not represented in the film but there are signs of young working-class 'age-specific' subcultures. I say 'subcultures' in the plural because part of being a Mod was to define the self against the Rockers, whose subcultural forms of differentiation where things like listening to rock'n'roll music, wearing leather jackets, jeans and white scarves and riding motorcycles (with the dream of hitting 100 miles an hour – hence they were known as 'ton-up boys'). Early in the film Jimmy meets an old school friend, Kevin, who happens to be a Rocker, and while there is antagonism between them they do share a sense of being from the same school and working-class area. While expressing themselves in alternative subcultures, they are united in their general background and rejection of authority.

As far as the **historical organization**, development and significance of leisure is concerned, *Quadrophenia* reflects the Mod(ern) tendency of youth to forge generational subcultural identities through consumption. However, it also reflects (minimally) the older ideological processes which worked upon working-class youth to inculcate the dominant values of good citizenship. This more traditional side of youth culture is reflected in the film when Jimmy goes to Brighton and sees the Boys' Brigade parading through the streets. In this way the film hints at how different forms of generational consciousness may come into being.

## Subculture and style

Dick Hebdige, in his contribution to *Resistance*, makes the point that the term Mod could refer to 'several distinct styles' associated with the 'myth' of 'swinging London' but restricts his usage of the word to 'working-class teenagers who lived mainly in London and the new towns of the South and who could be readily identified by characteristic hairstyles, clothing etc.' (87).

To get an idea of a fairly typical Mod style you only need to watch the beginning of *Quadrophenia* where Jimmy, wearing a Parka coat, small-collared shirt and narrow black tie, is seen riding his Lambretta scooter festooned with crash bars, extra lights, multiple rear-view mirrors, high-backed seat and long aerial protruding from the back. All these features helped to define a Mod style which, like so many subcultural styles, could be quite varied. For example, if you can get to see the film (or photographs from the period) you'll see that there was quite a lot of variation in the choice of shirts, coats, shoes and hair. For example, in *Quadrophenia* Ace Face, a character played by Sting, represents the height of Mod chic by being dressed in an impeccable light grey suit; a black Mod drug dealer, Ferdy, as well and Jimmy's friend, Dave, wear another Mod option - the pork-pie hat. The important point here, as reflected in the introduction to *Resistance*, is that subcultures **appropriate objects or commodities to their own ends**. Something known as **appropriation**.

## **help** FILE: appropriation

One way of theorizing appropriation is to adapt a concept associated with the work of Claude Levi-Strauss known as ***bricolage.*** This is described by John Clarke, another contributor to *Resistance*, as 'the re-ordering and re-contextualization of objects to communicate fresh meanings, within a total system of significances' (177). Simply put, Lambretta and Vespa scooters, Parka coats, amphetamine drugs and thin black ties etc. pre-existed the Mods but they appropriated these objects and made them fashionable symbols for their own particular subcultural way of life.

The important thing about style from the point of view of method is to try to understand what it *means* and how it functions within the subcultural group. Dick Hebdige's chapter in *Resistance* emphasizes this in its title: 'The Meaning of Mod'. While I can't go into all the possible meanings that Hebdige puts forward, a short description of some of his conclusions will give an idea of how new meanings could be generated from pre-existent objects and how these meanings functioned within the subcultural group.

## **help** FILE: appropriation and the meaning of style

The scooter, for example, is described by Hebdige as 'a formerly ultra-respectable means of transport' which was converted into a 'weapon and a symbol of solidarity'; pills used for medical purposes were 'appropriated and used as an end-in-themselves' (93). That is to say that amphetamines were used for their effect (they were called 'speed' because they gave the effect of constant nervous energy) but also had a symbolic value (served as another form of solidarity and gave kudos) to users within the group. Objects function to distinguish the group from the rest of society and commodities were adapted in unique and active ways as indications of subversion and **generational belonging** – the 'My Generation' mentality. ('My Generation' was the title of one of The Who's biggest hits and something of an anthem for many Mods.) Hebdige claims that Mods transformed the negative judgements made on them at school and work (for example, that they were lazy, arrogant and vain) into positive traits that were valued by their peers during their leisure time. The Mod style, he argues, was parodic of the consumer society in which they were located. Mods inverted and distorted respectable images like neatness and short hair, so valued by parents and employers, 'to create a style, which while being overtly close to the straight world was nonetheless incomprehensible to it' (93).

## Subcultural responses

Although subcultures are not limited to the working class, the authors of *Resistance* tend to put greater emphasis on this class, partly because many post-war subcultural styles (the Teds, Mods, Rockers and Skinheads) grew out of it. To analyse and understand a subculture it is necessary to be aware of **subcultural responses** (45f.). Some of these responses are:

- the winning of **cultural space**
- the establishment of **rituals** and key **locations for social interaction**
- the **focal concerns** of the group
- and **collective responses**.

### **notes** ON PRACTICE: Quadrophenia and subcultural responses

- The winning of **cultural space**. This includes using leisure time to mark out territory in the immediate locality which can be defended from other groups. In *Quadrophenia* Mods establish themselves on the street, in cafes and dance halls. Even the roads can become 'battlegrounds' where Mods and Rockers defend their subcultural ground.
- The establishment of **rituals** and key **locations for social interaction**. *Quadrophenia* reflects how social rituals and key locations are integrated in terms of social interaction. The Mods organize their subcultural lives around the consumption and use of commodities (music, clothes etc.) and activities for social exchanges (rituals) which are linked to key locations described above. The rituals, which range from meeting in cafes, riding scooters through the streets, taking amphetamines, listening and dancing to music, culminate in one of the most powerfully symbolic 'ceremonies' for Mods: the bank-holiday trip. The climax of the film is when Jimmy and his friends ride down to the seaside town Brighton and get involved in the famous 'battles' that took place there in 1964, when Mods and Rockers attacked one another and ran riot. Actually, the Brighton location reflects the working-class tradition of the bank holiday trip to the seaside: Brighton was a common destination for Londoners.
- These social interactions reflect the **focal concerns** of the group. These are related to the 'rituals' mentioned in the last point which generate a sense of group identity. The adoption and adaptation (the processes of *bricolage* mentioned above) and consumption of objects are also essential to establishing the style so important to subcultural identity. In *Quadrophenia* Mod music, clothes, scooters and drugs reflect focal concerns while helping to express rebellious group identity at the symbolic level. Part of this style involves a linguistic dimension – slang, swearwords, or forms of argot which help to maintain a sense of self and preserve the symbolic boundaries between inside and outside.
- All these factors can be understood as the **collective responses** of young working-class youths (mainly young men) which define subcultural styles and activities.

## Double articulation

In the introduction to *Resistance* the authors put forward the idea of **double articulation** which they see as useful to the understanding of working-class youth subcultures. The argument assumes that post-war subcultures, because they are a sub-set of general working-class culture, are **subordinate** to the dominant culture and come into being as a result of their location between the **dominant culture** and the **'parent' working-class culture**. Figure 8.1 illustrates these relations visually.

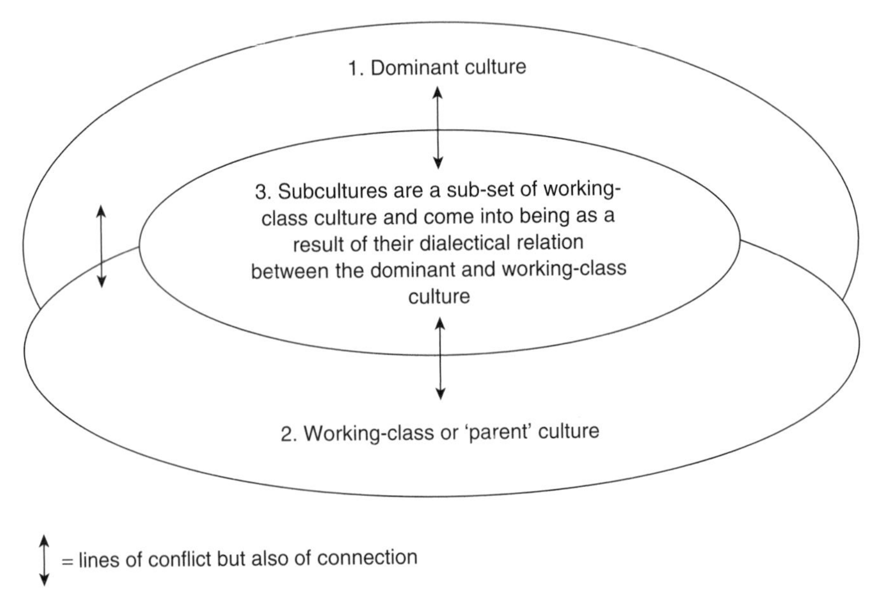


Figure 8.1 Double articulation

### notes ON PRACTICE: *Quadrophenia* and double articulation

Using *Quadrophenia* to illustrate this idea, Jimmy, as a symbol of Mod subculture, is in conflict with the values of the dominant culture. He works as a post-boy in an advertising agency but clearly has nothing in common with his middle-class colleagues. Much of his behaviour would be seen as anti-social by 'straight' society: Jimmy swears, takes drugs, gets involved in gang fights, robs a chemist, and uses his scooter to churn up a lawn when he leaves a party in a middle-class area. There are many lines of conflict, then, with relation to dominant 'official' culture – something emphasized by his relations with his bosses, the police, and later, the judiciary (the Mods who are convicted are called 'miserable specimens', 'strutting hooligans' and 'sawdust Caesars').

However, his relation to his 'parent culture' is more ambiguous because his sense of identity forged within Mod subculture is both in opposition to, and dependent on, his working-class environment. His parents fail to understand him – his mother telling him his behaviour is not 'natural' and his father laughing at his taste in music (and they eventually throw him out). Yet Jimmy and his Mod mates are very much working class and identify powerfully with the 'parent' culture. Here are some examples:

- All have fairly low-paid menial jobs (reflecting their educational background and limited opportunities).
- All have strong London accents, seem to delight in them, and use working-class Cockney expressions (avoiding the more formal registers associated more with middle-class forms of expression).
- They seem to enjoy upsetting their middle-class peers at a party, simply, I assume, because they are – middle class.
- They identify with the urban working-class communities in which they live (and defend their territory). As mentioned earlier, even though Jimmy is in subcultural conflict with an old school friend, Kevin (who has chosen another subcultural option, he's a Rocker), they still relate at the level of class, being able to communicate effectively when their friends are not around.
- The males, despite their 'clean', fashionable appearance, cultivate the macho image of the tough working-class street-fighter.

## Subcultures and young women

Having come this far, you might be wondering what subculture has to do with young women and girls. Angela McRobbie and Jenny Garber, in their contribution to *Resistance*, noticed that in studies dedicated to youth subcultures the role of young women was hardly mentioned or was completely invisible. When they were mentioned McRobbie and Garber argued that they either **reinforced stereotypical images of women** as passive and stupid, or they were **marginal**, or interest was reduced to their **physical appearance** (209). But what *was* the situation for young women? This is explored by a series of key questions which can serve as starting points for further analysis. (As McRobbie and Garber usually refer to young women as 'girls' I shall shuttle between the use of the terms 'young women' and 'girls' and balance the use of 'young men' with 'boys'.)

## Were young women and girls really absent from post-war subcultures?

In short, no. However, because the popular image of post-war subcultures in the media tended to emphasize male 'focal concerns' and masculine values, young women tended to be less noticeable.

### **notes** ON PRACTICE: *Quadrophenia*, subcultures and girls

Coming back to *Quadrophenia* for a moment, Mod girls are very much secondary. Neither of the two Mod girls in Jimmy's life, Steph and Monkey, owns a scooter or gets involved in focal concerns like fighting – the kinds of things that got Mods noticed in the media. While they adopt Mod fashion, take amphetamines, dance and 'hang around' with the boys, they confirm one of McRobbie's and Garber's assertions because their roles are very much constructed around whether or not they are attractive. An example of this is that Jimmy and his friends are attracted to Steph but not to Monkey, who can be picked up and put down at will – her nickname being indicative of her status.

McRobbie and Garber, however, do recognize that while young women *were* active members of subcultural groups, there were convincing reasons why subcultural options were not as open to many young working-class women. One is that young women's wages were generally lower than their male counterparts' and another is that working-class girls' lives were limited by being more focused on home and possible future marriage. For example, girls could try to have fun but those who were seen as sexually permissive suffered the consequences of the double standards applied to the sexes – boys could be respected for sleeping around but girls would be condemned for the same sexual licence. *Quadrophenia* reflects this more in the *absence* of female characters and thus only indirectly dramatizes these issues.

## Where young women were visible, what were their roles, and did these reflect the general subordination of women in the culture?

McRobbie and Garber argue that girls played very secondary roles in Teddy Boy and Biker cultures but were more visible in Mod and Hippy cultures. However, even in these latter subcultures they see the roles played by girls as less to do with the more 'aggressive and abrasive' aspects of subcultural life and more to do with appearance. This was especially true of girls who defined themselves as Mods because Mods (male and female) tended to put a great deal of emphasis on a highly stylized look, which was more associated with being feminine (hence the male Mod has often been seen as more effeminate than the Rocker) and less likely to provoke negative reactions from adults (217).

McRobbie and Garber affirm that where girls were visible their cultural subordination was 'retained and reproduced' (216). Significantly, they explain this with relation to the **restraining conditions** of the 'basic material and social structures predetermining the lives of the girls and limiting this relative visibility/autonomy/space' of being working class and female (218). That is, their lives were limited by the same kind of factors as their male peers - limited wages and career prospects - only these limits were more intensified because their wages were generally lower, their prospects fewer and social controls more pronounced.

### **notes** ON PRACTICE: *Quadrophenia*, girls and restraining conditions

*Quadrophenia* substantiates these claims in so far as the character, Steph, has a menial job as supermarket checkout girl, and it places the male Mod at the centre. However, it does not explore the material and social structures that limited the visibility, autonomy and space for girls.

In the case of Hippy subculture, which is associated more with the middle classes, the female student is seen to have more freedom and time to develop a personal style (owing to a generally longer education). However, despite opening up new cultural spaces for young women, there seemed to be little change in terms of the **traditional images and roles** played by women, the typical images being 'the Earth Mother, baby at breast, or the fragile pre-Raphaelite lady' (219).

## Did girls have alternative ways of organizing their cultural life?

The simple answer is yes. McRobbie and Garber emphasize that girls could participate in the teenage leisure market but more within **peer-centred** girls' culture. Here the main cultural space was the home, although girls could get out of the house by visiting one another and having parties. This avoided the riskier 'hanging around' in streets. Within the **culture of the bedroom** there were plenty of opportunities to partake of teenage consumer culture through make-up, listening to records, the reading of magazines etc. (213). There's a hint of this in *Quadrophenia* in the shape of Jimmy's sister who is only seen within the home – from this perspective she can be seen as a powerful symbol for domestic confinement.

This culture of the bedroom is associated with the 'Teeny Bopper' option which only required a record player, a space on the wall for photos of pop idols and a few friends. Despite being the most 'highly manufactured' of all subcultures, this enabled girls to negotiate leisure spaces of their own in which they could channel their own hopes, dreams, needs and desires (221). Because of its being home-based, Teeny Bopper culture can be seen as a **defensive retreat** protecting girls from risky sexual contact with boys, which could earn them a bad reputation and it offered self-sufficiency because a girl couldn't be excluded from participation by an 'in' group. In this sense, the Teeny Bopper option was not, properly speaking, a subcultural style. However, this does not mean that resistance could not be practiced both within the bedroom and outside it.

While a series of 'obsessions' for teen stars may not seem to be a very radical form of resistance, McRobbie and Garber argue that these 'obsessions' could function as meaningful reactions against the 'selective and authoritarian structures' that controlled the girls' lives at school, serving to alienate teachers and offer 'defensive solidarity', especially for those girls who thought of themselves as academic failures (220–1). Furthermore, Teeny Bopper culture could include 'quasi-sexual' rituals given that girls had 'no access to the masturbatory rituals common amongst boys' (220).

## Women take issue

These lines of research were considerably extended when the Women's Study Group at the Birmingham Centre published *Women Take Issue* (1978), which manifested feminist dissatisfaction with the largely male bias of cultural studies. This book helped to redress this very important imbalance and put feminist research on a more even footing. This book, while drawing on the kinds of concepts which guided *Resistance*, drew on complex psychoanalytic theory to

Figure 8.2 A Teeny-Bopper carves out her own subcultural space

theorize how gender was culturally constructed and argued; in the case of Angela McRobbie, that working-class girls were, at the same time, 'saved by' and yet, 'locked within' prevailing ideas of femininity (McRobbie in Women's Study Group, 1978: 108). Putting this very simply, this is to do with the way in which women are feminized within culture, through their constant exposure to images of themselves (in magazines, TV commercials, popular fiction, film and a host of popular cultural forms) yet can also derive considerable pleasure from these forms.

Extending these ideas, writers like Ehrenreich et al. (1992) have looked at teenage girls and the phenomenon of Beatlemania in the early 1960s to suggest that it was a sexually defiant consumer subculture. Despite the fact that Beatlemania can be seen as a well-managed media campaign, the authors found significant forms of female resistance: teenage girls, through what was described as **hysteria**, were screaming against the **systematic repression of female sexuality** and the double standards of female teen culture.

The authors argue that tens of thousands of teenage girls were, in small acts of defiance, defying the repressive role reserved for them by openly admitting potent, active sexual desire. Within this framework the authors explore the options open to teenage girls, and show how Beatlemania helped teenagers to define alternative values connected to independence and sexual desire and mark themselves off from the adult world. In short, despite its commercial character, Beatlemania is seen as the most significant (and dramatic) event in the female **sexual revolution**, before the advent of the woman's movement in the 1960s. Methodologically, these kinds of studies by and about women have been enormously important in helping to widen and reshape the field of cultural studies.

## Subcultures and questions of race and ethnicity

Cultural studies has also been widened by the inclusion of **questions of race and ethnicity**. Although *Resistance* is not dedicated to questions of race, it does touch on a number of very significant issues which would be broadened in the years following its publication. For example, Hebdige shows how Rastafarianism was translated from the Jamaican context into Britain (135f.), Chambers analysed what happens when black music is 'adopted and adapted to express the quite different experience of white American (and British) youth' (157) and Critcher offered a framework for understanding how mugging was related to black youth and crime (167f).

### help FILE: race and ethnicity

The words 'race' and 'ethnicity', while being useful to cultural studies (and many other academic areas) are enormously complex – so much so that one way of trying to understand these concepts is to turn to the *Dictionary of Race, Ethnicity and Culture* (Bolaffi et al., 2003), a 355 page book dedicated to the definition of these and related terms within the social sciences:

**Race** is generally associated with efforts (scientific or political) to establish groups of people connected by common descent. This usually involves the claim that these people share distinct physical, biological or genetic characteristics. This not only sets up the possibility of belonging to a race but being excluded from it and being defined negatively by a dominant group which sees itself as genetically superior. Not all definitions of race accept these assumptions and the concept can be used to focus attention on groups within society who are considered the victims of prejudice and inequality. Fighting against racial prejudice seems to assume that a society *is* divided by distinct races; however, cultural studies practitioners, while exploring the politics of exclusion and prejudice, generally see race as a social construction, rather than an objective description.

**Ethnicity** is sometimes used as a synonym for 'race' (Bolaffi et al., 2003: 99), which can lead to considerable confusion. Ethnicity is often connected to the idea of having a common, cultural tradition and often indicates origin by birth or descent rather than nationality. An 'ethnic minority' is assumed to be made up of people who recognize themselves (and who are recognized) as sharing certain beliefs, values and ways of seeing. Again, this sets up the possibility of insiders and outsiders with all the possible political problems resulting from these distinctions. Chris Barker has made the useful point that ethnicity is *relational*: 'What we think of as our identity is dependent on what we think we are *not*' (Barker, 2000: 195). Where the concept seems to differ mostly from race resides in not assuming that ethnic groups are the product of fundamental, genetic differences. Ethnic minorities are sometimes thought of as being non-native, but this is not necessarily true – think of aborigines in Australia or American Indians in North America. Their cultures pre-existed the dominant 'white' cultures.

Despite a certain ambiguity and even incoherence, these terms have proven useful in discussions of things like dominance, subjection, marginalization, prejudice, national identity and inequality. Raymond Williams (1983) provides a good starting point for looking at the evolution of these concepts with relation to intellectual history and Paul Gilroy's work provides an example of a black scholar who refuses the term 'race'. He sees it as negative, whether used by subordinating or subordinate groups, because (among other things) it fails to take into account the possible cultural diversity implied in being 'black' (Gilroy, 1987).

What I'll do in this section is to discuss, very briefly, what some of the writers mentioned above *do*, rather than put the main emphasis on the content of what they have to say. I'll use Hebdige to outline a number of themes which are relevant to this chapter and use Chambers and Critcher to sum up. Dick Hebdige's chapter, 'Reggae, Rastas and Rudies', starts by emphasizing the importance of slavery as a 'shaping presence' to black Jamaican experience (Hall and Jefferson, 1976: 136). This shadow of **colonial history** is important to an understanding not only of **Rastafarianism** and Reggae culture in Jamaica but to its transference into British subcultural life.

Hebdige examines the **transference** of Jamaican musical styles like Ska and Reggae (with their rich cultural heritage) into Britain. Doing this requires Hebdige to consider how these musical styles impacted on West Indian immigrant communities in Britain but also to examine how these styles were **appropriated** by white youth, particularly the Skinhead community who appreciated the music and the slick style of those associated with Ska.

### **help** FILE. Defining Ska

Ska was an earlier form of Reggae. Reggae, Hebdige reminds his readers, shouldn't be oversimplified, it being a complex, 'mosaic' form which inverted the rhythms of American soul music and incorporated things like African rhythms, Rastafarian values and beliefs, a sense of rebellion, the 'call and response patterns of the Pentecostal Church', the rhythms of Jamaican street talk, and the sexiness and cool of American Rhythm and Blues (140f.).

However, any promise of significant cultural integration between the black and white communities was short-lived. Firstly, racist attitudes on the part of the white population complicated significant integration. Secondly, the African character of Reggae with its distinctive religious beliefs, dress styles (and dredlock hair), its smoking of ganja (*marijuana*), arcane language and sense of oppression tended to alienate the white Skinhead community (152).

### **notes** ON PRACTICE: *Quadrophenia* and the influence of black culture

*Quadrophenia*, while reflecting the subcultural life of Mods rather than Skinheads, does reflect, in a minimal way, how black culture influenced 1960s Britain. The soundtrack is full of some of the black musical styles which appealed to the predominantly white Mod community (the Ronettes, The Crystals, Booker T. and the MGs, The Chiffons etc.). Before the Skinheads, Mod taste included Ska, Tamla Motown and Detroit Soul. There is a vague reference to the impact of Jamaican style in the shape of the black drug dealer Ferdy (a common racial stereotype) who wears an impeccable suit and the 'pork-pie' hat (mentioned above) which was appropriated by white Mods (like the character Dave in the film). The film can also be used to see how, despite the appropriation of black music, the white community represents black people. In one scene in the film when Jimmy and his mates visit Ferdy to buy amphetamines one of the gang reflects racist attitudes to the West Indian community when he says 'It's like Calcutta here'. While not all the Mods are depicted as being racist, Jimmy pointing out with disdain that Calcutta is in India, it does touch on the important factor of race relations in a multicultural society (for more discussion on this see chapter thirteen).

Ian Chambers' contribution looks at black music, mainly within the US context, locating its roots in the **historical experiences** of black slaves (157). He also shows how it is necessary to link the music to **black consciousness** which took its inspiration from black liberationist struggles in Africa but was a direct result of prejudice and discriminatory practices in terms of class and race, political deprivation and marginalization. Like Hebdige, he discusses how black working-class music was appropriated by poor white communities who **redefined** and **adapted** the music to their own ends (e.g. white blues, rock 'n' roll and rhythm and blues). However, Chambers points out that while the two communities are of the same **class**, the black community was **culturally subordinate** to the white community (160).

## **notes** ON PRACTICE: *Quadrophenia* and cultural subordination

*Quadrophenia* reflects these themes only in the most tangential way – again with relation to Ferdy. Methodologically, Chamber's point about the working-class black community's cultural subordination to the white community opens up the possibility of extending the idea of double articulation and suggests that the term 'working class' needs to be seen with relation to other contexts of subordination. Again, see chapter thirteen.

Chas Critcher's contribution to *Resistance* takes as its starting point the 20-year prison sentences given to three black youths from Handsworth who mugged (attacked and robbed) an Irish labourer in the early 1970s. Critcher explores the moral outrage provoked by muggings in Britain and the reason behind what he and other colleagues at the Birmingham Centre considered the 'extreme rigidity' of the sentences passed on the three youths. Critcher uses three main concepts to offer a framework for analysing why black youths may resort to criminal activity: **structures**, **cultures** and **biographies** – three aspects of the 'life situation of any individual' (168). In fact, these categories may be applied to *any* youth group (I would argue that they can be applied to any group – regardless of age).

- **Structures** These are aspects to do with the social structures that control the distribution of power and wealth, the availability of housing, type of work, levels of education and income etc. which are related to race and class status and largely beyond an individual's control. Although these do not cause crime (any more than race discrimination does) they may help to explain the turn to criminal behaviour.
- **Cultures** Any society has multiple 'cultures' associated with different groups which reflect ways of thinking and behaving which 'embody ideas, beliefs, values, [and] notions of right and wrong' (168). Of course, the law will reflect the values of those in authority but these dominant values may not be shared by other groups who may view things like property and violence in different ways (dependent on factors like youth, class and ethnic or geographical groupings). Again, although these 'cultural' factors will not produce criminality, they may need to be considered 'where the individual has little access to cultures which are law-abiding' and where individuals keep 'bad company', and are brought up in a 'bad environment' like a broken family (169–70).
- **Biographies** These describe the 'network of personal circumstances' (like poverty, anger, necessity etc.) within the general contexts of structures and cultures that may help to explain criminal activity (171).

Critcher argues that this framework can help to understand why certain criminal acts, like mugging, arise in specific communities. For an unemployed youth from an inner-city area, the turn to crime may offer some material gain while, at the same time, confer a certain social status on the criminal as delinquent. The general conclusion is that crime can only be understood as a social activity if the perpetrators of it are placed within these multiple contexts (172), something which requires new ways of thinking. The politics of this position is revealed when it becomes evident that this new way of thinking requires society to address **the distribution of wealth and power**, and the **unequal access** disadvantaged groups have to housing and employment: in short, those things which uphold the existing social order.

## **notes** ON PRACTICE: *Quadrophenia*, structures, cultures and biographies

Again, *Quadrophenia* only touches the tip of the iceberg in these respects, but there are many other films which can provide useful starting points for looking at the way structures, cultures and biographies may be used to understand the difficulties suffered by immigrant populations. At the end of the next chapter (in the section 'Exploring subcultures: possibilities for further study and practice') I have included some film titles which may help you explore these concepts. At a more general level, it is possible to use the concepts introduced here to explore how Jimmy ends up … (if you don't know what Jimmy's fate is you'll have to wait until near the end of this chapter). Incidentally, *Quadrophenia* would be more interesting to us if it explored how Ferdy became a drug dealer.

- Jimmy's situation can be explained with relation to **structures**. He was born in a working-class community in London and would therefore be less likely to excel educationally. His lack of higher qualifications means he is trapped in what he feels is a dead-end job. However, while his class positioning may limit his possibilities, being white and British he does not suffer systematic racial prejudice.
- Jimmy's life can be seen to be influenced by intersecting **cultures**. On the one hand, he has the influence of family, school and work, on the other, he has the values he shares with the subcultural group to which he belongs (double articulation). However, he identifies more with being a Mod so that robbing a chemist, taking pills, fighting, churning up a middle-class family's lawn on his scooter etc., while seen as delinquent by the dominant and parent cultures, are generally valued positively by his youth culture. As Albert Cohen has written, delinquent subcultures *invert* the norms of the wider culture thus conferring prestige on things like truancy, vandalism and theft (Cohen, 1976: 124).
- Jimmy's life also makes sense with relation to his particular **biography**. His life cannot only be explained with relation to structures and cultures but is also defined by how he responds to the situations in which he finds himself. That is to say, structures and cultures do not cause him to rob a chemist, take pills or riot: these acts are products of the choices he makes, or the situations in which he finds himself.

Just as feminists filled what was seen as a significant gap in cultural studies by publishing *Women Take Issue*, so black scholars at the Birmingham Centre organized a publication entitled *The Empire Strikes Back* (1982). This addressed what they felt were serious omissions within cultural studies with reference to 'racist ideologies and racist conflicts' in Britain (Centre for Contemporary Cultural Studies, 1982: 7) – even though *Policing the Crisis* (Hall et al., 1978) had made some headway in these areas. Again, as far as method is concerned, cultural studies would be enriched and broadened by these perspectives.

A final point, one of Hebdige's assertions is that Rastafarians in Britain are exiled from Jamaica, Africa and Britain and take refuge in 'some imaginative inner dimension' where 'solutions are religious rather than revolutionary' (Hall and Jefferson, 1976: 136–7). It might be said that Jimmy's solutions are 'quasi-religious' rather than revolutionary, and this brings me to the following section, which will sum up subcultural responses through the idea of imaginary solutions.

## Imaginary solutions

In carving out their own space, engaging in antisocial or delinquent behaviour and resisting the values and standards of the dominant culture, it seems as if subcultural groups really *do* make a difference. However, one of the basic tenets expressed in *Resistance*, inspired by the work of the sociologist Phil Cohen, is that subcultural lifestyles only offer **solutions at imaginary (symbolic) levels**. This is the **ideological dimension** (47). The basic idea here is expressed in Figure 8.3.

### **notes** ON PRACTICE: *Quadrophenia* and imaginary solutions

The idea of imaginary solutions which ultimately cannot solve structural problems is dramatized at the end *Quadrophenia*. Jimmy's search for a sense of authenticity in Mod subculture seems to come to fruition when he is arrested in Brighton and gets to share a police van and court appearance with Ace Face, who seems to be the epitome of the Mod rebel (when he is fined in court, he pays up immediately with an insolent sneer). When Jimmy returns home he argues with his parents who throw him out and he insults his boss and walks out of his job. His Mod friends do not respect him for giving up his job, effectively showing Jimmy that being a Mod is a leisure option, rather than an authentic way of life.

Faced with rejection and alienation from both family and friends (even the girl he thought loved him leaves him for one of his best friends), he returns to Brighton, the place where he most felt at one with his Mod ideals. However, Brighton has reverted back to an out-of-season, sleepy sea-side town full of pensioners. Jimmy's deception is completed when he discovers that Ace Face is working as a bellboy (a bag carrier) in a posh hotel and, despite some sneering, is ordered about by rich clients. This is the point where Jimmy fully realizes that his subculture has failed him. There is only one solution – suicide: he steals Ace Face's impeccable Vespa scooter and rides off the cliffs at Beachy Head.

Figure 8.3 Solutions at the imaginary level

## SUMMARY OF KEY POINTS

This chapter has introduced *Resistance through Rituals* and demonstrated how a number of writers at the Birmingham Centre approached the analysis of youth subcultures. Important approaches (that emphasize things like historical contexts, the forging of style, the winning of cultural spaces, the establishment of rituals, focal concerns and collective responses) have been introduced and illustrated. The chapter has also familiarized readers with terms like double articulation and imaginary solutions and shown how writers at the Birmingham Centre began to focus on themes of gender and race. The notes on practice focused on the film *Quadrophenia* have shown how all the major concepts may be used in practice.

From the point of view of methodology, the writers who contributed to *Resistance* abandon value judgements which either recommend or downgrade popular culture, preferring to develop a series of approaches which attempt to explain:

- The historical circumstances in which a subculture is forged.
- How subgroups appropriate clothes and other objects to create a sense of style, discussing the meaning of these styles and how they function within subcultural groups.
- What kinds of subcultural responses are typical to a subculture (the establishment of rituals and key locations for social interaction etc.).
- How subcultures operate with relation to categories like class, gender and race.
- A final point: the focusing on issues of gender and race helped to fill in important gaps and enrich, widen and reshape the field of cultural studies.

## References

Barker, Chris (2000) *Cultural Studies: Theory and Practice*. London: Sage.

Bolaffi, Guido, Bracalenti, Raffaele, Braham, Peter and Gindro, Sandro (eds) (2003) *Dictionary of Race, Ethnicity and Culture*. London: Sage.

Centre for Contemprary Cultural Studies (1982) *The Empire Strikes Back: Race and Racism in 70s Britain*. London: Hutchinson.

Cohen, Albert (1976) *Deviance and Control*. Englewood Cliffs, NJ: Prentice Hall.

Ehrenreich, Barbara, Hess, Elizabeth and Jacobs, Gloria (1992) 'Beatlemania: sexually defiant consumer subculture', in K. Gelder and S. Thornton (1997) *The Subcultures Reader*. London: Routledge.

Gelder, Ken and Thornton, Sarah (eds) (1997) *The Subcultures Reader*. London: Routledge.

Gilroy, Paul (1987) *There Ain't No Black in the Union Jack*. London: Hutchinson.

Hall, Stuart and Jefferson, Tony (eds) (1976) *Resistance through Rituals*. London: Hutchinson.

Hall, Stuart, Cricher, Chas, Jefferson, Tony, Clarke, John and Roberts, Brian (1978) *Policing the Crisis: Mugging, the State, and Law and Order*. London: Macmillan.

*Quadrophenia* (1979) dir. Franc Roddam.

Shiach, Morag, (1998) 'Feminism and Popular Culture', in J. Storey, *Cultural Theory and Popular Culture: A Reader* (2nd edition). Essex: Pearson Prentice Hall.

Storey, John (1998) *Cultural Theory and Popular Culture: A Reader* (2nd edition). Essex: Pearson Prentice Hall.

McRobbie, Angela (1978) in Women's Study Group, Centre for Contemporary Cultural Studies, University of Birmingham, *Women Take Issue: Aspects of Women's Subordination*. London: Hutchinson.

Williams, Raymond (1983) Keywords: *A Vocabulary of Culture and Society* (revised edition). London: Flamingo.

## Further reading

(see the end of chapter nine)

# Subcultures and Widening Horizons: Further Strategies for Practice

## Introduction

This chapter, the third on 'Consolidating Cultural Studies', is dedicated to developing and consolidating the practice skills explored in the last chapter. It will do this through the use of a simple heuristic. It will offer suggestions on how some of the ideas outlined in the previous two chapters can be used and adapted to study all kinds of cultures associated with groups, whether these be recognizable subcultures like Punk, pressure groups, or things like Internet Chats or the local chess club. This should help you see how the society you live in is made up of an enormous number of what might be called 'micro-cultures', which may or may not be in conflict with dominant or official cultural values. The chapter will also show how the approaches set out in *Resistance through Rituals* sets up a 'dialogue' with the social sciences and concludes with a detailed section on possibilities for further study and practice. Although this chapter has many notes on practice, it might be seen, in its entirety, as an extended note on practice.

### MAIN LEARNING GOALS

- To be aware of how the approaches explored in the last chapter can be used in practice and adapted to the analysis of subgroups in general.
- To recognize some of the problems that may arise from using the heuristic designed to help you adapt the ideas to other subcultures or subgroups.

*(Continued)*

- To understand how *Resistance through Rituals* set up a respectful but critical attitude towards approaches associated with the social sciences.
- To be aware of some further possibilities for further study and practice.

## From hobbies to subcultures: strategies for analysis

As mentioned in the introduction, this chapter is designed to help you develop your practice skills. The following heuristic sums up the basic categories explored in the previous chapter. Here I want to demonstrate how it can be adapted to the study of all kinds of social groups. Firstly, look at the heuristic (see next page) – then we'll look at how it can be used to prepare you for further practice.

## Notes on the use of the heuristic

To use this heuristic you need to place the name of the subculture (or subgroup) you wish to study in the centre, then consider the other contexts (adapting all the ideas to *your* particular cultural and geographical location). I have added '**sexuality**' and '**age**' to questions of gender and race, and the category '**technological and scientific changes that may facilitate the subculture**', to help adapt the ideas explored so far to more contemporary forms of culture (I shall return to this a little later). Sexuality has been added to take account of sexual choice and particularly Gay and Lesbian issues within cultural analysis. For example, using the heuristic, it is possible to analyse how groups within society define themselves against what Adrienne Rich has called 'heterocentricity' (1993: 203) – the ideological, political and cultural dominance of the (mainly male) heterosexual world.

Although *Resistance* does focus on the production of generational consciousness and belonging it does not take account of age in broader terms. For example, subcultures are not necessarily restricted to teenagers. It is worth remembering that the authors of resistance concentrated their efforts on *youth* subcultures and that I am using some of their ideas to analyse subcultures in more general terms. Returning to sexuality for a moment, the different Lesbian

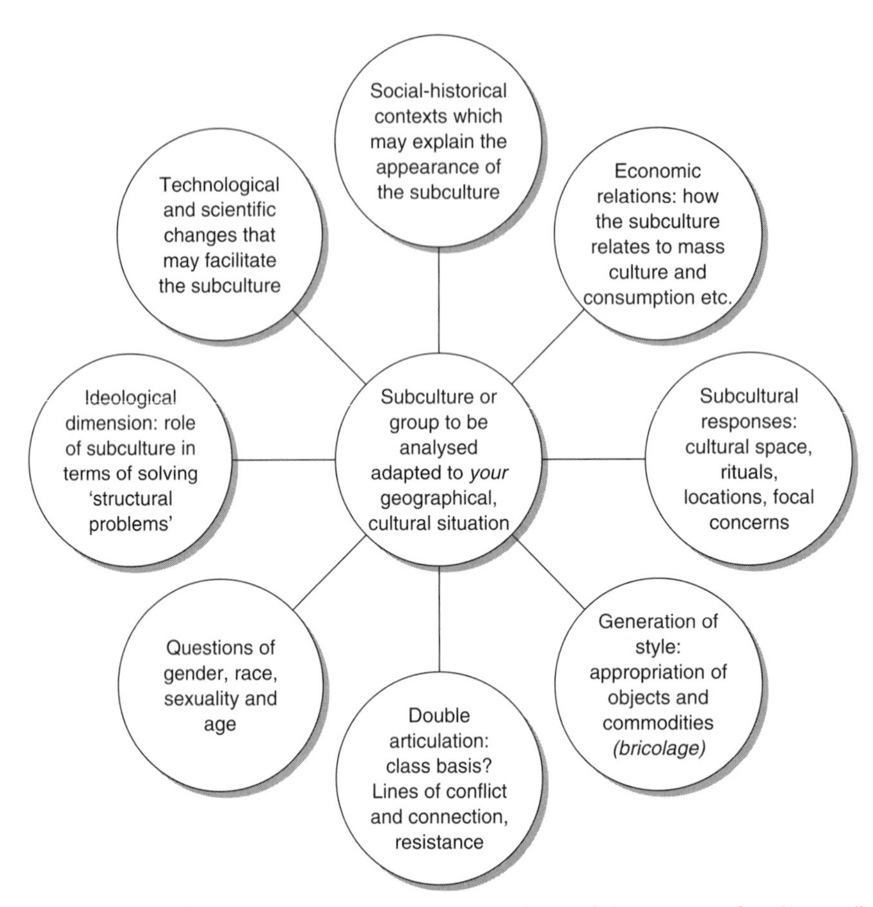


Further possibilities for analysis, (ir)relevance and criticisms of these ways of understanding.

Figure 9.1 A heuristic designed to explore subcultures

and Gay Liberation Movements which emerged from the end of the 1960s may be fruitfully analysed with relation to the concepts outlined in this section. However, forms of resistance cannot necessarily be restricted to a particular age group or generation. In these instances, generational belonging may have to be played down.

The inclusion of 'technological and scientific changes that may facilitate the subculture' is there to further emphasize the debate about the historical circumstances in which subcultures appear. For example, as *Resistance* makes clear, Mod subculture was very much dependent on the phenomenon of mass culture:

Mod fashion, the production of music and scooters etc. imply complex infrastructures and technologies which were the products of a fully industrialized society. Much contemporary cultural analysis needs to take account of constant changes with relation to micro chips and digitalization, whether this implies the storage of data or information, communications on the Internet, DVDs, or gadgets used in the production of music (like samplers). Take the case of chess: although the game may not require high levels of technological development at the local chess club, the game can now be played on the Internet, which opens up new possibilities for group behaviour and requires new forms understanding.

Using the above heuristic for broader analysis also requires some rethinking about the concept of 'double articulation'. Though it describes the complex ideological relations between working-class youth cultures and the dominant culture, it has to be adapted to discussions of subcultures associated with the middle classes or those which cut across class boundaries. For example, Hoggart was already aware in the 1950s that, while it made sense to talk of class at the level of sports, entertainment and other leisure activities, Britain was becoming increasingly 'culturally classless' (Hoggart, [1957] 1958: 342). Class wasn't disappearing but certain leisure-time pursuits, once seen as class based (cricket for the rich, football for the poor), were achieving wider appeal.

Another complication is when someone with a middle-class background becomes a Mod or Punk etc. (even if the origins of these groups were in working-class communities). In these cases subcultures are not simple sub-sets of working-class culture (even if, like the Mods, their origins are in working-class groups). Here the subculture comes into being as a result of a dialectical relation between the dominant culture and resistant sub-sets of the dominant culture itself. However, members of a subculture may be affiliated to one another in terms of activities and style but not in terms of class.

Let's take the Hippy movement for a moment – it was largely associated with the middle classes (although there were working-class Hippies). In this case a sub-set splits off into a middle-class counter culture setting itself up against the dominant values of its own 'parent' culture. Properly speaking, in this case there is no 'double articulation'; however, in the case of working-class Hippies 'double articulation' would still be relevant. Although Mods have been associated with the working-classes, there were middle-class Mods, which created the possibility for class conflict within the subcultural group. This requires special analysis, especially as the perception of class within groups may be ambiguous or negotiated. For example, someone from a more well-off working class family might be considered 'posh' by other members of a group and therefore excluded. On the other hand, if a member of the middle class had the right 'attitude' or was considered 'hard' s/he may be accepted into the group. All this necessitates not the erasing of class as an issue but a more careful handling of the notion of class, seeing that subcultures may be divided within themselves as far as class is concerned. (For more on reconsiderations of class and culture see chapter ten on Antonio Gramsci.)

Another significant detail that needs to be highlighted is that I have included '**class basis?**' as a question. This is because many groups (subcultural or otherwise) may not be closely identified with a particular class. Again, this does not mean that class issues can be ignored but that contemporary possibilities for the formation of subcultures have become enormously complex. An example is how different groups interact on the Internet. For example, in the virtual community of online communications traditional categories that were important to identity like gender, class and race may become less relevant or even become ambiguous or erased. On the other hand they may even become reinforced.

Finally, you will see there is the sentence which stands below the heuristic: '**Further possibilities for analysis, (ir)relevance and criticisms of these ways of understanding**' which is designed to get you to think about the way you are going about analysis, to consider alternatives, and to encourage a critical attitude towards the concepts and methods you employ (very much in the spirit of Hall and his colleagues in the Birmingham Centre).

I'm going to outline one possibility for analysis but without going into much detail – my aim is to offer a few starting points and further tips to aid practice. What I intend here is to offer ideas which can be explored by anyone with access to the Internet by looking at what are known as (Internet Relay) Chats. Although I imagine that a large number of my readers will already have experience of Chats, Blogs and all kinds of virtual forms of communication (and know more about them than I do), I will not assume that you already have detailed or specialized knowledge. I'll limit my use of technical terms and organize my ideas on the various possibilities for analysis according to the above heuristic. You will see that it is also influenced by Williams' approach: the phenomenon you study will be understood with relation to the culture (as a whole way of life) in which it has its existence. The idea here is to explore virtual spaces (or musical subcultures etc.), instead of reading *about* them – armed, that is, with a few concepts which may serve as a minimal tool kit.

## **notes** ON PRACTICE: using the heuristic – chatting in the cyber café

### Subculture

I am assuming that the groups who get involved in Chats are (cyber) subcultures or, if not, at least the concepts introduced in this chapter will be useful for their analysis. With in excess of 10,000,000 Chats available at the time of writing (2006), the possibilities for analysis and comparison are enormous.

### Social, historical, technological and scientific contexts

Here you need to be aware of the historical circumstances in which a particular culture emerges. When describing *Resistance* I outlined some of the dominant circumstances of post-war Britain; however, you will need to take account of the cultural space in which you are located. In Spain, for example, 'post-war' might be read as post Civil War or the Second World War, but a discussion of the significant rise of youth subcultures in Spain may make more sense with relation to the period of 'transition' after the Franco regime fell.

You will also need to focus on how changing technologies have opened up possibilities for new cultural practices but taking into account Williams' point that technologies do not *determine* cultural change or the way human beings perceive and understand reality (as McLuhan suggested), neither do they exist autonomously outside social, political or military needs. We saw that the World Wide Web was designed for military not commercial use, although it is now dominated by commercial interests. However, the culture in which you are working may have adapted to the Web in quite different ways.

You may also consider the uses of the Web with relation to notions of 'affluence' in a particular culture. That is, has the rise of cultures related to the World Wide Web coincided with significant changes in incomes and acquisitive power? (For further economic possibilities, see below.) Then there are questions relating to the levels of education and technical expertise required of users and providers and what these may imply about the societies in which they are used. You might also look at the rise and extent of Chats in a particular culture and look at the general themes explored in them (like, health, illness, sports, film, politics, pets, parenting, religion, sexuality, teen culture etc.) to get an idea of their composition and importance to a particular culture. You'll often find that Chats are 'transnational', to adapt Eliot's phrase, but may be dominated by certain nationalities.

### Economic relations (how the subculture relates to mass culture and consumption etc.)

The existence of the World Wide Web depends not only on technology and forms of expertise but huge financial investment, and can be seen as a further way in which consumer

*(Continued)*

*(Continued)*

society has been able to extend itself with relation to mass culture. The regular (and often irritating) pop-up advertising banner is a constant reminder of the economic imperatives that underlie it. Even though you may not have to pay to enter a Chat, this does not mean that there aren't considerable costs which make using the Internet possible in the first place (buying computers, screens, modems, paying monthly telephone lines etc.).

Even if you use the Internet for what you see as subversive purposes, the whole system already depends on mass consumption. However, even this point might have to be rethought because, although in many cultures owning a computer and having access to the Internet is considered 'ordinary', this may not always be the case. In other cultures navigating on the Internet may be considered a luxury and therefore have class associations. The use of credit cards in a kind of pay-as-you-Chat has led to new forms of expenditure and exclusivity, with the possibility for controlling who participates.

**Subcultural responses: cultural space, rituals, locations, focal concerns**

This is where you get to explore how subcultures can now be located not only in the 'physical spaces' like streets and bars but virtual spaces. Chats open up (leisure?) spaces which may be prolonged or very sporadic in terms of how people use those spaces – Chats, for example, may be accessed during work time introducing an element of leisure into more formal work situations. Also, while you can only be in one bar at a time, you can negotiate more than one Chat at the same time (with people from many different parts of the world) so that the use of both time and space may be significantly different from pre-Internet cultures.

You might explore how these virtual spaces are organized through 'operators' who may have the power to include and exclude participants according to certain rules. The typical conventions for using Chats may be fruitfully analysed by asking questions about 'rituals' (the conventional ways of interacting) and 'focal concerns' (what issues or interests dominate a particular kind of interaction). Most Chats have basic rules governing politeness, introducing yourself into a conversation and prohibiting advertising, putting limits on swearing, insults, racism and aggressive sexual advances etc. If you type 'Chat etiquette' into a search engine you'll get a whole list of do's and don'ts. Even 'listening in' to conversations may be considered unacceptable, which raises ethical issues about whether or not researchers should 'spy' on other users without their knowledge. One way of resolving these problems of 'netiquette' would be to start a Chat about Chats or limit observation to your personal experience of Chat interactions. And then there are questions about collective responses which help to knit the virtual sub-group together.

**The generation of style, appropriation of objects and commodities (*bricolage*)**

It may seem odd to introduce questions of style with relation to Chats; however, there are many ways in which styles are produced in virtual spaces. One is the use of 'avatars' – 'personalized' images which represent the user (although users may draw on a common

*(Continued)*

stock so that more than one user has the same avatar). Added to the avatar is the nickname, which can help establish a virtual identity. Then there are the use of colours and scripts and the adaptation of language to the medium. For example, the written language of Chats resembles that of the SMS of the mobile phone, where abbreviations and acronyms make communications faster and more efficient in terms of the space needed to express ideas.

In English, if you don't know what abbreviations like afk (away from keyboard), bbl (be back later), lol (laugh out loud) mean it would be hard to negotiate Chat environments. There is the possibility of seeing these devices as forms of creative linguistic *bricolage* which can also serve to preserve 'insider/outsider' relations, reinforce group identity and create a sense of style. For example, chats dedicated to specific issues (like parenting) or illnesses (like cancer) often have topic specific abbreviations negotiated by members. As I'm sure you already know, further expressive possibilities are facilitated by the use of capital letters (a kind of RAISING THE VOICE for emphasis), stretched words ('cooool') and the use of 'emotions': smilies and a host of other faces expressing common emotions, which can be chosen from pre-existing images ☺, or typed. The typical typed versions for happy, angry and ironic wink :-), x-(, ;-) require a new convention of reading where readers have to read as if their heads were leaning to the left.

All this can be seen as a form of appropriation at the level of language – and hence educators (representing the official organs of power) often complain of falling standards and the decline of literacy and an impoverishment of emotional life without necessarily recognizing the creative sides of elliptical forms (in this respect it would be interesting to compare conservative responses to digitalized communications to the dominant values found in Leavisism). Considering these factors it is possible to see how symbols are adapted to a particular group or subcultural ways of life and how meanings and identities are negotiated.

**Double articulation: class basis? Lines of conflict and connection, resistance**

As suggested earlier, questions of class may be implied, erased, buried or even the main topic of a Chat. You may have to accept, however, that double articulation may be extremely hard to explore in Chats where there is no clear sense of a working-class group in conflict and connection with parent and dominant cultures. However, the concept of resistance is enormously flexible and may be manifested in multiple ways. What kinds of resistance do you find? What kinds of subversion are possible? Who is resisting whom? Subversion against whom or what? The notion of double articulation may be adapted to forms of resistance, subversion and delinquency. The Internet is full of people illegally downloading music and images, hackers, spies, hatchers of viruses, illegal porn sites, pederasty, snuff movies and a host of other illegal practices. Yet they may intersect with different value systems in distinct ways. Are there ways of re-reading 'parent' culture and 'Internet' cultures to analyse these issues?

*(Continued)*

*(Continued)*

**Questions of gender, race, sexuality and age**

In virtual spaces identity can be enormously fluid in so far that gender, race, sexuality, age etc. can be adopted as choices. This doesn't mean that all contributors will deliberately hide factors like gender, but virtual spaces do offer this possibility. Each of these factors may be the main topic of a Chat or, like class, may be implied, erased or buried. How relevant are gender, race, sexuality and age to the Chats you have explored, especially in those which are not dedicated to critical assessments of these issues? You might go back to the sections on subcultures, girls and race to reconsider the questions posed there in the light of internet culture.

Caroline Bassett, analysing the text-based virtual space known as LamdaMOO (a variation on a Multi User Domain or MUD), takes up the question of how gender functions in online worlds. If you are not familiar with these environments this will give you an idea of what you might find. Lambdans not only chat, argue and flirt, in up to 8,000 different 'rooms', but are able to 'dance', 'eat', 'drink' and engage in 'cybersex'. They can swap gender and appearance at will so that appearances are assumed to be deceptive, 'unfaithful iterations of players' Real Life identity' (Bassett [1995] in Gelder and Thornton, 1977: 538).

Drawing on Judith Butler's work, Bassett says that gender is 'performative' – put simply, it is the product of ways of behaving. I act *as* female, therefore I *am* female. Butler radically questions sexual identity as something fixed; Bassett finds the idea especially suggestive when examining virtual environments. Although in Lamda gender can be complex with neuter and mixed options, Bassett observes that most users choose between male and female (a highly dramatized affair, which may or may not resemble their Real Life status) and that (despite ambiguities) men often switch gender (to call attention to themselves) while women 'gravitate to neutral positions' to avoid unwanted attention (546). However, despite the 'morphing' between genders, especially where cybersex is concerned, many users still show an interest in the Real Life status of their 'partner'.

As a conclusion, Bassett reaffirms Butler's idea that gender is 'mobilized by gender norms, rather than gendered essences' thus 'cyberspace demands a reconsideration of the workings of gender and identity' (549). This is a project that anyone with access to the internet can explore and these points can be adapted to the analysis of other categories like race and age and open up debates about how far virtual identities are based on or differ from the dynamics of identities outside virtual spaces.

**Ideological dimension: role of subculture in terms of solving 'structural problems'**

Chats may not lend themselves very easily to an analysis of how group members tend to solve structural problems at an imaginary level. It could be argued, in the style of Adorno, that virtual culture is just another way that citizens can be immobilized, pacified and generally depoliticized (something which, if too simplistic, may be considered seriously). It is

*(Continued)*

possible, however, to recognize that the more politicized Chats often attempt, within the virtual community, to mobilize users to act both inside and outside virtual spaces. The circulation of petitions is very common and Chats are useful for organizing demonstrations in the non-virtual world. In this way groups within the virtual community may address structural problems and even become, as Thompson or Williams might have said, active agents of change. Of course, the effort doesn't constitute change, it only potentiates it. For example, in Spain, when the Aznar government decided to send troops to Iraq, there was an attempt to get Internet users to send so many e-mails to the Ministry of Defence that the messages themselves would paralyse their operating system. As far as I know, this e-warfare didn't have the intended effect: the system never seized up and, even if it did, the Aznar government didn't change its position (although, eventually, it did get voted out).

Finally, once you start looking into some of these issues, you'll realize that much more could be said and that the concepts you have been exploring, while useful, need considerable extension and refinement to understand the complexity of virtual communities. This, then, is the first stage in what could be a long journey ...

Figure 9.2 Creative linguistic bricolage

Before I go on to offer advice on further practice, here are a few comments on the way *Resistance* interacted with approaches associated with the social sciences.

## A dialogue with the social sciences

One important aspect of *Resistance* which would characterize much of the work which came out of the Birmingham Centre under Hall's directorship was a constant, respectful, but critical, dialogue with the social sciences. While I have not designed this book as an introduction to the social sciences, I would like to emphasize that what is known as cultural studies is multidisciplinary. This means that there are constant crossovers between cultural studies, Sociology, Media Studies, Political Economy, Literary Studies and Film Studies etc. Sometimes the debates that arise between these areas can be conflictual, and even dismissive, but there is also much healthy mutual interest. The longest section of *Resistance* is entitled 'Ethnography' but many contributors either do not draw on ethnographic theory or, when they do, maintain a critical relation to it. While I in no way do justice to the complexity of the arguments, my aim here is to indicate some of the main areas of contention between the contributors of *Resistance* and the sociological tradition (with its rich sources of theories and research methods).

For example, Geoffrey Pearson and John Twohig discuss in *Resistance* the use of drugs with relation to subcultural contexts but, at the same time, offer a critique of an **ethnographic method** associated with Howard Becker's **sociology of deviant conduct**. One of the main problems of this approach for Pearson and Twohig is how Becker's work was 'passed down by sociologists as gospel' (Hall and Jefferson, 1976: 124) when, for them, there are too many unquestioned assumptions in his work which avoids moral-political questions. The failure of sociologists to fully engage with youth cultures at the political level is also explored by Paul Corrigan and Simon Firth (231f.).

*Resistance* tends to reflect an ambiguous relation to the use of sociological method. On the one hand there are writers who are committed to sociological enquiry, but feel it needs to be revised or extended, on the other, there are others who, like Pearson and Twohig, are very sceptical of some of the assumptions behind it. For example, Graham Murdock and Robin McCron discuss consciousness with relation to class and generation, appreciating and taking into account much sociological theory (192f.). They clearly respect **empirical method** (which assumes that knowledge should be based on observation and experiment) but conclude by insisting that the sociology of youth needs to be revised and shouldn't be reduced to a single method.

Steve Butters rehearses, within the sociological tradition, some of the main arguments against **scientific empiricism** which assumes that there is an 'objective social reality' which can be captured by the sufficiently 'careful observer' (254) through an **inductive method**. Again, he questions methods based on induction (constructing hypotheses on observed data) insisting on the need for Sociology to constantly revise its ways of understanding in the light of its own insights – thus avoiding scientific dogmatism. Butters contribution is

*(Continued)*

particularly valuable for anyone interested in an informed overview of the way sociological method relates to the analysis of subcultures in the 1970s.

Similarly, Brian Roberts questions what he saw as the dominant positivism of mainstream Sociology – **positivism** aiming at, to quote Brian Roberts, 'objective scientific completeness' and certainty through quantification, analytic method, the search for 'objective causality' and the 'adoption of an a-historical standpoint' (243). He notes that the sociology of deviant subcultures tends to stand outside the positivism of orthodox Sociology. Without writing off sociological approaches, Roberts recommends **participant observation** where researchers have to introduce themselves into the social groups they wish to understand, rather than stand at a (positivistic) distance, and a more radical, politically aware method than mainstream Sociology normally allows. Butters, while recognizing the value of participant observation, offers an analysis of its shortcomings and assumptions.

## Exploring subcultures: possibilities for further study and practice

One way of 'cutting your teeth', in terms of using the ideas outlined in these chapters on subcultures, is to choose a film (like I did with *Quadrophenia*) to see how these theories might work. Of course, a film can never be mistaken for a subculture or subgroup but it may help to get you on the road to practice without requiring a great deal of background study. Below I offer a short list of films in the English language that you might use; however, I would also advise you to explore films in other languages. This list is by no means exhaustive but each one relates to a subculture and is available in DVD at the time of writing. They are listed in order of appearance.

*Easy Rider* (1969) dir. Dennis Hopper. Classic bikers' road movie that can be used to explore the US counter culture of the later 1960s.

*This is Spinal Tap* (1984) dir. Rob Reiner. This is a parodic, 'mockumentary' of heavy rock dinosaurs, full of irony and tongue-in-cheek humour. It can be used to see how some of the concepts we have been looking at might be applied.

*Sid and Nancy* (1986) dir. Alex Cox. Gives insights into the subcultural world of Punk through the rise and self-destructive fall of Sid Vicious of the Sex Pistols.

*Do the Right Thing* (1989) dir. Spike Lee. Just one example of US Black independent cinema which explores racial prejudice and tensions between different marginalized immigrant communities. Most of Lee's cinema explores issues relevant to subcultures including, in *Malcolm X* (1992), the rise of 'The Nation of Islam', which also gives insights, by drawing on Malcolm X's autobiography, into drugs and jazz subcultures.

*Priscilla Queen of the Desert* (1994) dir. Stephan Elliot. This film imaginatively creates a subcultural camp world of drag queens and transsexuals – and all in the Australian desert.

*Trainspotting* (1996) dir. Danny Boyle. Through a group of Edinburgh heroin addicts, Boyle offers the possibility of testing insights into drug subcultures and addiction.

*Velvet Goldmine* (1998) dir. Todd Haynes. It's possible to use this film to gain insights into the Glam Rock styles, attitudes and posturings of the 1970s, especially those associated with David Bowie and Iggy Pop.

*East is East* (2000) dir. Damien O'Donnell. This is just one of many British films that can be used to explore themes like race, racism, integration, subordination and generational difference. This film is in the tradition of a long history of films which deal with black and Asian communities in Britain. The first film of this kind was Horace Ové's *Pressure* (1975), which, unfortunately, is not yet available on DVD, although you might be able to get a copy through your library. See chapter thirteen for an in-depth analysis of *East is East*.

*Ali G: Indahouse* (2002) dir. Mark Mylod. Sacha Baron Cohen's parody of US-style gang warfare mediated through gangasta rap and translated into the quiet suburbia of West Staines (England) can be used (with a sense of ironic fun) to explore many of the concepts introduced in this chapter.

Documentaries are particularly useful sources for testing ideas, although many made for TV do not reach DVD. 'Rockumentaries' like *Woodstock* (Michael Wadleigh, 1979) and *The Filth and the Fury* (Julien Temple, 2000) which give insights into Hippy and Punk subcultures are, because of their continued popularity, still widely available. Again you should check your library resources. There are many books published on popular styles of music which, while not written for an academic reader, may prove to be informed and useful. For example, to limit myself to a couple of titles that deal with women and resistance in music, Lucy O'Brien's *She Bop* (1995) offers a history of women in music from blues to Rap, while Simon Reynolds and Joy Press's *The Sex Revolts* (1995) take up the theme of rebellion with relation to gender and, like O'Brien's, draw on some feminist theory.

An alternative is to raid your bookshelves and search out novels that deal with subcultures or subgroups to explore some of the concepts I've been exploring. To get an idea of the sheer range of possible subcultures, you might type the word 'subcultures' into a search engine and see what comes out. In my experience you'll get everything from the youth subcultures discussed here to things like Sado-Masochism and Satanism. If I had to recommend just one book as a follow-up it would be Dick Hebdige's *Subculture: The Meaning of Style* (1979), a study which explores the subversive implications of style in British youth subcultures as varied as Teds, Mods, Rockers, Skinheads, Punks and Rastas (I offer some further suggestions below).

## SUMMARY OF KEY POINTS

The aim of this chapter has been to help you develop your practice skills through the use of a simple heuristic. It has suggested how a number of key ideas developed in the previous chapter can be adapted to study all kinds of cultures associated with different social groups. Practice has been illustrated by referring to Internet Relay Chats. This chapter has also indicated how the authors of *Resistance through Rituals* set up a 'dialogue' with the social sciences. The chapter has been concluded with a detailed section on possibilities for further study and practice. I will not conclude this chapter with a list of methodological implications of this approach because they are already summed up at the end of the previous chapter (this chapter's theoretical companion).

## References

Bassett, Caroline (1995) 'Virtually Gendered: Life in an on-line world', in K. Gelder and S. Thornton (1997) *The Subcultures Reader*. London: Routledge.

Gelder, Ken and Thornton, Sarah (eds) (1997) *The Subcultures Reader*. London: Routledge.

Hall, Stuart and Jefferson, Tony (eds) (1976) *Resistance through Rituals*. London: Hutchinson.

Hebdige, Dick (1979) *Subculture: The Meaning of Style*. London: Methuen.

Hoggart, Richard ([1957] 1958) *The Uses of Literacy*. Harmondsworth: Penguin.

O'Brien, Lucy (1995) *She Bop: The Definitive History of Women in Rock, Pop and Soul*. London: Penguin.

Rich, Adrienne (1993) *Adrienne Rich's Poetry and Prose*. New York: W.W. Norton.

Reynolds, Simon & Press, Joy (1995) *The Sex Revolts: Gender, Rebellion and Rock 'n' Roll*. London: Serpent's Tail.

## Further reading

Many of the critics coming out of the Birmingham Centre would follow up the idea of resistance, linking it to popular styles of music. As indicated above, Dick Hebdige's *Subculture: The Meaning of Style* (1979) has become a standard work. However, if your first language is not English you might find some of the theoretical sections rather difficult. Nonetheless, it is well worth exploring.

Brooker, Will (1998) *Teach Yourself Cultural Studies*. London: Hodder & Stoughton. For such a concise publication Brooker gives a surprisingly broad view of how writers inspired by the Birmingham Centre focussed on, theorized and disagreed about subcultures. See especially chapter four 'Birmingham and Beyond'. See also Brooker's last chapter which gives very useful advice on surfing cultural studies' websites on the internet.

Butler, Judith (1990) *Gender Trouble*. London: Routledge. In this book Butler outlines the idea of gender being 'performative' which was so important to Caroline Bassett's argument. While this book has become a classic of feminist theory, given its complexity, it may prove difficult to students whose first language is not English.

Castells, Manuel (1996) *The Rise of the Network Society, Vol. 1*. Oxford: Blackwell. A standard introduction to the network society.

Chambers, Ian (1985) *Urban Rhythms: Pop Music and Popular Culture*. London: Macmillan. Chambers explores the diverse histories of rock music in Britain and the US from Johnny Ray to Johnny Rotten, and beyond, contextualizing the music with relation to the social-political background.

Chambers, Ian (1986) *Popular Culture: The Metropolitan Experience*. London: Methuen. Generally accessible and generously illustrated study of popular culture as a product of urban life with constant references to youth styles of music. The book also offers suggestions for further work.

Davis, Helen (2004) *Understanding Stuart Hall*. London: Sage. This is an accessible introduction to Hall's approaches to culture and is much more wide-ranging than the account I give in this book.

Evans, Liz (1994) *Women, Sex and Rock 'N' Roll: In their Own Words*. London: Pandora. A series of revealing interviews with women about being musicians in an industry dominated by men. Like O'Brien (1995) (see references above) and Reynolds and Press (1995), it helps to widen perspectives in terms of gender.

Gelder, Ken (2006) *Critical Concepts in Media and Cultural Studies*. London: Routledge. If you are really interested in subcultures this four volume set will prove to be an invaluable source. It includes many key texts from a variety of disciplines such as Cultural Studies, Sociology and Criminology. The volumes are very wide in scope ranging from essays exploring subcultures and history to work associated with important schools such as Birmingham and Chicago. Theoretical essays are juxtaposed with case studies on popular forms like jazz, punk, metal, hip hop, disco and clubbing. The last volume looks at subcultures and sexuality, virtual communities and new age communities. If your interest is less specific, Gelder and Thornton's *The Subcultures Reader* (1997), referenced above, is an excellent collection of diverse writings taking in the sociological tradition as well as studies more closely associated with cultural studies.

Goldstein, Dan (ed.) (no date) *Rappers Rappin*. Chessington. Surrey: Castle Communications. This was cited in chapter two but would adapt well to the study of subcultures, especially with relation to race issues.

Grossberg, Lawrence (1984) 'Another Boring Day in Paradise: rock and roll and the empowerment of everyday life', in Gelder and Thornton (eds) (1997). This essay pushes the analysis of subcultures that bit further by insisting on the 'affective power' of rock music. Grossberg addresses two main questions: How does one describe the specific effects (and popularity) of particular forms of rock and roll? How does one describe the consistency which constitutes rock and roll as a determinate cultural form? (477–8).

Haskins, James (2000) *The Story of Hip-Hop*. London: Penguin. This book, like Goldstein (no date), was mentioned in chapter two and is useful if you want to practise a kind of ethnogRAPhy.

McRobbie, Angela (1991) *Feminism and Youth Culture: From* Jackie *To* Just Seventeen. London: Mcmillan. In this book McRobbie sets out some of the main feminist criticisms against the male bias in previous studies of youth subcultures, while considering important issues concerning the methods that may be most appropriate to carry out these studies. She also offers a very in-depth analysis of how girls consumed the comics and magazines aimed at them and how they negotiated their own leisure spaces through things like romance fiction, fashion and music.

Porter, David (1997) *Internet Culture*. London: Routledge. A very useful book to help grasp what kinds of cultures are evolving on the internet.

Rojek, Chris (2003) *Stuart Hall (Key Contemporary Thinkers)*. Cambridge: Polity. One way of exploring Hall is to read Hall; another is to read Rojek or Davis (above) on Hall. Yet another, which would give you an insight into Hall's continued relevance and impact, would be to read what critics have to say about Rojek on Hall. Bill Schwarz reviewed Rojek's book in 'Stuart Hall' in the journal *Cultural Studies* (19(2) 2005) and indicated how he disagreed with Rojek's account. Rojek defended his book in 'On a rant by a little musketeer: a reply to Bill Schwarz' (in *International Journal of Cultural Studies*, 8(4) 2005). These two positions reveal that cultural studies is not a unified field. This argument also helps to remind us that different critics will understand their sources in different ways or place emphasis on distinct parts of a source. These differences of opinion also help to define what is at stake for different practitioners of cultural studies.

Storey, John (1998) (ed.) *Cultural Theory and Popular Culture: A Reader* (second edition). Essex: Pearson Prentice Hall. This reader contains many essays of great interest to those interested in how subcultures or subgroups make sense of what they consume. You might start by looking at Paul Gilroy on music and Black Power, Will Wright on the Western, Ien Ang and Christine Geraghty on the Soap Operas, Janice Radway on reading Romance and Yvonne Tasker on Crime Writing.

van Dijk, Jan (1999) *The Network Society: Social Aspects of New Media*. London: Sage. This is a very accessible introduction to how new media have impacted on contemporary culture.

# 10 How to Dominate the Masses without Resorting to the Inquisition: Antonio Gramsci and Hegemony Theory

## Introduction

This chapter and the next make up the fourth and fifth chapters dedicated to 'Consolidating Cultural Studies'. They are closely related in terms of their theoretical heritage and in the way they help to develop the thematic concerns associated with popular culture explored in the previous three chapters. This chapter, and its counterpart (chapter eleven), will introduce you to Antonio Gramsci and Louis Althusser, two Marxist thinkers who have been of particular importance to cultural studies, especially in Britain. Both these writers have helped to revise the way ideology is understood within cultural analysis.

The present chapter will begin with a consideration of an influential Marxist notion of ideology as an introduction to Antonio Gramsci's theory of hegemony, which will be introduced through a fictional dialogue between Gramsci and a prison doctor. This introduction will be complemented by advice on how hegemony theory might be practised (with full examples drawing on contemporary events) and how it can be adapted to the analysis of popular culture. The chapter finishes with ideas for further practice.

## MAIN LEARNING GOALS

- To appreciate how the work of Gramsci has been a fertile source of ideas with relation to the analysis of how political groups gain power through alliances, negotiation and compromise.
- To understand why cultural critics like Raymond Williams preferred Gramsci's approach to more simplistic interpretations of Marx and Engel's notions of ideology, and to appreciate why there was a 'turn to Gramsci'.
- To be able to see how some of Gramsci's principle ideas can be put into practice through the interpretation of contemporary politics and how they can be adapted to the analysis of popular culture.
- To understand how culture can be seen as a site of struggle.
- To recognize the role hegemony theory has played in helping to create a theoretically informed and politically engaged form of criticism.
- To work towards interpretive independence.

## Cultural studies and ideology

I want to begin this chapter by outlining an enormously influential model of **ideology** that has informed many forms of Marxist criticism and has often been the starting-point for much discussion within cultural studies. Marx and Engels, in an often-quoted passage, claimed that the class which rules at the social, economic, political level would also establish its view of the world as the 'ruling *intellectual* force' (Marx and Engels, [1846] 1970: 64). According to this way of thinking, ruling ideas as put forward by the ruling class are 'the ideal expression of the dominant material relationships' (64). This means that a dominant class does not only subordinate non-ruling groups at social, political and economic levels but also in terms of how individuals understand the world they live in. Read in terms of **capitalism**, the **bourgeoisie** establish industrial capitalism as the basis of their social, economic and political power which necessitates the **subordination** of the working class (the **proletariat**) whose economic inferiority and belief in the system is vital to the maintenance of the high profits necessary to sustain the capitalists' way of life.

Marx and Engels took this basic argument a stage further when they asserted that when a ruling class establishes itself it must, if it wishes to maintain its position, represent its own interests as if they were the common interests of everyone in society. Furthermore, these ideas have to be presented as if they are the 'only rational, universally valid ones' (66). This model of ideology assumes that the relations of subordination in the material base must be justified at the level of ideas and beliefs: that is, at the ideological level (of consciousness). Unless subordinate groups like the proletariat and the rural worker etc. believe that this system is the best possible for them, capitalist society would be under constant threat.

This has often been associated with the idea of **false consciousness**: that is, the working class, instead of seeing their subordination and exploitation, is led to see the world in a distorted way. (Incidentally, this idea does not have its origin in Marx's writings. Engels did use it, but very sparingly and it is open to various interpretations (Eagleton, 1991: 89f.)). The idea of false consciousness assumes that subordinate groups see the world through the eyes of their oppressors. The laws and values of the ruling class, as well as their way of organizing money, government, people and resources, are falsely assimilated and understood as the necessary prerequisites for the good of all.

In terms of methodology, this opens up the possibility of exploring in what ways dominant groups might create false ways of seeing and understanding in order to perpetuate a given social, political, economic system. As we saw in E.P. Thompson's work, this model is one which posits conflict between two fundamental classes: the rulers and the oppressed. Although this way of understanding ideology has been enormously productive, and may still be of use, much cultural studies has refined, argued with or moved beyond it. One of the main ways in which cultural studies has tried to refine and move beyond this approach to ideology is through Antonio Gramsci's theory of hegemony, which will be the subject of the following sections.

### Oversimplification
**WARNING**

My introduction to Marxist notions of ideology is only scratching the surface of a very big iceberg. The rest of this and the next chapter, as well as the chapters dealing with the Frankfurt School and E.P. Thompson should indicate that Marxist thought is enormously varied and there are considerable differences in the approaches to, and understanding of, the texts of Marx and Engels. However, even these references by no means exhaust all the possible approaches. See further reading for more possibilities.

## Introducing hegemony theory: a dialogue with Antonio Gramsci

In order to explore some of the main themes of hegemony theory I shall resort to another dialogue (which reflects the situation in which Gramsci had to develop his ideas). It is 1937 and Antonio Gramsci has been in confinement under the Mussolini regime for the last 11 years. Given his ill health, Gramsci is under police guard at a clinic in Formia (Rome) where he now awaits release, for he has finally been granted conditional liberty. What Gramsci doesn't know is that he will never enjoy freedom because, by the time his sentence is complete (April 1937), his body will give in to the long-term illnesses that have not been treated adequately in prison. Later that same month, at the age of 46, he will die from a massive cerebral haemorrhage.

Here we find Gramsci talking to a young doctor. At first Gramsci was reluctant to speak to him, suspecting that he was a government spy but the young man's sensitivity, intelligence, attitude and interest have gradually won him over. The doctor has asked Gramsci many questions about the notebooks that he keeps (he has been writing them since being given permission to do so some eight years ago in 1929). At first Gramsci only speaks about themes he feels are of no real interest to the prison authorities but after a number of conversations with this doctor he allows the man to probe other questions. Gramsci is wary but feels he can trust him. We break into the middle of a conversation (by the way, the following dialogue is entirely imaginary and only a vehicle for introducing a few important ideas).

DOCTOR: (speaking in hushed tones) I think I understand what you have been saying up to now about the need for the poor, the agricultural and industrial worker to unite against the Fascists, but look around you! Mussolini's leadership goes from strength to strength and we are not only dealing with the bourgeois classes – there seems to be massive support from the classes you tried to unify in the Communist Party before you were imprisoned. That is to say, from the very classes you argue have the least to gain from aligning themselves with the fascists. How can you explain this?

GRAMSCI: Over the years I have given this matter some thought and I think the most effective way to describe this situation is to refer to the term '**hegemony**'.

DOCTOR: Ah, through dominance! While I agree that the regime has, if you'll forgive a metaphor drawn from my own profession, surgically removed all those seen as contrary to its own values and beliefs and has silenced many through violence, prison and coercion, there are still those workers who seem entirely convinced by the fascist 'solution'.

GRAMSCI: Yes, but I think I ought to explain to you what I mean by hegemony. Traditionally hegemony has been understood in terms of domination through the open exercise of power or naked aggression but I am arguing that hegemonic control is more subtle than this. Of course, the fascists are able to bully, compel, imprison and kill but their power is not only dependent on this. The way I understand hegemony is that the exercise of political power cannot only be understood in terms of violence, it is also a question **of moral and intellectual leadership** (Gramsci, 1971: 57). This is particularly relevant in modern democratic societies (unlike ours) where the use of overt coercion and violence are generally underplayed. Of course, they are always there to be used – the army, police, courts and prisons are a social-political reality of democratic life.

DOCTOR: Doesn't this relate to a distinction you made in an earlier conversation between the **State and civil society**.

GRAMSCI: Yes, my idea is that direct coercive power is associated with the political power of the State, whereas the art of persuasion, the winning of consent, that is, hegemonic leadership, takes place in civil society. Hegemony, however, doesn't only relate to civil society, it also operates through state institutions.

DOCTOR: By civil society you mean what might be called 'private life' – that which is not subject to direct State control?

GRAMSCI: That's more or less what I meant – but these are complex questions that are not always easy to theorize. Put simply, hegemony relates to civil society with relation to things like the church, the family, political parties, clubs, the trade unions and the media. Although all these are subject to the laws of the State they are not (in democratic societies) directly controlled by governments – they are the cultural terrain upon which ideas, values and beliefs are discussed and fought out.

DOCTOR: So *how* does a dominant group manage to exercise moral and intellectual leadership? I mean, how does a political party which represents, for example, the interests of powerful capitalists manage to win the favour of large parts of the rural poor and the industrial proletariat?

GRAMSCI: A complex question, Doctor, which would require many years of painstaking thought! However, I'll try to give you an idea of how I deal with these issues. The starting point is Marx's idea that the dominant ideas governing society will be those formulated by the ruling class (in this case the capitalists) and they will, of course, be used to represent and defend its ways of seeing, its consciousness and interests. However, in order to win consent from other groups, the **dominant power bloc** must already exercise **leadership** before it can hope to govern – this is the source of its prestige, confidence and power (12 and 57). It must, once in power, negotiate and, where necessary, make concessions to the groups with whom it seeks allies, or over which it wishes to exercise control. Of course, the core values and interests of industrial capitalism cannot be seriously undermined, but it has to be prepared to make some compromises (161). In this way the dominant political grouping can claim to represent the other potentially antagonistic groups and thus absorb their interests, hopes, and claims as part of its own political projects. Thus, the interests of the dominant group can be presented as the 'motor force of a universal expansion' (182). Ideological domination, then, is dynamic: we don't have a model where the dominant power bloc ignores other groups – the groups are not isolated from one another, they **interact**. These are some of the workings of hegemony!

DOCTOR: (looking to see if any guards are within hearing distance) Hmm, I see what you mean. Those classes who may, on the surface, seem to have no reason to support a political party are effectively bought off and disarmed by these concessions. Hegemony is a form of leadership, or social control, where the masses are dominated but where the rulers do not need to resort to the Inquisition!

GRAMSCI: (smiling) Well, they are not my words, but you might put it like that. Socialism (he lowers his voice) must break the hegemony that effectively reproduces the class base of society and preserves, as much as possible, the dominant and subordinate roles upon which it is constructed.

DOCTOR: You have explained how hegemony may function but, how might subordinate groups counter these hegemonic tendencies?

GRAMSCI: Precisely through new forms of intellectual and moral leadership. As a Marxist I conceive of the possibility of a radical transformation of society through class struggle. In the case of the Bolshevik Revolution in Russia (1917) we can talk of a '**war of manoeuvre**' where power could be seized quickly and effectively. However, where this is not possible this would be a question of what I have called '**passive revolution**' or '**the war of position**' (108f.) where the working class would align itself with other subordinate groups to create a new and convincing collective will that can, at the appropriate moment of crisis, weaken and eventually overthrow capitalist domination. Just as the capitalist bourgeois classes have their intellectuals (understood in the widest sense of anyone involved in the creation and circulation of ideas) then so the revolutionary class needs its own creators and propagators of ideas and values which may coalesce into a powerful form of counter hegemony. Yet these **organic intellectuals** (6, 12 and 15) must grow from within the working class itself – not be imported from outside (although intellectuals from other classes may ally themselves to the cause). This counter hegemony, then, involves winning the support and exercising effective leadership not only over the working class but other classes – including those associated with the dominant power bloc. I am talking about people like you yourself, doctor ...

DOCTOR: (looking nervous and leaping away from Gramsci) Oh dear, Mr Gramsci, I really think we had better stop here. Is that a guard I hear approaching? It has been a most illuminating and stimulating talk but you really must rest for you are looking rather pale – and exertion isn't at all good for you. Besides I have many other patients to attend to ...

## The turn to Gramsci

This is a highly simplistic account and there is much that I have left out. However, it should give you an idea of how Gramsci argued that hegemonic forces may exercise a decisive influence over large groups of people at the level of civil society. As mentioned in the dialogue, Gramsci's notion of hegemony is related to the way power is exercised in democracies although, as you can see, it may be applied in useful ways to dictatorships (and other forms of rule). For cultural studies there are a number of important methodological implications in Gramsci's theory of hegemony, so much so that critics like Tony Bennett have talked about a 'turn to Gramsci' in British cultural studies (Bennett, in Storey, 1998: 217f.).

## Marxist notions of base and superstructure and, why turn to Gramsci?

To answer this question I'll start by referring to Raymond Williams. One reason that Raymond Williams was resistant to Marxist theory until quite late in his career was that he found the way that many writers had understood Marx's distinction between the **economic base** and the **superstructure** too simplistic. But what did Marx mean by these two phrases?

Very simply put, Marx distinguished between two levels of society: the base and the superstructure. The base describes the **material conditions** of production. In capitalist society, for example, the productive base is a system which implies certain relations of dominance and subordination between capitalist investors, entrepreneurs, factory owners etc. and the industrial proletariat who have but one commodity: the power of their labour. As we saw earlier, the industrial-economic system, being dependent on this politics of subordination, needs to be able to preserve these relations for its survival. This is achieved at the level of the superstructure.

Marx theorized, in the interests of practical revolutionary ends, that the superstructure was **determined** by the relations established in the base. The superstructure refers to things like the law, politics, religion, art, science and philosophy. That is, elements which help to organize society at the level of ideas and influence consciousness – what is established as right and wrong, the potentialities and limits of power, the possibilities for belief, creativity, and understanding. The idea is that in a feudal system the superstructure will reflect the interests, beliefs and consciousness of monarchs; in capitalism the laws and social and political freedoms will be adapted to the interests of the bourgeoisie. This means that any change in the base, or the mode of production, will be, sooner or later, reflected in the superstructure. A neat summary of these ideas can be seen in Marx's famous phrase: 'It is not the consciousness of men that determines their being, but on the contrary it is their social being that determines their consciousness' (Marx [1859], 1976: 3f). To prepare us for an exploration of why writers like Williams were dissatisfied with the way this distinction had been interpreted (and thereby facilitated a 'turn to Gramsci'), let's do a short practice exercise.

### **practice** EXERCISE: interpreting with the base and superstructure model

This simple distinction has been enormously suggestive to Marxist writers and, I would argue, it is still very useful. To explore the ideas outlined above you could think about how different forms of society might imply or require distinct relations between the material base and the superstructure. I shall base this exercise on Marx's distinction between the five stages of historical development, and give a few tips on the first category to help you think these relations through. The idea here is not to give 'a right answer' but just think about Marx's distinctions.

| **Material base**<br>What kind of social, economic and political relations do you think characterize each of these stages? | **Superstructure**<br>What forms of social organization do you think would be necessary to perpetuate the relations established in the base? |
|---|---|
| **Primitive (pre-literate) tribal communities**<br><br>Social relations: tightly-knit family/tribal affiliations.<br><br>Economic relations: no significant economic organization. Hunter-gatherer community dominated by survival rather than profit.<br><br>Political relations: no significant institutionalized government. Possibly forms of direction or leadership based on strength, skills or family ties and mystical beliefs. | Law: no institutionalized law but, being a preliterate society, probably organized around rituals and customs.<br><br>Politics: no organized politics, although this does not exclude the possibility of the domination by individuals or clans etc.<br><br>Religious belief/ethics: no organized religion but the beliefs of tribal life probably dominated by what would now be called magic rites and ceremonies, and possibly conducted by priest-like individuals (of either sex?).<br><br>Art: no institutionalized forms of art. Hard to know what things like cave |

| | |
|---|---|
| | paintings signified or if they reinforced dominant ways of seeing.<br>Science/Philosophy: again no institutionalization of knowledge but belief systems probably based on practical knowledge of the environment and magic rites etc. |
| You might think through how the social, economic and political relations may change with relation to states dominated by:<br><br>• **Slavery**<br>• **Feudalism**<br>• **Industrial capitalism**<br>• **Socialism** (which assumes the end of exploitation and subordination) | Try to imagine how the laws, political systems, religious/ethical beliefs, art and science and philosophical ideas might change with relation to the different societies. |

The problem, however, for writers like Williams was that this relation between the base and the superstructure was often assumed to be mechanical, and Williams was not at all convinced that the base was so easy to define. You may have concluded this yourself from thinking through the previous practice exercise. Williams saw the base as **a dynamic process** which had its dominant tendencies and characteristics but did not lend itself to simple description – it could be better envisioned as setting limits and exerting pressures on the superstructure (Williams, 1980: 34). Along with writers like Stuart Hall (in Morley and Chen, 1996: 266f.), Williams believed that Gramsci's theory of hegemony helped to challenge the idea that the base determined the superstructure in a simple way – even though it had to be admitted that a significant change in the base would have to have repercussions in the superstructure. If the base wasn't as static or monolithic as it seemed, then this would question any straightforward determinism (Williams, 1980: 34).

Another problem for Williams was where Marxist criticism assumed a simplistic relation between ideas generated by the dominant capitalist classes and their effect on the subordinate working classes. In *Marxism and Literature* Williams stated his belief that Gramscian hegemony theory went beyond the

Marxist notions of **ideology**, outlined at the beginning of this chapter, where 'a system of meanings and values is the expression or projection of a particular class interest' (1977: 108). Hegemony theory implies that political dominance or leadership can no longer be seen as the simple imposition of the ideas, beliefs and values (ideology) of a dominant group, but that this 'ideology', while rooted in the interests and intentions of the dominant class, is also the product of **negotiation and allegiances** (Williams, 1980: 36). Tony Bennett neatly summed the importance of the 'turn to Gramsci' when he wrote that it has been influential in both disputing the assumption that cultural forms can be assigned an essential class-belongingness and contesting a simply 'bourgeois versus working class' conception of the organization of the cultural and ideological relationships (Bennett in Storey, 1998: 226).

These ideas help to explain how particular ways of seeing and understanding society are so persuasive and become so ingrained that they are converted, as Gramsci insisted, into unshakeable **common sense**. This entails the kind of mentality that Marx and Engels had recognized that assumes that the existing social, economic and political arrangements are the only viable ones. Alternatives are represented as mere fantasy and doomed to failure. This is one of the ways Gramscian theory links to political change: organic intellectuals need to be able to break down the persuasive power of this common sense by developing **counter-hegemonic strategies**. However, if hegemony is based on negotiations, alliances and compromise then this suggests that any political consensus is always open to further negotiation and change. Here, subordinate groups which are, nevertheless, important to maintain the status quo, can attempt to win more rights and recognition. Political parties, unions and pressure groups etc. have a space in which they can move and attempt to gain advantages for their members.

In this context Stuart Hall has stated that one of the intentions of the Birmingham Centre when he was director was the production of organic intellectuals who could both theorize culture but, at the same time, attempt to transmit counter hegemonic ideas to a wider public – outside, that is, the confines of academic institutions (Hall, 1996: 267–8). Although Hall has been very modest about the success of the project, it does indicate how those in academic establishments may try to make their work politically relevant. As Gramsci insisted, the organic intellectual cannot rely on eloquence but has to be 'in active participation in practical life' as a constructor, an organizer and a 'permanent persuader' (Gramsci, 1971: 10).

The 'turn to Gramsci', then, was a way of assuming that those working in cultural studies could be theoretically informed but, at the same time, **politically**

**engaged**. As Hall made clear, this didn't necessarily mean becoming a revolutionary Marxist, but it did mean seeing '**intellectual practice as a politics**' (Hall, 1996: 272). This has become one of the key assumptions in much of cultural studies and has very important implications for practice – because now cultural criticism is not only politically *informed* but can be understood as being linked to political *action*. You might remember the words I quoted from Marx in chapter two on the Leavises: 'The philosophers have only interpreted the world, in various ways; the point is to change it'. I would argue that it is this way of thinking that makes cultural studies attractive to many people: now there's the possibility of not only analysing the world but being involved in efforts to change it.

## Practicing cultural studies with hegemony theory

One of the most effective ways of using hegemony theory is to look at what's happening in the political world around you. For example, when I began writing this book a number of members of the European Community were voting on whether or not to adopt the European Constitution. The unity of the European Community was thrown into disarray when both France and the Netherlands voted against it. On 5 June 2005, the German Chancellor, Gerhard Schröder, met with the French President, Jacques Chirac, in Berlin to see how the European Community might overcome the crisis caused by these defeats. They decided to ask colleagues in other member countries to accept a period of reflection on ratification, rather than abandon the possibility of agreement. The fact that France, seen as one of the prime movers of the Constitution, voted against it was seen as particularly damaging to the idea of a fully united Europe. Taking this incident, how might hegemony theory be applied to understand it?

### Oversimplification

**WARNING**

There is much simplification in what follows and much has had to be left out. Much more, for example, might be said on Chirac's changing attitudes toward the European Union (after all, in France he is known as La Girouette – 'the weathervane'), and not all political analysts would necessarily agree with the way I interpret the events. My main aim here, though, is to indicate in a rough way how hegemony theory might help to interpret a particularly difficult moment for the European Union.

The following heuristic breaks down hegemony theory into a series of five simple areas that can be used to ask questions about a given political situation. This can be added to other concepts taken from Gramsci's work, where they may be appropriate, like the role organic intellectuals and 'war of manoeuvre' and 'war of position' etc.

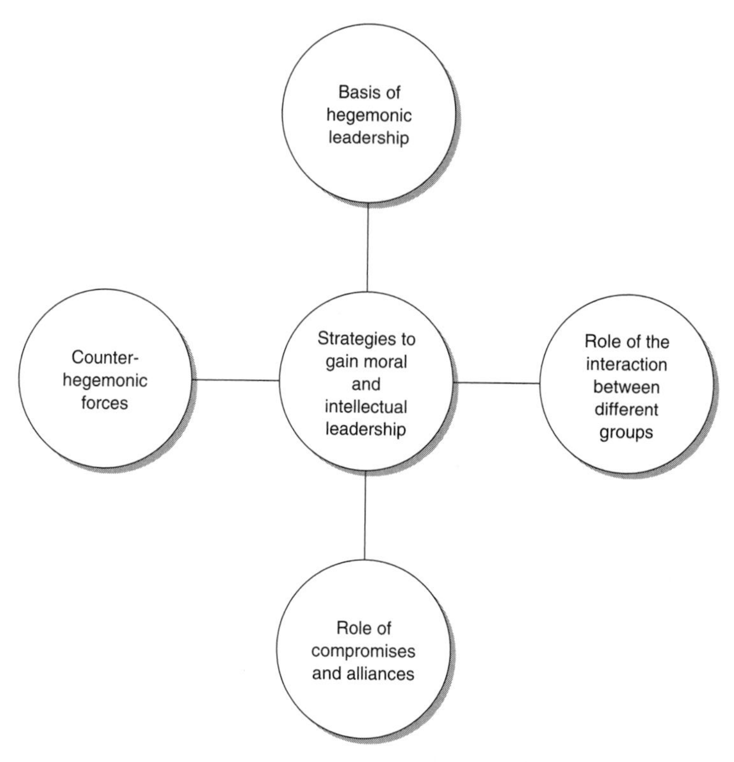


Figure 10.1 A heuristic to explore Gramsci's theory of hegemony

Let's see what kind of interpretation may result from these basic ideas.

## **notes** ON PRACTICE: using the heuristic. Reading contemporary politics with hegemony theory

Let's look at and interpret some of the factors which led up to, and followed, the defeat of the referendum in France.

- The French President, Jacques Chirac, was clearly for the European Constitution and closely allied with one of the other prime movers, Gerhard Schröder (who had already achieved a positive vote in Germany – albeit at parliamentary level and not as a result of a popular referendum). Here we can define the basis of hegemonic leadership within the Community and, through the two leaders, important hegemonic forces at national levels.
- However, the strength of the Franco-German hegemonic alliance was questioned by the failure of a positive vote in France, which threatened the existing hegemonic power with its basis in the unity of the two nations. It is worth noticing that the two leaders, despite the fact that Chirac had lost the hegemonic battle for a positive vote in France, attempted to maintain hegemonic leadership over the 25 members of the Community by claiming there was no alternative to European unification. This can be seen as an attempt to construct a form of 'common sense'. Hegemony, though, has to be won; thus they called for a new consensus.
- The French rejection of the proposed Constitution not only questioned Franco–German hegemonic power in the European Community but also revealed Chirac's, and the pro-constitutionalists', failure to exercise sufficient leadership (hegemonic power) over politics at a national level. The main political forces in France – the Socialist Party (PS), the Union for a Popular Movement (UMP) and the Union of French Democracy (UDF) – were originally united in their support for the European Constitution, which meant that objections from less powerful groups (both Right and Left) would not seriously challenge the outcome of the referendum. Hegemony, in this instance, clearly cut across traditional party interests.
- Yet the failure to obtain a majority was also the result of a hegemonic breakdown within the French Socialist Party. Against party policy (the ex-Prime Minister) Laurent Fabius, was part of an influential sub-group that campaigned for the rejection of the European Constitution. He, and other senior members of the party who supported the 'no' vote, were considered traitors and consequently dismissed from the leadership. Fabius justified his defiance by claiming that he was acting in the interests of the French people and fighting for socialist unity, thus challenging the current leadership. Many within the Socialist Party believe that Fabius acted out of self-interest in a move to consolidate his position to make a bid to become President in the 2007 elections (*El País*: 2005: 4). If this is true, it helps to demonstrate the complexity of hegemonic forces within a single party.
- One of the ironies of the rejection was that very different political parties were involved in marshalling public opinion against the Constitution. One of the ways the Socialist Party tried to convince other left-wing groups to vote for it was to emphasize that they would, if they insisted on influencing the public against the Constitution, be in coalition with extreme right-wing groups like the National Front. In this way two hegemonic forces representing two political poles were, in practice, united.

- Yet, once the referendum rejected the Constitution, *both* political wings claimed victory, thus staking a claim to effective leadership.
- In the days following the failure to lead the public towards an acceptance of the European Constitution, the international press was full of speculation as to *why* the French public voted as it did. Political analysts have offered many reasons to explain these events, from the public perception that belonging to the European Union has not benefited France, to fears that a European Constitution would open the floodgates for more immigration, and thus more unemployment. (*El País* 2005: 4). These circumstances, imagined or real, are not necessarily confined to one class but are factors which can be played upon by any political group attempting to win hegemonic control.
- Hegemony theory, then, can help to highlight that the rejection of the Constitution could not be reduced to a simple form of class belongingness.
- One other theme that appeared in the press directly after the French referendum was the idea, put forward in the European press by Timothy Garton Ash, that with the possible fracture of the Franco-German alliance a country like Britain may end up providing a different kind of leadership in Europe – more in line with the social and economic reforms associated with the Tony Blair Government (Garton Ash, 2005: 13). This hegemonic turn, which could overturn the prevailing economic agreements, was reinforced by Britain's presidency of the European Union.
- This brings a further element into the hegemonic equation: alternative power bases moving into perceived power vacuums offering alternative hegemonic possibilities.

This by no means exhausts the possibilities for analysis, but it should show how some of the basic concepts associated with hegemony theory can be adapted to an analysis of contemporary politics. You can also see that I've extended the use of hegemony theory from the national to the larger alliances (and 'dis-alliances') of the European Union.

## Hegemony theory and popular culture

The use of hegemony theory within cultural studies, however, has gone beyond applying it to the machinations of contemporary political life. As Stuart Hall once commented, Gramsci's notion of hegemony is an 'enormously productive metaphor' (Hall, 1996: 267). One of the areas where hegemony theory has proven to be most fruitful is in the way it has been used to analyse forms of **popular culture**. Before discussing its use it is necessary to reflect for a moment on the idea of the popular. Of course, popular culture may be defined in many ways, from that which is consumed by large masses of people, to anything that describes the 'distinctive way of life' of 'the people' (Hall, 1998: 446f.).

However, Hall has offered a definition of a particular approach to the 'popular' that has won wide currency (particularly within British cultural studies):

> This looks, in any particular period, at those forms and activities which have their roots in the social and material conditions of particular classes; which have been embodied in popular traditions and practices. (449)

You may notice that Hall's use of hegemony theory does not lead him to abandon the notion of class – although he recognizes, with Gramsci, that affiliations *cut across* class distinctions. Furthermore, he insists that what is essential to the definition and study of popular culture is the recognition of how popular cultural forms are **in tension with the dominant culture** (449). What this means in practice is that the critic needs to take account of:

> what belongs to the central domain of elite or dominant culture, and the culture of the 'periphery'. It is this opposition which constantly structures the domain of culture into the 'popular' and the 'non-popular'. (448)

These categories are not fixed – a novel, film or play can be popular at one moment in history and considered 'Art' at another – but it is possible to analyse the relationship between cultural practices and forms in terms of how they relate to, or are in conflict with, the dominant values of the power bloc at a given historical moment.

Seen in this way, popular forms of culture, rather than lead to the manipulation of the masses, can be seen as sites of ideological struggle, where hegemonic battles are won or lost. Cultural forms, then, are not *essentially* class based but subject to valuations which associate them with particular groups or classes which have the power to accord them official or non-official status. This idea of popular culture as a **site of struggle** has been repeated many times and has proven to be very suggestive for cultural analysis. What is of paramount importance for Hall and those influenced by his ideas is '**the class struggle in and over culture**' (449). What constitutes popular culture, then, is the culture that is associated with those who are **excluded** and **oppressed**; the key relation to take into account is that between these groups and those alliances that make up the power bloc (452). Popular culture is that place where **consent** and **resistance** are expressed, where 'the struggle for and against a culture of the powerful' is staged (453).

Popular forms of culture, rather than lead to the manipulation of the masses, can be seen as sites of ideological struggle, where hegemonic battles are won or lost.

Figure 10.2 Hegemony and popular culture

## **notes** ON PRACTICE: reading popular culture with hegemony theory

This kind of 'turn to Gramsci' can be illustrated by referring to the last chapter on subcultures, where the authors of the introduction to *Resistance Through Rituals* see working-class (youth) subcultures as winning cultural space for the young. We saw that this involved factors like establishing rituals and locations where social interaction can take place, creating structured relations which establish a sense of group identity, and the exploration of 'focal concerns' which become central to the inner life of the group.

If we come back to the film *Quadrophenia*, we can see how the Mod subculture attempted to establish itself against the dominant values of 'straight' society – that is, win some cultural space for itself. Mod culture can be seen as a space where meanings and alternative value systems are fought out for members of a subordinate class.

Taking this a little further it is possible to analyse any form of culture which poses some challenge to the dominant political order at any given moment. Some of the common categories in which challenges are articulated are the following:

- Gender
- Class
- Race/ethnicity
- Sexuality

Any one of these categories may be in contradiction with one or more of the others. For example, Mod subculture may have been oppositional in its rejection of what was considered the 'straight' world around it and carved out a space in which young people (mainly from the working class) could affirm themselves. However, as we saw in the last chapter, as a working-class movement, it offered fewer possibilities for young women and could actually be seen as complicit in many respects with the way women were generally treated and (under)valued in the wider culture. We also saw that *Quadrophenia* reflected certain generalized racist attitudes and, if you watch the film carefully, you'll also notice that part of the banter between Jimmy and his friends involves what is now described as **homophobia**: hostility towards same-sex relations. An example is when Jimmy and his mates go to the barber's for haircuts and refuse to have lacquer put on their hair on the grounds that it's for 'poofs'. Heterosexual masculinity often asserts itself through hostility towards what can be called a **significant other** that has to be reviled in order to preserve its own integrity.

The same process can be seen to function when a Rocker asks the character Monkey (who wears her hair very short) if she is 'the boy or the girl' and when the Rockers associate the motor scooter with a hairdryer – it is downgraded through its common association with women. This makes reference to the sound of the scooter's two-stroke engine, with its hi-revving, high-pitched sound regarded as effeminate with relation to the deeper, 'gutsier' sound of the large four-stroke motorcycle (more often than not British) favoured by the Rockers. Conclusion: while Hall's notion of the popular is enormously useful, we should avoid idealizing it.

If you look at chapter thirteen (on race, ethnicity and sexuality) you'll see that I show how a popular cultural form like film can represent and explore those who are subordinated excluded or oppressed. The kind of analysis I offer is very much in line with Hall's notion of popular culture because the popular form I choose represents a challenge to dominant notions of racial and national identity. Chapter twelve (on Virginia Woolf and feminism), while not based on a 'popular' form of culture, also explores related issues in so far as feminist writings are involved in hegemonic struggles against male oppression.

## Oversimplification

### WARNING

Although, according to this model, popular culture is seen as the site of struggle for meanings and cultural value, this does not mean that official forms of 'high' culture cannot be in conflict with the values or ways of thinking of the classes associated with hegemonic control. A simple example would be what is now considered to be the 'serious' novel (literature with a capital 'L') which has often been regarded as an essentially bourgeois form: a cultural product of the rise of industrialism and the middle classes. However, many novels can also be seen as repositories of fierce criticism against bourgeois ideas, values and practices. Hall's ideas, without discarding this possibility, help to focus on the idea of the popular as oppositional, marginal and suppressed but, as we have seen, the popular may be understood in other ways. It is also worth taking into account that the multiple definitions of, and approaches to, 'popular culture' have rendered it a deeply ambiguous and even confusing concept (Bennett, 1980: 18f.).

## Hall's adaptation of hegemony theory to popular culture

Before looking at how you might go about practising Hall's adaptation of hegemony theory to popular culture, I'd like to make a few preliminary points. To begin with, you might go back to the conversation in chapter seven and imagine how the ideas expressed in the present chapter might compare with the ideas Hall and Whannel were putting forward in *The Popular Arts*, and how Hall's conception of the popular outlined above might change the direction of the debate. As a preparation for practice let's get clear what kind of method Stuart Hall felt was necessary to study popular culture:

1. It assumes that **the domains of cultural forms and activities are constantly changing**.
2. It studies **the relations which structure the cultural field into dominant and subordinate**.
3. It tries to be aware of **how these relations are articulated by treating them as the process through which some things are singled out so that others can be excluded or devalued**.
4. At its core is an interest in '**the changing and uneven relations of force which define the field of culture**' – that is, cultural struggle.
5. Finally, its main focus is on '**the relation between culture and questions of hegemony**' (Hall, 1998: 449).

### **notes** ON PRACTICE: Hall's adaptation of hegemony theory to popular culture

Let's see how you might put some of these ideas into practice. Although Hall's emphasis is on the popular, you will see that this only makes sense with relation to the way 'high' or official forms of culture are established.

1. Hall's first point assumes that any cultural form may be upgraded or demoted according to the hegemonic forces in place – certain Hollywood films might be considered entertainment when made but elevated to the 'seventh art' at a later date. Certain kinds of jazz may be considered of little worth at one period of history but worthy of study and funding by public institutions at another.
2. Moving on from the first point, you might try to get an idea of *how* different cultural forms may be organized into dominant and subordinate. It is a good idea to look at the roles played by arts councils and influential private organizations (like independent art galleries) to see how these relations are established.
3. A consideration of point three should help you to become more aware of the processes through which certain forms of culture are singled out. A very useful article by Paul DiMaggio (in Storey, 1998) may help you to focus on the kinds of processes and conditions which may establish certain cultural forms or practices as dominant and valued. DiMaggio describes how a notion of 'high culture' was established in nineteenth-century Boston (USA) through the establishment of the Museum of Fine Arts and the Boston Symphony Orchestra. What DiMaggio shows is that both the museum and orchestra were the products of a particular upper-middle-class group, 'not separate products of different segments of an elite' which managed to dominate and centralize the 'high cultural' life of Boston at the expense of other groups (468). Of course, this is not always the case and you might explore local situations to see how they reflect or differ from this model. DiMaggio, for example, recognizes that in Europe the processes were often more complex involving both aristocrats and the bourgeoisie.

4 & 5. DiMaggio could be said to expose 'the changing and uneven relations of force' which defined the field of culture in nineteenth-century Boston because the establishment of the orchestra involved a certain amount of rivalry, downgrading and exclusion of other efforts to found what was considered a worthy musical culture. That is to say, Henry Lee Higginson, the man who was largely responsible for founding the orchestra, was 'forced to wrest hegemony over Boston's musical life from several contenders'. This was made possible because of his 'centrality to Boston's economic and social elite' (464).

We see here, in line with Hall's way of thinking, that cultural hegemony intersects with questions of class and power. What would be of particular importance to Hall's notion of the popular would be to study how other forms of culture (especially those of subordinate groups) are excluded, devalued or ignored and what efforts were being made to establish alternatives. DiMaggio's conclusion is worth summing up to explore how the relations between class and culture may function. For DiMaggio, the creation of the Museum of Fine Arts and the Boston Symphony Orchestra and comparable organizations all over the United States 'created a base through which the ideal of high culture could be given institutional flesh'. Thus, an alliance between class and culture emerged that was intimately bound up to its 'organizational mediation'. The consequence is that a distinction between high and popular culture is only understood in the double sense of 'both a ritual classification and the organizational systems that give that classification meaning' (471).

**Notes on further adaptation: exploring the cultural field in your locality**

- The ideas expressed above are only some ways you might explore hegemony theory. The possibilities, however, are huge – you might recall that Hall makes the point that Gramsci's notion of hegemony is an 'enormously productive metaphor'. With relation to DiMaggio's ideas, you might look at what kinds of culture are sponsored in your local area, town, or city to get an idea of what cultural forms or practices are drawn into official notions of culture. You might also try to get an idea of which kinds of 'culture' are well established and which are in a process of reconsideration. That is, you might sketch out what you think is the cultural field in your locality.
- You can look at how non-governmental organizations construct a sense of official culture and look at the way local councils and ministries use their resources. That is, what kinds of cultural activity do they sponsor? You will often find that sponsored cultures are, in practice, quite wide and not always predictable. Therefore, three more simple questions might be asked. How much space or money is dedicated to what? What percentage of resources is dedicated to each category? What kind of prestige is associated with different cultural activities?
- Another way you might practise hegemony theory would be to go back to the last chapter on subcultures and consider how different youth movements oppose or challenge at different cultural levels.
- In fact, every organizational structure can be read from the point of view of hegemony theory. As we've seen, the dynamics of power can be analysed in terms of the internal functioning of a group (how leadership is won) and in terms of how that group may attempt to influence other groups or events in a wider sense. Apart from political parties and youth subcultures, you might explore other groups like trade unions, religions, environmental groups, peace movements, gay and lesbian rights, anti-globalization, animal rights, human rights, and pro- and anti-abortion movements etc. You might even analyse groups *you* belong to.
- You can now go back to the chapters that deal with other Marxist thinkers, like Adorno and Thompson, and consider the strengths and weakness of each approach and how far the theories might benefit from hegemony theory.

## SUMMARY OF KEY POINTS

This chapter has outlined how Gramsci's work helped cultural critics to challenge some of the more simplistic notions of Marxist ideology. Hegemony theory has been seen to give a much more complex account of how political power is exercised and has shown how leadership is more than just a question of the use of force. The 'turn to Gramsci' has been explained as a way cultural studies could be theoretically informed but, at the same time, politically engaged. Gramsci's ideas have been shown to be flexible enough to be applied to contemporary politics and the chapter has shown how hegemony theory has been, and can be, adapted to the analysis of popular culture (understood as cultures of the 'periphery'). In the final part of this chapter advice has been given on how Gramsci's ideas may be used to interpret the processes through which different cultural products are valued into 'high' or popular forms. The methodological importance of this way of thinking can be summarized in the following ways:

- It helps to us to understand that the exercise of political power in democratic states is highly dependent on negotiation, alliances and acts of persuasion linked to moral and intellectual leadership.
- Without abandoning the idea of class, it helps us to see it in more complex ways. Gramsci's ideas have also helped critics to visualize the relations between the Marxist notions of base and superstructure in more subtle and dynamic ways which avoid more deterministic ways of seeing. Hegemony theory also challenges the idea of essential class-belongingness, questioning the simpler working- versus ruling-class opposition.
- Recognizing the role of organic intellectuals in counter-hegemonic struggles, it offers the possibility of 'intellectual practice as a politics'.
- Stuart Hall's use of hegemony theory has helped to provide a strategy for the analysis of popular culture which sees cultural forms as sites of struggle where battles are won or lost in terms of what counts, and what is valued, as culture.
- As a method this can help cultural critics to appreciate how subordinate groups fight against and are in conflict (or negotiate or collude) with the dominant power bloc.

## References

Bennet, Tony (1980) 'Popular culture: a teaching object'. *Screen Education*, 34.

Bennett, Tony (1998) 'Popular culture and the "turn to Gramsci"', in J. Storey (ed.), *Cultural Theory and Popular Culture: A Reader* (2nd edition). Essex: Pearson Prentice Hall.

DiMaggio, Paul (1998) 'Cultural entrepreneurship in nineteenth-century Boston: the creation of an organizational base for high culture in America', in J. Storey (ed.), (2nd edition) *Cultural Theory and Popular Culture: A Reader*. Essex: Pearson Prentice Hall.

Eagleton, Terry (1991) *Ideology: An Introduction*. London: Verso.

Garton Ash, Timothy (2005) 'Que se puede hacer' ('What one can do'). *El País* (Supplement), 5 June.

Gramsci, Antonio (1971) *Selections from Prison Notebooks*. London: Lawrence & Wishart.

Hall, Stuart (1996) 'Cultural studies and its theoretical legacies', in D Morley and K-H. Chen *Stuart Hall: Critical Dialogues in Cultural Studies*. London: Routledge.

Hall, Stuart (1998) 'Notes on deconstructing "the Popular"', in J. Storey (ed.), *Cultural Theory and Popular Culture*: *A Reader* (2nd edition). Essex: Pearson Prentice Hall.

Marx, Karl and Engels, Friedrich ([1846] 1970) *The German Ideology*. London: Lawrence & Wishart.

Marx, Karl ([1859] 1976) *Preface and Introduction to A Critique of Political Economy*. Peking: Foreign Languages Press.

Morley, David and Chen, Kuan-Hsing (eds) (1996) *Stuart Hall: Critical Dialogues in Cultural Studies*. London: Routledge.

*País, El* (2005) 'Fabius es expulsado de la dirección de los socialistas franceses' and 'Algunas razones inconfesables del "no"', 5 June.

*Quadrophenia* (1979) dir. Franc Roddam.

Storey, John (ed.) (1998) *Cultural Theory and Popular Culture: A Reader* (2nd edition). Essex: Pearson Prentice Hall.

Williams, Raymond (1977) *Marxism and Literature*. Oxford: Oxford University Press.

Williams, Raymond (1980) *Problems in Materialism and Culture*. London: Verso.

## Further reading

Bourdieu, Pierre (1984) *Distinction: A Social Critique of the Judgement of Taste*. London: Routledge. This highly influential sociological study looks at the politics of taste. Bourdieu argues that cultural value, based on taste, is a question of social power rather than something essential to cultural products or the product of disinterestedness. Bourdieu coined the term 'cultural capital' to describe how social and aesthetic values coalesce in works established as official high culture. For more studies that relate to the politics of taste, see de Certeau, Michel (1988), Fiske (1989a and 1989b) and Jenkins (1992).

de Certeau, Michel (1988) *The Practice of Everyday Life*. California: University of California Press. This book explores ways in which ordinary people resist or subvert dominant meanings. Like Hoggart, de Certeau is interested in how ordinary people (rather than members of counter cultures) negotiate paths through dominant, official or hegemonic culture. Like Fiske and Jenkins (see below) this study helps to counterbalance the negative readings of mass popular culture found in the work of the Leavises and the Frankfurt School.

Eagleton, Terry (1991, see references above) gives a thoroughgoing, critical introduction to the uses of the term ideology within Marxist debate.

Fiske, John (1989a) *Understanding Popular Culture*. London: Routledge. Fiske, like Hall, is primarily interested in what he calls 'the political potential of popular culture' (159) and its ability to disrupt or subvert hegemonic power structures. Fiske has often been criticized because he is seen to celebrate popular mass culture, rather than condemn or be more critical of it. Fiske, however, justifies his celebration of much popular culture because he sees it as an oppositional force resisting the power bloc. Fiske's last chapter is well worth reading to understand the politics of the popular.

Fiske, John (1989b) *Reading the Popular*. London: Routledge. This is the companion volume to *Understanding Popular Culture* (1989a) and shows how ordinary people make meanings out of popular cultural forms and practices. Fiske engages with European cultural theory to show how meanings are generated in and around popular cultural forms and practices like shopping in malls, going to the beach, playing in video arcades and listening to Madonna. The book illustrates, through wide references to English-speaking cultures, the politics of the popular.

Frow, John (1995) *Cultural Studies and Cultural Value*. Oxford: Oxford University Press. This book explores and questions, in a very cogent way, the relations between so-called 'high' and 'low' culture and what has often been seen as the class basis of different cultural forms. It engages with Hall's arguments about popular culture and Bourdieu's idea of cultural capital and puts forward a series of arguments of its own. This is a key study for all those interested in questions of cultural value.

Jenkins, Henry (1992) *Textual Poachers*. London: Routledge. Another study that emphasizes that consuming popular cultural forms can be active, creative and socially relevant. Jenkins' book, very much influenced by de Certeau, focuses on how fans of popular TV series respond in highly complex ways, pointing out that alternative readings are not necessarily resistant or progressive. While he tends to see Fiske's claims about audiences as exaggerated (see above), he does insist, however, that fans of *Star Trek* and other series have exercised interpretive power by sharing their readings on web pages, re-editing episodes, and systematically campaigning TV networks to reshow or revise content.

Storey, John (1998, see references above) includes his 'Rockin' Hegemony: West Coast Rock and America's War in Vietnam', a very useful essay which effectively demonstrates how you might apply hegemony theory to an understanding of the 1960s West Coast counterculture. Storey's reader includes short extracts from Marx and Engels, Gramsci, DiMaggio and Bourdieu and many other writers relevant to the themes explored in this section. An excellent source of reading if you do not have access to the original texts.

Storey, John (2001) *Cultural Theory and Popular Culture: An Introduction* (3rd edition). Essex: Pearson Prentice Hall. In his first chapter, Storey offers a very useful, instructive and constructive overview of definitions of popular culture.

Strinati, Dominic (1995) *An Introduction to Theories of Popular Culture*. London: Routledge. This introduction has useful sections on Marxist uses of ideology and Gramsci's contribution to the analysis of popular culture.

Tudor, Andrew (1999) *Decoding Culture. Theory and Method in Cultural Studies*. London: Sage. Tudor's introduction is useful to those who want to see how Gramsci's ideas have been absorbed into British cultural studies.

Turner, Graeme (1996) *British Cultural Studies: An Introduction* (2nd edition). London: Routledge. Like Tudor, above, offers an accessible and historically informed overview of how Gramsci's ideas have made an impact on the British cultural studies tradition.

# A Few Ways you might Adapt Louis Althusser's Ideas to Cultural Studies: A Dialogue with Dr Jekyll and Mr Hyde

## Introduction

We now arrive at the final chapter in the section on 'Consolidating Cultural Studies'. It extends a number of themes introduced in the last chapter by introducing a series of important concepts taken from the work of Louis Althusser. Through a dialogue between Jekyll and Hyde, the concepts are introduced and illustrated in detail. This chapter also shows how Althusser's ideas can be adapted to the analysis of popular culture and ends with suggestions for further practice.

### *MAIN LEARNING GOALS*

- To see how Louis Althusser's ideas can help students of cultural studies to interpret what Althusser saw as the gaps and silences in texts.
- To be aware of how to go about adapting some of Althusser's ideas to rudimentary forms of cultural analysis.
- To see how Althusser's ideas might be used to reflect on how audiences may be positioned in important ways in order to respond to cultural forms.
- To work towards interpretive independence.

As stated above, I shall now move on to the Marxist critic Louis Althusser, who has also exercised considerable influence over cultural studies (particularly the British variety). This is partly because a number of his ideas have been adapted to political analyses beyond their original applications, and partly because his theories concerning ideology, like Gramsci's, challenge the simplistic determinism governing the relations between the base and the superstructure (outlined in the previous chapter). I shall not discuss every aspect of ideology in Althusser's work but concentrate on those features I feel can be used for relatively simple forms of practice.

**Oversimplification**

**W A R N I N G**

The introduction offered here adapts a number of Althusser's ideas which can be, and have been, used to interpret various forms of (especially) popular culture. It also ought to be kept in mind that these adaptations often extend their use in ways that might have surprised Althusser.

Through a dialogue between Jekyll and Hyde, I shall suggest ways in which a number of concepts may be used to interpret popular culture (including advertising). Jekyll isn't involved in cultural criticism but is interested in the kinds of issues it discusses. I shall suggest ways of practising the concepts as they are introduced. We break into a conversation held in a bar somewhere in Britain near to where an important academic conference is being held. While reading this dialogue you might think about why I have chosen these names.

## Introducing Althusser through Jekyll and Hyde: the problematic and symptomatic reading

JEKYLL: Now, the other day I was talking to this guy about Marxist interpretation who kept going on about '**the problematic**' and '**symptomatic reading**'. I just nodded my head wisely but, to be honest, I hadn't the faintest idea what he was talking about. For that reason I've invited you here to explain these things to me.

HYDE: Ah, well, I hope you've brought a lot of money because this is going to cost you a few beers. This man was referring to concepts associated with the French Marxist philosopher, Louis Althusser. He came up with the concept of the problematic in a book called *Reading Capital* (1970), based on his interpretations of one of Marx's key works, *Das Capital* (began in 1865). The basic idea is that it is possible to read all kinds of texts with relation to their theoretical or ideological limits.

JEKYLL: Whoa, you're losing me already! What does he mean by reading texts with relation to their theoretical or ideological limits?

HYDE: Let's take an example, it could be a book on philosophy, history, economics or a novel or a film etc. What Althusser says is that a text (understood in the widest sense) is limited by its subject matter which, in turn, limits the kinds of questions that can be asked about it – and this circumscribes the answers that can be given. In this way we can talk about a text's ideological limits which are its 'problematic'. For example, we might be watching a reality TV programme where we look into the lives of an artificial community. We can observe how the different members of that community interact and we may know things that they do not know, like the things we are told by presenters. However, we only see what the programme makers choose to allow us to see. The programme is like a novel, a philosophical tract, a history book, or a film in this respect: the reader, viewer etc. can only respond to what is presented. But there's a lot behind a book, film or programme etc. which could be said to make it possible but which is not part of what readers or viewers can experience directly.

JEKYLL: Wow, I could have worked that out for myself – without Althusser's fancy concept to help me!

HYDE: Hold on a moment, I haven't finished yet (oh, and get the beers in). This is just the problematic but it's linked to another idea which is 'symptomatic reading'. A symptomatic reading is one which asks questions which demand answers which can only be found in the text's **silences, gaps or absences**.

JEKYLL: Symptoms! Answers to be found in what is absent! Sounds like Althusser had been reading Freud ...

HYDE: Precisely, my dear Jekyll. Althusser, like the Frankfurt critics, combined Marxism with ideas taken from psychoanalysis, among other things. Just as Freud worked back from symptoms to their causes in the unconscious, so Althusser works from the text (as symptom) to that which is unstated but which is fundamental to the way a text is structured in the historical moment in which it was produced – namely its ideological underpinning. Symptomatic reading is a kind of **double reading**: it reads the surface but also reads beyond that surface to open up significant gaps and silences. There's also an interesting variation on this idea that Althusser called the '**invisible problematic**' where it is possible to perceive answers which do not correspond to any question posed in the text (Althusser, 1970: 28).

JEKYLL: What? Er, well, yes, but ... I'll just get a couple of beers in (he returns, still perplexed). Cheers! But, concentrating criticism on what's not in the text, this symptomatic reading based on the ... problematic ... isn't it a bit loony? I mean, isn't the idea to read and interpret what you can see and experience *directly*?

HYDE: Of course you can do this, but this is only part of double reading. Some really interesting cultural criticism can come out of reading gaps and silences. (Jekyll is still looking confused and gulping his beer to settle his brain.) Look, I can see you haven't really understood this. Let me give you a few simple examples. Can you think of an advertisement? We'll use it by way of illustration.

## **notes** ON PRACTICE: practising symptomatic reading: the Marlboro Man and Nike sports wear

JEKYLL: Yes, what about those old Marlboro cigarette ads that had the cowboy riding out on the prairies – I liked those.

HYDE: (looking at Jekyll suspiciously) You're not *still* smoking, are you?

JEKYLL: Well, only from time to time ...

HYDE: Whatever. Let's take the first part of double reading. Why don't you interpret *what you see.*

JEKYLL: Well, there was the lone cowboy figure herding cattle on a fine brown horse. He's the rugged, strong, silent type – looks to me like he enjoys freedom and is in complete control, and he's out there in nature – breathing in that fresh air ... I reckon the audience is supposed to identify with this – it's like saying 'smoke these cigarettes and you, too, can enter Marlboro country and enjoy something akin to the experiences of the Marlboro Man'.

HYDE: We may not all read it in the same way but I think you're basically right. It's a fictional world which is an invitation to consume. In terms of the problematic it's a world which will only admit certain very limited and rather banal questions like 'what's Marlboro country?' 'How am I supposed to feel as a Marlboro Man?' (Notice there aren't any Marlboro women.) A symptomatic reading would get behind this simple fiction to ask other questions which the advertisement, as it stands, couldn't answer.

JEKYLL: Like what?

HYDE: For example, the man on the horse is rather ironic when you think that cigarette manufacture is an industry. By representing the product out in the middle of the mythic West the product couldn't be more divorced from the modes of production that make it possible. This is normally the case in advertising but not always (some car ads feature the factory but it is an idealized hi-tech environment). The silence here is one which may be filled by human beings involved in mass production with all the mechanical and economic relations that this entails. From here you could ask questions about wage structures, working conditions and industrial strife etc. Then there's the idea of the strong, mean, independent cowboy. Yet other gaps to do with health issues might be explored here. Is smoking likely to promote things like strength and independence?

*(Continued)*

JEKYLL: (looking uneasy and fiddling with the packet of cigarettes he has in his pocket) Well, no, I'd say more like poor health, addiction and even serious cases of eye, mouth, throat and lung cancer (shivering). And I remember reading a report of one of the Marlboro men, I think his name was Wayne McLaren, who actually died of lung cancer (Marchese, 1992).

HYDE: Yes, a vicious irony, and he wasn't the only Marlboro Man to die in that way, there was also David McLean, whose family have been trying to sue Philip Morris, the owners of Marlboro, ever since (*The Wall Street Journal*, 1999). And to think, the Marlboro Man in the ads is always breathing in all that fresh air! But then, you might ask questions about this 'fresh air'. Given the dominant systems of production in the land of Marlboro and the US's record on environmental issues, how fresh is the 'fresh air'? Then there are issues to do with passive smoking and from here we might look at addictive substances which are alleged to be deliberately added, how manufacturers have deliberately targeted the third world and young women. There have been allegations that big tobacco companies smuggled products into Iraq during the embargo on that country ...

JEKYLL: Well, at least manufacturers provide health warnings on cigarette packets.

HYDE: Well, only because they have to! This is an interesting detail because it has obliged tobacco companies to open up one of the silences traditionally smothered in advertising campaigns. Although it is now very difficult for tobacco companies to advertise in many countries, you can see that there was a lot of what we might call ideological 'scaffolding' holding up the image of the Marlboro Man.

JEKYLL: And what might that mean?

HYDE: The Marlboro Man can be seen as an example of how images function within consumer societies like masks or screens – which hide more than they show. Take many powerful contemporary icons like Coca-Cola, Disney, Nike, McDonalds, Microsoft etc., each one can be analysed to see in what ways the dominant advertising images are in contradiction with, or disguise, what might be seen as some of their more 'questionable' business practices. Just take Nike, as an example. This company, like all companies, keeps its manufacturing costs down in order to maximize profits but this has meant transferring their manufacturing bases to lower wage regions. Over the years they have had manufacturing bases in Japan, South Korea, Indonesia, the People's Republic of China and Vietnam, abandoning one country in favour of another when wages threatened to get too high for their profit margins. In 1996 the company was at the centre of a scandal when it was discovered that they were using child labour in Pakistan (Goldman and Papson, 1998: 6f.). In the ads we're welcomed into the Nike club to share sports with the greatest athletes in the world who are young, strong, super healthy and stylish. Nike

*Continued)*

*(Continued)*

offers one positive symbol of North America, but once we look into the gaps and silences behind these images, into where and how these products are made, and by whom, we find a history of shoddy work conditions, child labour, poor wages, the suppression of unions – exploitation at many levels.

JEKYLL: The 'Just do it!' slogan now sounds as much like an authoritarian command as a friendly encouragement to amateur and professional athletes! In terms of Althusser, am I right in thinking that the work, sweat, endurance and struggling at the limit which are positive signs in the ads can be read, then, as symptoms that actually reveal iniquities in Nike's manufacturing base?

HYDE: Yes, that's it! Although I'm not sure that Althusser would have anticipated quite this use of his theories. However, even though what I'm putting forward here is an adaptation of Althusser, this way of thinking has been very suggestive for cultural criticism. If you look at the end of this chapter you'll see our author has some suggested further reading there. A point that's worth making here is that the interpretation of a text (as book, film, advert etc.) is really an excuse for opening up gaps and silences – I would argue that the value of this approach is not so much in the contribution it makes to the interpretation of the text itself but in how it encourages questions about the social, political, economic and cultural world in which the text is produced.

JEKYLL: OK, but what about the 'invisible problematic', how might a form offer answers to questions that aren't formally posed?

HYDE: Althusser's inspiration for this idea was the way Marx read the work of the British eighteenth-century economist, Adam Smith. Very simply put, Marx noticed that Smith, in order to preserve the ideological structure of the text, had to remain silent on certain issues that might threaten the integrity of his overall arguments, or offer what he thought of as 'deformed' answers to the questions which are ignored or absent. Again, this idea has been adapted in ways which can be practised in fairly easy ways. One suggestive example has been given by ... wait, the author is sitting over there. (Shouting) Hey, John, over here! Jekyll's getting the beers in! (Jekyll gets the drinks and John Storey comes over and Hyde asks him to explain how the 'invisible problematic' might be adapted to the analysis of popular culture).

STOREY: (after a little small talk) Take car advertisements where cars are shown off-road in the desert or on the beach etc. It's possible to see these ads as implicit responses to criticisms of pollution and congestion. 'In this way, the criticisms are answered without the questions themselves having been formally posed'

*(Continued)*

| | |
|---|---|
| | (Storey, 2001: 97). So, questions not posed in the ads themselves are implied in the assumptions which organize them. |
| HYDE: | Thanks, John ... (a man taps him on the shoulder). Can I help you? |
| FIRST STRANGER: | Excuse me, but I couldn't help overhearing your conversation and I thought I might be able to help your friend. It's just that I'm Pierre Macherey ... |
| HYDE: | Not *the* Pierre Macherey, the famous Marxist philosopher who adapted Althusser's ideas to argue that the 'unconscious' of Jules Vernes' science fiction fantasies can be read to reveal the contradictions of French colonialism? |
| MACHEREY: | The same. You might recommend your friend read my *A Theory of Literary Production* (1978). |
| HYDE: | I will ... (a woman taps him on the shoulder). Can I help you? |
| SECOND STRANGER: | Excuse me, I couldn't help overhearing your conversation and I thought I might be able to help your friend. It's just that I'm Judith Williamson. |
| HYDE: | Not *the* Judith Williamson who wrote *Decoding Advertisements: Ideology and Meaning in Advertising* (1978) which shows how Althusser's ideas can be used to explore ideology within advertising? |
| WILLIAMSON: | The same. I thought you might recommend it. |
| HYDE: | I most certainly will ... especially as my approach here is very indebted to your work (another woman taps him on the shoulder). Can I help you? |
| THIRD STRANGER: | Excuse me, I couldn't help overhearing your conversation and I thought I might be able to help your friend. It's just that I'm Catherine Belsey ... |
| HYDE: | Not *the* Catherine Belsey who, in *Critical Practice* (1980: 109f.), drew on Macherey's ideas to offer a feminist analysis of the Sherlock Holmes stories? Not the critic who showed how the scientific rationalism in the stories was undermined by its inability to contain female sexuality? |
| BELSEY: | The same. I thought you might recommend it. |

To save Hyde from further taps on the shoulder we shall leave him in the bar and put further references at the end of the chapter. I think it might be clear now why I chose the names Jekyll and Hyde for this dialogue. The two sides of symptomatic reading are like Jekyll and Hyde because it is assumed that there is always the visible symptom to be read and that which is hidden behind the

Figure 11.1 Marlboro men discuss symptomatic reading

symptom but which can be revealed. Like Mr Hyde, what stands behind is considered to be the unattractive face of the problematic.

## Further practice: symptomatic reading

Practising symptomatic reading through the problematic requires the kind of steps that Hyde performed in the above dialogue. You can see that advertisements of all kinds, regardless of whether they are based on static or moving images, are particularly useful to experiment with these ideas. As you can see from the dialogue, these ideas have also been very useful when applied to literary texts, although they serve just as well when applied to film or TV programmes. You might take a series of films or TV series and try to see how they might be interpreted in terms of problematics and perform symptomatic readings on them. The more you know about the historical period and cultures in which the object of your analysis is situated the easier it will be to use these ideas. The use of the ideas, despite their names, is not that difficult; however, being informed enough to perform a reading of this kind may take considerable preparation.

## **practice** EXERCISE: exploring the problematic through Quadrophenia

Referring back to *Quadrophenia*, consider how the ideas presented in this chapter might be applied to it. Once you've applied the ideas to one film you should find it easier to apply them to others.

## **notes** ON PRACTICE: how might the problematic be applied to Quadrophenia?

One way of reading *Quadrophenia* would be to explore ways that the film could be said to stage the failure of the cultural ideals of capitalism. As we've seen, the film follows the tragic life of a young man who expresses himself, and tries to find meaning, in Mod subculture. He cannot adapt himself to the life outside his chosen subculture and when that subculture ultimately fails him his disillusionment is so great that he commits suicide. This is the visible aspect of a symptomatic reading (notice that this is still an interpretation and may not receive general agreement). The problematic might be seen in what the film does not state overtly.

The film's main focus is on Mod subculture but the source of Jimmy's discontent can be found in the general background that makes that subculture possible and, for some, necessary. Jimmy's need for an alternative way of living can be explained through reference to the social, economic world in which he lives. As a working-class youth, Jimmy's life seems limited. His menial job supplies him with enough money to engage in subcultural activity but cannot satisfy him in any meaningful way. Official culture does not offer

*(Continued)*

*(Continued)*

him what he needs and his dissatisfaction is expressed in various acts of delinquency. Mod culture ultimately fails Jimmy, because his friends and even his idol, the Face, cannot live up to his idealized expectations of it. They live the subculture as consumers; he tries to live it as an 'authentic' way of life.

Mod subculture might be seen as a symptom of youth subcultures as they are lived in capitalism. Capitalism turns rebellion into a commodity and thereby manages to contain it. From here it is possible to explore how the film never fully states this failure because it is beyond its problematic; it merely hints at it through Jimmy. The problematic can be found in how the film exposes this contradiction. We could say that youth subcultures open up rebellious spaces in capitalism but they are limited because they tend to be 'contaminated' by the system in which they are made possible. Jimmy's friends never reach Jimmy's level of disillusionment because their lives are not fully dependent on their subcultural life: they treat it as a commodity to be consumed during appropriate moments of leisure. Jimmy, however, is taken in by the lures of a youth subculture. When he rides his scooter to the edge of the cliffs at Beachy Head, it is like he metaphorically reaches the ideological limits of Mod culture. As we saw in chapter eight, youth subcultures can only offer solutions at symbolic levels. Asking more of a subculture brings Jimmy to the brink of the abyss. His only solution is dis-solution.

You might also reconsider the section on subcultures and girls. Female Mods in *Quadrophenia* are secondary to the males and their lives and difficulties are hardly explored. Using McRobbie and Garber you might think about the significance of these absences. You should now be able to see how this way of reading can dovetail quite neatly into the approaches we explored in the chapters on subcultures. You might also think about how these ideas reflect other Marxist approaches, particularly the work of Adorno.

## Althusser and interpellation

To finish this section on Althusser I want to introduce another idea that has had considerable influence on cultural studies: the notion of **interpellation**. This is a concept designed to help explain *how* ideology works. Let's follow Jekyll and Hyde into a quiet bar where they cannot be disturbed.

JEKYLL: (who has provided a large jug of beer to keep Hyde well oiled enough to prolong the conversation) You know the other day we were talking about Althusser? Well, I mentioned him to one of my academic mates and, at one point in the conversation, he used the term 'interpellation'. He got so carried away with other things that I didn't get a chance to ask him what it meant.

HYDE: Ah, yes, a very interesting idea and I suppose you nodded your head sagely to suggest you understood it! To begin with it is worth keeping in mind that Althusser saw ideology not only as ruling or dominant ideas but as **material practice** (Althusser, 1971: 155f.).

JEKYLL: Ideology as material practice, I'm afraid you've lost me already!

HYDE: OK. What he meant by this was that **ideology is contained in the practices of everyday life**. Ideology here is related to Gramsci's idea of hegemony (of which Althusser was aware): it resides in all those things which tend to go without question. Take the case of holidays. These can be seen as ideological practices. They offer pleasure and relief from the difficulties or boredom of work and make life for those unhappy with their jobs a bit more bearable. However, holidays help to keep us exactly where we are. Christmas, for example, is a time for celebration, relaxation, worship etc. but also helps us to cope *and* spend lots of money. This reflects a general idea we've seen a number of times within Marxist thought: that everyday life functions to reproduce the unequal social relations necessary for the perpetuation of capitalism. At the domestic level, you might ask, who cleans? Who cooks? Who gets up to clear the dishes? Who throws out the rubbish? Who cleans the car? And so on. From the answers we receive we can ask if common forms of the division of domestic labour suggest anything about the way society is engineered and gendered.

JEKYLL: Er, right (remembering that he left his dirty dishes for his girlfriend to clear up). So, what's interpellation about then?

HYDE: It's about how individuals become subjects of, and in, ideology. Althusser argues that ideology functions like a **summons** – like when a policeman shouts 'stop!' He reckons that it's always the suspect who's addressed who looks round.

JEKYLL: What? That's not always true! And I still don't get it!

HYDE: Well, let me give you an example of my own. Have you seen the Hitchcock film *North by Northwest* (1959)?

JEKYLL: The one where Cary Grant gets mistaken for a secret agent?

HYDE: Yes, that's the one. Well, he plays Roger Thornhill who happens to call a waiter at just the moment when a waiter has been asked by a couple of criminals to call out the name 'George Kaplan' – the name of a non-existent agent invented by the secret services to deflect attention away from their real agent. This leads the criminals to kidnap Thornton and treat him as if he really were Kaplan.

JEKYLL: I remember how, despite the fact that Thornhill denied being Kaplan, he was never believed, and in his efforts to clear his name he ends up being blamed for murder.

HYDE: That's right. You could see Thornton as a symbol for how Althusser argues individuals become subjects – how they are interpellated. Notice how Kaplan answers a call and is then completely defined and shaped by forces outside himself (we could say that this is like someone being born into a particular culture). Despite all resistance, he is caught in networks which give him identity and meaning. This reflects Althusser's idea that ideology has the function of 'constituting' individuals as subjects (Althusser, 1971: 160).

JEKYLL: It's like we come to recognize ourselves in ideology then?

HYDE: I reckon that's a useful way of looking at it. We might think that we are free of dominant ideas, beliefs, ways of doing things that characterize capitalism but we are actually *products* of cultural systems. Society is full of 'subjects' who live the illusion of feeling like they are free 'individuals' but they aren't. Thornhill, of course, is not typical in this sense. At another level we could think of him as a kind of Althusser, because he sees through the system.

JEKYLL: So how come Althusser isn't a victim of ideology?

HYDE: Good point. The only way to see through ideology is through what he regarded as Marxist science.

JEKYLL: (smirking) Oh, I get the idea, through Althusserian Marxism!

HYDE: Exactly! Take a look at this – it's a sketch a friend of mine did to explain interpellation (he hands him the image).

Figure 11.2 Interpellation

HYDE: Anyway, these ideas had a great influence on film and media studies in Britain in the 1970s. You might get an idea of how this works in practice by discussing advertisements (which simplifies the theory) but can lead to some interesting forms of interpretation. For example, imagine you are a teenager again. You wake up one morning and there, staring at you from your face, are a load of spots. There's an especially prominent one on the end of your nose ...

JEKYLL: Hey, you've been looking at old photos of me!

HYDE: (ignoring him) Later in the day you are watching TV and see an advertisement where someone looking like a scientist asks: 'Do *you* suffer from greasy skin, acne or spots on the face?' When you relate to the object pronoun ('you') in this question you see yourself addressed as an individual, or as a member of a recognizable group. You are invited to take up the role of possible consumer created by the discourse of the advertisement. You could say you are positioned by the advertisement as a consumer (in this case as a spotty one). You are implicitly constructed as a subject (someone who can freely choose between products) and subject *to* the persuasive power of the discourse of the advert. Also relevant is *how* you are positioned with relation to the ad. Typical of this kind of ad is the 'before and after' device where the dystopia of the pitted face is replaced by a utopian vision of the happy, smiling zit-free individual finally freed from the tyranny of hormones and recalcitrant skin. The ad, in turn, serves as one of the main pillars of capitalism which is to persuade potential customers to engage in one of its principal material practices: consumption. Thus, you can see how the idea of interpellation might help to interpret the world of advertising.

## **notes** ON PRACTICE: interpellation and further practice: making yourself a 'mock reader, viewer or listener'

HYDE: As you can see, advertisements are a good place to start because they are short and you can investigate how you are being invited to take up a position with relation to it. I say 'invited' because there is no determined relation between experiencing an ad and accepting the subject position it seems to imply. It's possible to think about this with relation to Althusser's theory of interpellation and consider up to what point you think individuals can be interpellated by capitalism.

*(Continued)*

*(Continued)*

JEKYLL: Hmm, that's an interesting question. But what other possibilities are there for using the idea of interpellation?

HYDE: Well, moving on from this simple exercise, you might try things like watching films, reading novels, listening to songs, reading political propaganda etc. and asking yourself if they, like advertisements, seem to create fictional spaces into which readers, viewers etc. are, explicitly or implicitly, invited into. The critic Walker Gibson came up with the idea of the **mock reader** which I think is very useful in this context.

JEKYLL: Wasn't he a literary critic?

HYDE: Yes, but I think we can adapt his idea to cultural criticism (after all, literature is a form of culture). Now, Gibson argued that there are two readers during the experience of reading: the actual flesh and blood reader who is holding the book and the 'mock reader' which corresponds to the role that the reader is invited to play during the reading experience (Gibson, in Tompkins, 1980: 1f.). To take the example I used above, if a viewer puts him or herself in the position of a spotty person, then s/he has accepted the role of the mock reader. I would argue that what makes Gibson's idea interesting to cultural analysis is his assertion that by taking up the position of the mock reader (in our case the mock reader, viewer, listener etc.) it is possible to construct a dialogue between the text and the actual reader to try to uncover what values and assumptions seem to be required by a text (we need to interpret 'text' in the widest possible sense).

## Oversimplification

**W A R N I N G**

Gibson assumes actual readers can state what responses are required of readers and what values and assumptions these imply. He also argues that readers can decide on the value of the book they read: a bad book is one whose mock reader we refuse to become. Here I do not assume we can get back to the values and assumptions in a straightforward way or predict exactly what responses may be required. I would also abandon the idea of deciding if something is good or bad on the grounds of the mock reader or viewer etc.

However, I would argue that if care is taken not to oversimplify the 'text', these ideas can help to illuminate all kinds of cultural forms, especially with relation to interpellation.

HYDE: Let's explore and adapt these ideas with relation to different cultural products. Why don't you tell me a joke and we'll see if we can mix Althusser's theory of interpellation and Gibson's idea of the mock reader.

*(Continued)*

JEKYLL: OK, right, here's a joke I really like, it's a variation on one which was circulating in 2001 after the United States had attacked Iraq and removed Saddam Hussein:

Albert Einstein dies and goes to Heaven. He arrives at the Pearly Gates and asks to be let in. St Peter says, 'You look like Einstein, you sound like Einstein, but can you prove you're Einstein? People will do anything these days to get in here'. Einstein meditates for a few moments and asks for paper and a pen. St Peter conjures them out of thin air and hands them to him. Einstein jots down all kinds of arcane mathematical symbols which St Peter recognizes as his General Theory of Relativity. Suitably impressed, St Peter exclaims, 'You really ARE Einstein! Come in.'

The next to arrive is Pablo Picasso, who knocks on the door and asks to be let in. Once again, St Peter is sceptical and asks Picasso to prove his identity. Picasso picks up the pen and pad and, with only a few strokes, creates a version of his famous painting *Guernica*. 'No one but Picasso could do that', cries St Peter, and welcomes him into Heaven.

Much later St Peter is confronted by a man claiming to be George W. Bush who asks to be let in. St Peter scratches his head saying, 'Einstein and Picasso both managed to prove their identity, can you prove yours?' Bush looks bewildered and asks, 'who on Earth are Einstein and Picasso?' St Peter sighs and says, 'Come on in, George!'

Not bad, eh?! So, how can we analyse it according to the theories we've been looking at?

HYDE: It is possible to use this joke, in the same way as those which are directed against women, nations, the non-heterosexual community etc., to see how it creates a position for the listener who, through laughing at the joke, can share in a certain view of an American President. It might be said that to enjoy the joke one has to be interpellated into the space created for the mock reader or listener. On the other hand, if you are a staunch defender of this particular President or sympathetic to his role in world politics, you may find the joke objectionable and refuse the space opened up for laughter.

JEKYLL: Now I can see what you mean. I'd never thought about jokes, satire or humour like that. Actually, I think much humour functions in this way, to laugh *at* something or somebody will often require a certain disposition to accept that the butt of the joke is a legitimate object of fun or mockery.

HYDE: So, you see that to laugh at a person or community etc. you are required to take up a position. Those people who hear a joke against people or groups and refuse to laugh are overriding the invitation to laugh and recognizing that the values or assumptions

*(Continued)*

*(Continued)*

behind the joke are offensive. In refusing interpellation, you might say they are practising a form of active cultural criticism – a form of resistance. This exercise does not necessarily assume that individuals are passively and unconsciously interpellated, and, again, you might consider up to what point interpellation can be said to be involuntary. We might explore these ideas by choosing a dozen different jokes and subjecting them to these concepts.

JEKYLL: Oh, no! I think we'll leave that until another time!

HYDE: OK, but let me just make the point that its possible to analyse all kinds of cultural products by asking yourself if you are being positioned in a particular way in order to partake in or enjoy something. The literary critic Wayne C. Booth once made an interesting point about Mickey Spillane's detective stories involving Mike Hammer. Booth claimed that when the tough detective beat up a black American he was more brutal than when beating up a Jew, and considerably less brutal when beating up a white Anglo-Saxon American. Booth argued that the enjoyment of the novels was based on this kind of 'vicious morality' which suggests that the hero 'discriminates his punishment according to the racial worth of his victims' (Booth (1961) in Lodge, 1972: 576). You may or may not agree with this, but I think it does suggest a relevant critical perspective for cultural analysis that you can experiment with.

JEKYLL. Hey, I've just had an idea, based on what we've been talking about. Take a look at this (he pulls out a magazine from a small rucksack).

I think another way of using this idea of interpellation might be to look for significant exclusions.

HYDE: That sounds interesting. We'll make a cultural critic of you yet!

JEKYLL: Look, here's part of an advertisement selling a Triumph motorcycle (pointing it out). It's the one accompanied by the photo of a woman with a sad look on her face (he reads):

> From the moment I met him I knew he was different. He was warm, affectionate and funny. People said he was difficult because he did things his way. But he knew what he wanted from life and from me. Perhaps I shouldn't have been surprised when I discovered I had a rival for his time and affection. A striking and sensuous rival; a classic beauty – a Thruxton 900. I knew he appreciated great design and that the Thruxton is inspired by the racing Triumphs of the Sixties. But its appeal transcends aesthetics. (*Torque*, 2005)

And look, the advertisement has the words 'If it was another woman at least I could compete' written across it. What do you reckon of that?

*(Continued)*

HYDE: I like your idea of looking for exclusions because it seems to me that a potential buyer is represented in positive ways but the fiction of the worried female partner interpellates the reader in such a way that it excludes, in its gender bias, all possibility of a woman buying the bike. Women are positioned as potentially jealous rivals rather than active agents who may buy into a fantasy space which may challenge their partners. And here you see a heterosexual form of positioning which assumes sexual rivalries between men and women. It's interesting, though, that the woman, although not interpellated as a buyer, seems to show extraordinary knowledge about the history of Triumph Motorcycles! The Triumph ad reminds me of an advertisement I saw the other day for an Vauxhall Vectra which functioned in a similar way. Standing by the car, was the image of what looked like a tough, nononsense business man. Over the photo' was written 'New Vauxhall Vectra: power and control without argument' and then: 'The man who controls all situations needs a car with power and response' (*El País*, 2006, translated from Spanish).

JEKYLL: But, of course, Vauxhall and Triumph are in the business of selling cars and motorcycles, not challenging sexual stereotypes – after all, the ads play to the perceived market!

HYDE: OK, I take your point. It's true, although more women are buying motorcycles and scooters, most buyers are male and the ad links into the macho culture which associates powerful motorcycles with heterosexual men. Of course, some car ads are directed specifically at women – but the cars tend to be much smaller. I think it's quite revealing to look at *how* different products are positioned with relation to gender. I suppose the reverse of this kind of advertisement is where a cultural form positions the audience in such a way that traditional, orthodox ways of seeing are challenged. The clothes manufacturer Calvin Klein, for example, has recently played on sexual ambiguity or same-sex relations to sell underwear ... (Jekyll, however, is no longer listening; he's staring at the ad and dreaming of a new motorcycle).

## Some final tips on practice

Having begun on jokes and ads, you might look at how films, novels, soaps, reality TV etc. may challenge dominant beliefs by offering 'alternative' representations for mass consumption. Again, this takes interpellation a long way from Althusser's formulation, but this way of looking might help to give you insights into contemporary popular culture. Another fairly simple exercise is to look at the way various media create a sense of being young, a teenager, a rebel, middle aged, old, a parent etc. For example, how are age groups interpellated into the various categories, and for what ends? How important are popular representations of teenagers, for example, to what it means to be a teenager? How dependent is the idea of the teenager on media representations? (You might remember that in chapter six Hall and Whannel saw the rebellious teenager as a media construction.)

From here it's a question of reading the world according to interpellation to explore ideological questions and see how it might help to theorize how individuals are positioned and how these positions may either reinforce or challenge traditional forms of representation. As far as symptomatic reading and the problematic are concerned, you might take a popular study on a well-known corporation and see how it might be re-read through Althusser's concepts (see Goldman and Papson (1998) and the further reading section for other references).

### Oversimplification
**W A R N I N G**

Here we come to the end of the section dedicated to the consolidation of cultural studies. However, I don't want to suggest that these were the *only* ways in which British cultural studies (or any national variety) has consolidated itself. While these approaches have been of great importance, and I hope that I have shown how they have benefited studies dedicated to the understanding, interpretation and politicization of popular culture, they shouldn't mask the fact that there are many more approaches that could have been listed under 'consolidation'. The following chapters are designed to fill in some of the blanks and the final chapter (chapter fourteen) will take up some of the difficult issues associated with the identity of cultural studies.

## SUMMARY OF KEY POINTS

Althusser's contribution to cultural studies has been illustrated through concepts like the problematic and symptomatic reading where critics look into the gaps and silences of cultural forms to establish their theoretical and ideological limits. In this way, critics have been seen to be able to offer double readings which take into account the cultural form but also take account of history and attempt to expose the ideology of colonialism, globalization, sexism and

*(Continued)*

questionable business practices etc. Althusser's notion of interpellation has also been outlined and illustrated to show how he claims individuals, although they may feel free, are actually products of cultural systems. This basic idea has been used to show how audiences or individuals may be positioned by different kinds of cultural products. The chapter ends with advice on how to take these ideas in further directions.

In methodological terms, Althusser's work can be seen as significant in the following ways:

- It offers a series of useful concepts to treat cultural forms as symptoms which can be interpreted to reveal how they are ideologically structured.
- The idea of double reading, enables critics to read the surface of things but then examine what Althusser considered the necessary gaps and silences which reveal hidden ideological structures.
- Althusser's method helps critics to reveal what he understood as the 'problematic': the theoretical and ideological limits of the form which invariably reflect on the contradictions and iniquities of capitalism.
- The concept of interpellation helps critics to become aware of how individuals are products of ideology and implicated in the political, economic and cultural system in which they are brought up. This helps critics to reflect on the limits of personal freedom.
- Interpellation can provide a method that can make cultural critics more aware of how different forms may ideologically position audiences which may reinforce dominant ideas, values and ways of understanding the world.

## References

Althusser, Louis (1970) *Reading Capital*. London: Verso.

Althusser, Louis (1971) *Lenin and Philosophy and Other Essays*. New York: Monthly Review Press.

Belsey, Catherine (1980) *Critical Practice*. London: Methuen.

Booth, Wayne (1961) 'Objectivity in Fiction' in, Lodge, David (ed.) (1972) *20th Century Literary Criticism: A Reader*. London: Longman.

Gibson, Walker (1980) 'Authors, Speakers, Readers, and Mock Readers' in, Tompkins, Jane (ed.) (1980) *Reader-Response Criticism: From Formalism to Post-Structuralism*. Baltimore: Johns Hopkins University Press).

Goldman, Robert and Papson, Stephen (1998) *Nike Culture*. London: Sage.

Lodge, David (ed.) (1972) *20th Century Literary Criticism: A Reader*. London: Longman.

Macherey, Pierre (1978) *A Theory of Literary Production*. London: Routledge.

Marchese, John (1992) 'A Rough Ride'. *The New York Times*, 13 September.

Munns, Jessica & Rajan, Gita (eds) (1995) *A Cultural Studies Reader: History, Theory, Practice.* London: Routledge. In the section on Gender Studies, this reader features Mulvey's article as well as other influential essays focussed on gender and sexuality.

*North by Northwest* (1959) dir. Alfred Hitchcock.

*País, El* (2006) Advert for Vauxhall Vectra, 28 January.

*Quadrophenia* (1979) dir. Franc Roddam.

Storey, John (2001) *Cultural Theory and Popular Culture: An Introduction* (3rd edition). Essex: Pearson Prentice Hall.

The Munns and Rajan reference needs to be edited to erase references to homophobia because I do not review homophobia in this chapter (sorry!). The reference should read:

Tompkins, Jane (ed.) (1980) *Reader-Response Criticism: From Formalism to Post-Structuralism.* Baltimore: Johns Hopkins University Press.

*Torque* (2005) Official magazine of the Riders Association of Triumph. Issue 36 (back cover).

*Wall Street Journal, The* (1999) '"Marlboro Man" Suit Against Tobacco Goes to court of Appeals', 30 August.

Williamson, Judith (1978) *Decoding Advertisments: Ideology and Meaning in Advertising.* London: Marion Boyars.

## Further reading

Althusser, Louis (1971, see references above). One aspect of Althusser's work I have not reviewed here, and which you might follow up, is his distinction between ideological and repressive state apparatuses. These help to explain the functions of ideology with relation to the material base of capitalist societies. Althusser also explains how relations between the base and superstructure are 'overdetermined'. Rather than see society governed by simple deterministic forces, Althusser's notion of overdetermination, allows cultural forms a certain autonomy, rather than be the determined products of the material basis of society. This is one of the reasons William's found Althusser's work of interest. Storey (1998, below) includes sections which relate to these concepts.

Eliot, Mark (1993) *Hollywood's Dark Prince.* New York: Birch Lane. A very accessible non-theoretical exposé of the seedier side of the Disney Corporation which could serve as a simple source for preparing an Althusserian symptomatic reading that could help to reveal very significant gaps and silences.

Mulvey, Laura, in Munns and Rajan (1995, see below) 'Visual pleasure and narrative cinema'. This essay is difficult to read for the beginner because it demands not only an understanding of Althusser but some knowledge of both semiotic theory and psychoanalysis. This essay is of great interest because of the way Mulvey uses Althusserian theory to study the way women have been represented in classic Hollywood films. To reduce her complex arguments to the banal, Mulvey sees the Hollywood heroine as serving a largely ornamental function to satisfy the erotic needs of a male audience. This essay is well worth studying if you want to see how interpellation and feminism may function to create an engaged form of criticism. See Storey (2001: 114f., references above) for an accessible introduction to some of Mulvey's main ideas. Mulvey's article was originally published in *Screen* in 1975, a film journal which was a rich source for articles inspired by Althusser's ideas.

Munns, Jessica and Rajan, Gita (eds) (1995) *A Cultural Studies Reader: History, Theory, Practice*. London: Routledge. This reader includes Mulvey's article and a section on Gender Studies in which you can explore the theme of homophobia. Of particular interest is Jonathan Dollimore's 'Homophobia and sexual difference' (519f.).

Pendergrast, Mark (1993) *For God, Country and Cola-Cola*. London: Phoenix. An accessible, non-theoretical and highly critical history of Cola-Cola that could serve as an effective source if you are thinking of planning a symptomatic reading of the soft drinks manufacturer.

Storey, John (1998) *Cultural Theory and Popular Culture: A Reader* (2nd edition). Essex: Pearson Prentice Hall. This reader includes useful extracts from Althusser's work.

Strinati, Dominic (1995) *An Introduction to Theories of Popular Culture*. London: Routledge. Although he does not discuss the problematic or symptomatic reading, Strinati gives a very clear overview of Althusser's theory of ideology and offers some very effective and balanced criticism of it (46f.).

Tudor, Andrew (1999) *Decoding Culture: Theory and Method in Cultural Studies*. London: Sage. Tudor offers a critical introduction to Althusser and shows how his ideas have been absorbed into British cultural studies in distinct ways through the Birmingham Centre for Contemporary Cultural Studies and the film journal *Screen*.

Turner, Graeme (1996) *British Cultural Studies: An Introduction* (2nd edition). London: Routledge. Turner offers an accessible and historically aware overview of Althusser's ideas and discusses the impact they have had on British cultural studies.

# PART IV

## Probing the Margins, Remembering the Forgotten: Representation, Subordination and Identity

# Crying Woolf! Thinking with Feminism

12

## Introduction

We now come to part four of the book: two chapters focus on 'Probing the Margins, Remembering the Forgotten: Representation, Subordination and Identity'. These chapters will explore different ways of approaching the multiple themes expressed in the title – the first chapter serving as a theoretical and practical introduction to the second. You may notice that this chapter does not have notes on practice. This is because I explain theory and practice together as I go along and the following chapter shows, in considerable detail, how you can go about adapting the strategies and ideas outlined in this chapter to other contexts.

Through a dialogue, I am going to start the present chapter with a discussion of some basic approaches to feminism. Particular emphasis will be put on what is known as the 'images and representations' approach to feminist criticism. The dialogue will develop into a discussion of Virginia Woolf's *Three Guineas* which will be used to give insights into a number of key feminist issues and to demonstrate what cultural criticism might look like from a feminist perspective. The chapter will show how Woolf develops a series of critical strategies to critique and challenge the structures of patriarchal power that severely limited (and still limits) women's lives. However, this introduction also serves to introduce a number of key concepts (like 'difference', 'the other', 'representation' and 'signifying practices') which can be used to explore other contexts of subordination. In short, this chapter will work towards developing a heuristic which will serve as the basis for the following chapter.

## MAIN LEARNING GOALS

- To be aware of how Woolf develops a powerful cultural critique with relation to how women were systematically subordinated and excluded within the British culture of her day.
- To appreciate how Woolf not only calls for equality but insists that feminist demands must also require important cultural changes.
- To see how Woolf develops a series of concepts to explore contexts of marginalization and repression and how she weaves into her critique concepts which focus on representation, sexual difference, patriotism and national identity.
- To understand not only the content of Woolf's *Three Guineas* but to be aware of what she *does*, with a view to seeing how a source can be used to extrapolate concepts that can be adapted for further interpretation and analysis.

In this chapter I want to extend some of the ideas outlined in previous chapters. We saw in chapter ten that Stuart Hall has a very particular way of defining popular culture as a site of struggle. What this implied was that popular cultural forms are of analytical interest only in so far as they are in tension with the dominant culture. This meant taking account of what belongs, at any given historical moment, to the periphery. This, in turn, was related to who is oppressed and who or what is excluded from official versions of culture. It also concerned a form of analysis of *how* certain kinds of culture come to be official or dominant. This very distinctive definition of popular culture was informed by hegemony theory because it places great emphasis on resistance and consent, where cultural criticism could analyse struggles for and against the dominant cultures of the power bloc.

If you look back at chapter ten you'll see I stated, in the section on 'reading popular culture with hegemony theory', that it is possible to analyse any form of culture which challenges the dominant political order through categories like **gender**, **class**, **race**, **ethnicity** and **sexuality**. Here I want to offer some more ideas to help you engage with issues arising from these categories. I think it should be fairly clear from the previous chapters that cultural studies has demonstrated great interest in analysing groups considered marginalized, oppressed or silenced. This is one of the reasons why cultural studies can be thought of as a highly politicized area of study.

In chapter eight I indicated how feminists and critics interested in race manifested their dissatisfaction with the lack of interest that was being shown in sexist and racist ideologies and conflicts in Britain. Since then much work has been done and these areas have become fundamental to what it means to do cultural studies. Added to these two important areas of analysis is the interest shown in sexuality: that is, how it is socially constructed, represented and understood. The development of these ways of looking has also been a result of work done by critics who have manifested their frustration at having these issues ignored.

I am going to introduce this first section through a conversation between George and Eliot. As you may know, George Eliot was the pseudonym used by the nineteenth-century British novelist Mary Ann Evans (later known as Marion). Evans' choice of name can be read as a kind of cultural criticism in itself – a comment on the age in which she lived. She was responding to the following historical circumstance: during her lifetime (1819–80) female literacy was on the increase and women both produced and consumed literary works. However, while women were not excluded from literary production, they were generally felt to produce inferior work. Thus, to have her ideas taken more seriously, Mary Ann Evans chose to adopt a name that would encourage the literary establishment to assume she was a man. In the following dialogue Georgina talks to Eliot, a friend of hers. Georgina, however, is known as George to her friends.

## Basic approaches to feminism: a dialogue between George and Eliot

### Learning from 'femenism'

GEORGE: Hi, Eliot. What's the big fuss? Why did you ask me to come so urgently?

ELIOT: Ah, George, glad you could make it. I've been asked to write an essay on how a feminist might approach the analysis of culture and, as I haven't had much time to think about it, I wanted to bounce a few ideas off you.

GEORGE: OK, I'll try and help you think it through. Before I begin, however, I'd like to make the following observation. The author who has breathed life into us told me that he once received an essay from a student who wrote 'femenism' for feminism. Thus, placing men right at the centre of the concept! This struck him as a very ironic and revealing slip given the historical problems that we women have had in terms of making our voices heard, having our ideas taken seriously, and having our demands for **equality** and **basic rights** incorporated into everyday 'democratic' life.

Traditionally, it has always been men who spoke for 'mankind' – representing both men and women. However, I reckon the slip is also revealing in the present context, given that it is a male writer who is giving voice to ideas developed within feminism. Thus, what is being offered here is another kind of 'femenism'!

ELIOT: Do you consider that a bad thing?

GEORGE: No, because I believe (or I am being made to believe) that one of the successes of feminism is to have argued that no one should be excluded from any debate on the grounds of gender.

AUTHOR: Hey! Can't you just get on with the explanation and leave me out of this conversation?

GEORGE: Certainly not! You can't pretend that you're somehow above your own discourse and beyond questions of things like gender, race, class and sexuality. If these perspectives have taught us anything it is that we have to recognize, following writers like Jordan and Weedon (1995: 4), 'who is representing whom and on what basis'. It's not enough to represent others and think that's OK, you have to recognize that while you can summarize or express a view and interpret what others say, you can't ever speak *for* others.

AUTHOR: OK. I think I get the message! (He fades into the background.)

ELIOT: But is 'femenism' really possible?

GEORGE: Well, not all feminists are in agreement about quite what kind of feminism might be practised by men (or if it's possible or desirable). However, Toril Moi has argued that the main theoretical undertaking for male feminists is 'to develop an analysis of their own position, and a strategy for how their awareness of their difficult and contradictory position in relation to feminism can be made explicit in discourse and practice' (Moi, 1989: 71).

ELIOT: From what you're saying I can see that this problem is related to and complicated by one important element within feminism, which is to do with women's struggle to be able to speak for themselves, rather than have men speak for them?

GEORGE: Exactly, the early history of feminism in the West can be seen in this way, linked to the all-important political project of demanding equality with men. There's a rather clichéd word which helps express this which is known as the problem of *her*tory. It may be something of an overused term, but it's a useful starting point. *His*tory needed, needs, and will need, to be balanced by *her*story.

ELIOT: What would this kind of *her*story look like?

GEORGE: Well, there are many approaches, and too many to go into here. To speak in very general terms, Lana Rakow has distinguished between four feminist approaches to popular culture: the recovery and reappraisal approach, the images and representations approach, the reception and experience approach, and the cultural theory approach (Rakow, in Storey, 1998: 275f.). What she says is that feminists have generally tried to recover works written or made by women but which have been ignored. Some have analysed how women have been represented by men and by themselves, and others have put the emphasis on how women consume cultural forms. Finally, there's the possibility of taking a general theory developed within feminism and applying it to a popular cultural form.

ELIOT: That sounds like a tall order!

Figure 12.1 The Fate of Women under Patriarchy

GEORGE: It is! And we can't cover all those possibilities here. I think we could concentrate mainly on the images and representations approach and try to make a few passing comments about the other approaches. To give you an example of what *her*story might look like I'll refer to one of *the* figures within feminism: Virginia Woolf.

ELIOT: Woolf! I've read a number of her novels like *Mrs Dalloway* (1925) and *To the Lighthouse* (1927).

GEORGE: Here, however, I want to mention her critical essay of 1939 entitled *Three Guineas* because it may help you to see what cultural criticism might look like from a feminist perspective. Also, it hasn't received that much emphasis within cultural studies, which I think is a pity. It was also very controversial, Q. D. Leavis calling it 'nasty', 'dangerous' and 'preposterous' (in Woolf, [1939] 1992: xxvii). Later, you'll see why. I hope to persuade you that Woolf merits a place in the pantheon of early British cultural critics and some of her critical writings deserve to be anthologized in cultural studies readers along with Arnold, the Leavises, Hoggart, Thompson and Williams.

ELIOT: So, why do you think she was such an effective cultural critic?

GEORGE: To give you an answer I'll limit myself to *Three Guineas*, rather than her *A Room of One's Own* (1929 – Woolf ([1939] 1992), which most writers focus on. In *Three Guineas* Woolf imagines she is replying to a letter sent to her by a successful and respectable barrister asking her how the daughters of educated men might help to prevent war. Actually, Woolf discusses the general question of how these 'daughters' might help to prevent war within the context of three imaginary requests seeking support and money for different causes (each asks for a guinea). Woolf practises feminist cultural criticism by offering three replies:

1. To a treasurer asking for money to rebuild a woman's college.
2. To a treasurer asking for a subscription to a society to help the daughters of educated men to obtain employment in the professions.
3. To the barrister mentioned above who is appealing to the daughters of educated men to sign a manifesto pledging themselves to protect culture and intellectual liberty, and join his society, which is also in need of funds.

Woolf's replies are written in the form of a long open letter.

ELIOT: Doesn't this look like creative criticism?

GEORGE: I would say it is and this 'question and answer' technique helps her to develop a dialectical style which is important to method. She constantly balances one way of looking with another – effectively contrasting different views in order to subject them to criticism. In general terms what she does is to refuse to donate money or support a cause unless those petitioning her agree to certain conditions. Look (taking a copy of *Three Guineas* out of her pocket), I'm going to lend you my copy of the book. Why don't we meet up in a couple of days and discuss it?

ELIOT: (takes the book) Thanks! Great idea! See you in a few days.

## **help** FILE: the historical context of *Three Guineas*

It is important to recognize the historical circumstances in which *Three Guineas* was written in order to understand both its significance and controversial impact. It was written on the eve of the outbreak of the Second World War, when Fascism was perceived as a real threat to world peace. In Spain the Civil War (1936–1939) was raging where Republicans were defending themselves against Franco's fascist forces (Woolf reflects this in numerous references to photos) and fascist dictatorships had now taken hold of Germany and Italy under Hitler and Mussolini. Questions of whether or not war would break out in Europe, whether it should be fought, or how it might be prevented were of paramount importance.

Note: **A guinea** was a coin in circulation in Britain worth 21 shillings (one pound and one shilling).

## A few notes on how to read the following section

Two days later the two friends meet again to talk about Woolf's essay. You will notice that they possess prodigious memories although, even though they remember an extraordinary amount from one reading, they do not exhaust the essay's extent or interest. Also, rather than criticize the essay and look for its possible shortcomings, they emphasize how it might contribute to cultural criticism.

You will notice that as the dialogue evolves so too will the names of the participants. When you see a new name you might like to underline it. Each new pair of names will represent an important voice within feminist debates within cultural studies (if they are not concepts introduced as voices). I will not include feminist writers already mentioned in this book or introduce the new feminist writers here. The names mentioned *are by no means exhaustive* of important contributors to cultural analysis, just a few you might follow up. If you do not recognize a name, you could try looking for references to it in the Internet. All the writers have work published and some even have pages dedicated to them. Alternatively, you can look at basic introductions to cultural studies to find the name there and get an idea of some of the writer's main concepts.

## *Three Guineas* 1: from exclusion, subordination and patriarchy to patriotism, national identity and sexual difference

GEORGE: Well, have you read *Three Guineas*?

ELIOT: Yes, I really enjoyed it and have learnt an incredible amount from it.

GEORGE: Good! Shall we begin by discussing how Woolf addresses the general question of how the daughters of educated men might help to prevent war?

ELIOT: OK, but you begin!

GEORGE: Well, her basic answer is that they can't! Why? Firstly, the basic instinct for waging war with other countries seems to be confined to the male sex – she asks, when have the women of her class taken up arms? Also, men have been able to influence other people's thoughts and actions through their involvement in every area of public life. She explains that up until 1919, twenty years before *Three Guineas* was written, men had exclusive access to and control of politics, education, Law, the Stock Exchange, the Civil Service and the Diplomatic Service and yet in the late 1930s women's access to these areas was very limited and still discouraged (Woolf, [1939] 1992: 172f.).

ELIOT: Yes, she explains how it took upper-class women over a century of exhausting and often humiliating struggle to achieve the vote (170). As for the Armed Forces, women had no access whatsoever and the Church had systematically relegated them to insignificant positions. Even though women were not barred from writing, thus they *could* write articles or send letters to the Press, the decisions about what was printed was in male hands (166–7). How, then, could women be expected to prevent war if their sphere of influence was so impoverished? The consequences of all this are that if women were to try to help prevent war, then the whole present political, economic, legal and cultural arrangements would have to be changed. Let women fully enter into public life and then there might be some hope of women influencing contemporary life.

GEORGE: I really enjoyed the fact that Woolf's reply to the question enables her to mount this powerful cultural critique of **exclusion** and **systematic subordination**. Many men argued that upper-class women should not have the right to earn a living, that working in the professions wasn't dignified and only another kind of slavery. Woolf replies that 'to depend upon a profession is a less odious form of slavery than to depend upon a father' (173), thus bringing out what she saw as the '**patriarchal**' basis of British life (246f.).

ELIOT: She helped me see that the patriarchy she talks of is related to **patriotism**. For example, she analyses men's attitudes towards war and notices that patriotism is put forward as a legitimate reason for taking up arms (161). Patriotism, she notices, includes the idea that men claim to fight out of a love of freedom and are driven by the pride they feel for their country. These justifications enable Woolf to ask what patriotism might mean to the daughters of educated men (162f.). What possible reason might the women of her class have to defend freedom, when it is the freedoms and privileges of men they would be protecting? Later in her essay she raises the question of **national identity** (although she doesn't refer to it in this way) when she claims she has no wish to be 'English' under the present conditions (301). She suggests she has no country because it has made women of her class wholly dependent and treated them as slaves (313).

GEORGE: I loved that part where she asks 'What does "our country" mean to me an outsider?' She says that the daughters of educated men would have to analyse the meaning of patriotism for themselves, asking questions involving the relative position of her sex and class, how much land she owns, how much legal protection the law offers and has offered in the past etc. (311). I liked also the fact that **sexual difference** for her, at least in this work, is not a question of something laid down by 'nature' but a product of how the sexes experience the world through the culture and opportunities available to them. Her identity as a woman is very much a product of *cultural* differences constructed by a society historically dominated by men.

ELIOT: Yes, she makes this clear from the very start by imagining the kind of man she is addressing. He is middle-aged, distinguished, very comfortably off, has risen in the legal profession and has an excellent education. What she says is that their different educational backgrounds are the cause of difficulties of communication and that although they are of the same class, speak with the same accent and share all kinds of things in common, there is a great gap in terms of their educational and professional opportunities.

GEORGE: Furthermore, she says the consequence is that although men and women of her class look at the same things they see them differently. Men see inside and experience the expensive schools and universities; women only stare in frustration from the outside. We could say that Woolf recognizes that the men and women of her class are divided by **a sense of perspective**, and it is this that constitutes their difference. All these themes are connected with the other question she addresses in the first part of her essay, where she answers a treasurer asking for money to rebuild a woman's college.

## *Three Guineas* 2: from history, representation and autobiography to audience, irony and signifying practices

MARY: I think it significant that Woolf **historicizes** what she has to say. This means she continues to summarize the struggles that were involved for upper-class women to win the very restricted right they had to study from about 1870 (188). Of course, it had been influential men who had stood in the way of the financing of women's colleges and their rights to study. Then these same influential men were reluctant, even when women finally proved themselves capable of passing the necessary exams, to allow women to use letters after their names. Woolf also showed great interest in what we now call **representation**, making clear how men had constantly represented women as intellectually inferior and better fitted to domestic duties than learning. This historical perspective is something she tries to offer with relation to everything she discusses, whether it be education, the control of publishing, or the entry into the professions, including the Church. This helps to contextualize her arguments and means that she doesn't fall into unsubstantiated generalizations.

WOLLSTONECRAFT: Yes, she has a very wide range of reference. She constantly uses literary texts and seemed particularly fond of biography, memoirs and quoting from newspapers. In terms of method, **(auto)biography** has been of particular importance to feminist approaches to the understanding of culture.

MARY: Yes, I think this autobiographical tendency has at least two important consequences. One, the use of the singular voice recognizes itself as personal, rather than making large claims about being 'objective' and speaking for all wo-mankind; thus avoiding what is seen as the universalizing tendency in much writing by men. Two, many analyses of popular cultural forms associated with women, like soap operas and romance novels, have used interviews to try to understand *how* women understand, interpret and use these forms. This puts the emphasis on individual consumption and the **particular responses and experiences** of members of a collective **audience** not just on **production** (see further reading).

WOLLSTONECRAFT: She also used *Hansard* (the official reports from Parliament) and statistics from sources like Whitaker's famous *Almanack*, which collected together all kinds of data from public life. She calls what she takes from the almanac 'facts'. Of course, today these statistics would have to be presented with great care and we would want to ask who put them together, for whom and how reliable they are. However, in fairness to Woolf, I think she presents this information in a slightly tongue-in-cheek way, to emphasize that it is the official statistics of *men* who are providing her with just the incriminating information she needs to condemn them!

MARY: Yes, there are quite a few examples of **irony**. I think it would be possible to write an essay that only focused on the use of irony as an effective critical tool. Just to mention one example, which brings us back to the idea of representation, Woolf explores the way men represent women as vain and dominated by fashion. She cites Justice MacCardie.

JUSTICE MACCARDIE: 'women cannot be expected to renounce an essential feature of femininity or to abandon one of nature's solaces for a constant and insuperable physical handicap ... Dress, after all, is one of the chief methods of women's self-expression ... In matters of dress women often remain children to the end' (373: footnote 16. The ellipses are Woolf's).

MARY: Listen, I hear a voice ...

THE OUTRAGED VOICE OF VIRGINIA WOOLF: Your clothes 'make us gape with astonishment'. Look at the clothes worn by the educated man in his public capacity! 'Now you dress in violet; a jewelled crucifix swings on your breast; now your shoulders are covered with lace; now furred with ermine; now slung with many linked chains set with precious stones. Now you wear wigs on your heads; rows of graduated curls descend to your necks' (177).

WOLLSTONECRAFT: Yes, Woolf offers a thoroughgoing exposé of male vanity describing how men not only attach symbolic meanings through dress to express their position in the hierarchies of church, university, armed forces etc. but how dress interacts with other objects like mitres and medals and ceremonies that also function to gratify vanity, please the eye and 'advertise the social, professional, or intellectual standing of the wearer', apart from attracting the admiration of other men (179). She also compares male dress to the tickets describing goods in a grocer's shop! But instead of saying this is margarine, this is pure butter, this is the finest butter the 'ticket' says this is a clever man, this is a very clever man and this is the most clever man (179). The full extent of her irony is revealed when she says that all these forms of vanity are a 'barbarity which deserves the ridicule which we bestow upon the rites of savages. A woman who advertised her motherhood by a tuft of horsehair on the left shoulder would scarcely, you will agree, be a venerable object' (179–80). We could say that Woolf is interested in what is now known as **signifying practices**: that is, how, within given contexts, things are made to mean. These practices are often called **signification**, which may sound complex, but it describes how meanings are created, made possible, rejected etc.

Figure 12.2 Woolf offers a thorough going exposé of male vanity

## **help** FILE: signifying practices and structuralist theory

**Signifying practices** are often discussed with relation to what is called **semiotics**. Semiotics uses **structuralist theory** to account for not so much what **signs** mean but *how* they mean. Very simply, semiotics uses the linguistic theories associated with linguists like Ferdinand de Saussure (1966) to analyse the nature of signs (anything that can have meanings attached to it – words, traffic lights, photographs, Braille, Morse code etc.) – and the laws and conventions that govern how meanings are made possible.

If you look back at the chapter on Althusser, it may serve to give you an idea of one of the ways in which structuralism tends to understand culture. In that chapter I referred to Hitchcock's *North by Northwest* and suggested that Thornton could be seen as a symbol for how Althusser argues individuals become subjects – how they are interpellated. Notice how he answered a call (a bit like someone being born into a particular culture) and was then completely defined and shaped by forces outside himself. Despite all resistance he was caught up in networks which give him identity and meaning. This reflected Althusser's idea that ideology has the function of 'constituting' individuals as subjects (Althusser, 1971: 160). Notice that instead of putting the emphasis on *agency* (as Thompson did) Althusser argued that we do not *precede* ideology or cultural systems but are actually *products* of them. This privileging of systems as a means to explain phenomena is a typical feature of structuralist ways of understanding culture.

E.P. Thompson was not convinced by Althusser's structuralist approach arguing that it was insufficiently historical and, as a method, wholly 'self-confirming' – 'a sealed system in which concepts endlessly circulate, recognize and interrogate each other' (Thompson, 1978: 208). These criticisms resulted in an acrimonious debate between Thompson and critics who defended structuralism. As Graeme Turner has argued:

> Structuralism encouraged cultural studies theorists to see Thompson's (and, for that matter, Williams') concentration on individual experience and agency as romantic and regressively humanist. Since consciousness is culturally constructed, why waste time dealing with its individual contents when we can deal with its constitutive processes – language, for instance? Culturalists, on the other hand, saw structuralism as too abstract, rigid and mechanical to accommodate the lived complexities of cultural processes. Structuralists saw culturalists as lacking theory; culturalists saw structuralists as theoreticist. Culturalism was a home-grown movement, while structuralism was foreign. In the discipline of history, the controversy became quite specific: historians claimed, with some justice, that structuralism was ahistorical and thus denied the very processes historians examined; conversely, structuralists saw culturalist historians as theoretically naive in their understanding of cultural processes. (Turner, 1996: 65)

To get a fairly accessible idea of how these theories work with relation to representation you might start with Roland Barthes' *Mythologies* (1972), which outlines the general theory and interprets, in a non-technical way, cultural phenomena as diverse as wrestling, margarine, soap powders, detergents, plastic, striptease, Greta Garbo's face and even the meaning of preserving Einstein's brain. Barthes' chapter on theory is reprinted in Storey (1998), and Johnson et al. (2004: 157f.) offers an accessible approach to reading popular narratives through structuralism.

SIMONE: So we could say that Woolf not only shows how culture relates to its patriarchal basis but indicates how it manifests itself in ritual and symbol. In this she is a little like a feminist cultural anthropologist describing beliefs, attitudes and social relationships but reading culture through gender.

DE BEAUVOIR: Woolf is not only demanding equality but goes a step beyond this by getting women to consider whether it is a good idea to aspire to the same world that dominant men have constructed.

SIMONE: As hinted above, Woolf insists that if she's to give a guinea to a cause she wants to establish the terms on which she will give it. In the present context she insists that if a college for women is to be rebuilt then it must be on different principles from those in existence for men. The reason is that when she looks round at the kind of social order produced in and by male educational establishments, far from creating a society characterized by generosity, magnanimity and peace, it actually seems to produce the opposite. She only sees men protecting their own interests and advantages at the expense of women (195). If she is to give a guinea the college must teach respect for liberty and the kind of things that will inspire hatred of war, not the arts of acquiring land and capital, of ruling over and killing others (199).

DE BEAUVOIR: Yes, segregation, specialization, competition, all the old teaching methods would be abolished (200f.). And with what art she dovetails all these ideas into her answer to the treasurer asking for a subscription to a society to help the daughters of educated men to obtain employment in the professions! Woolf adapts the same point she has already made, arguing that before she agrees to give her support she would like to establish a number of provisos. In a provocative tactical move, she asks if it is such a good idea if women enter the professions. The reason is that once people enter them they become 'possessive, jealous of any infringement of their rights, and highly combative if anyone dares dispute them' (249).

ELAINE: The problem for Woolf is that if the women of her class are encouraged to enter the professions they may well, ironically, evolve into the belligerent individuals the barrister's society is at such pains to confront (237–8). Thus, she insists that she will only give a guinea to the cause if the treasurer agrees to do all in her power to persuade any woman who wants to enter the professions to abide by the following rule. She must promise that she will not oppose anyone suitably qualified, regardless of sex or colour, from entering the professions, but do all in her power to help (249–50).

SHOWALTER: Quite! And while acknowledging the dangers, Woolf recognizes that unless women fully participate in education and the professions etc. they can never hope to have any influence over society. Thus, one of her strongest arguments is that the only way women can help to prevent war is for men to allow women this **full participation**.

## *Three Guineas* 3: from poverty, chastity and derision to intellectual liberty, dictatorship and the tyrannies of the Fascist state

ELAINE: Precisely, and she has a recipe for women to enter the professions 'and yet remain civilized human beings' (269). These are **poverty**, **chastity**, **derision** and **freedom from unreal loyalties**.

THE VOICE OF POVERTY: I teach women that they must earn just enough money to become independent of others (especially men). Women can then buy the health, leisure, knowledge etc. that is needed for their development (270).

THE VOICE OF CHASTITY: I am not the traditional Christian imperative to abstain from sexual intercourse! I demand that women, once they have earned enough money to live on, must not sell their brains for money as men have so often done to their own detriment. Do things 'for the sake of research and experiment' (270).

THE VOICE OF DERISION: Avoid advertising your own merits and choose obscurity, ridicule and censure over praise and fame.

THE VOICE OF FREEDOM FROM UNREAL LOYALTIES: This means freeing yourself from the kind of pride, so often felt by men, that results from identification with family, religion, school, sex or nationality.

SHOWALTER: And this brings us to the final part of *Three Guineas* where Woolf replies to the barrister who is appealing to her to sign a manifesto pledging herself to protect culture and **intellectual liberty**, and join his society, which is also in need of funds.

GERMAINE: Here Woolf makes a number of very telling points. She points out, and here's another example of irony, that the women of her class have already contributed to male intellectual liberty for centuries, because all the money that could have been spent on the education of women has been spent on men.

GREER: Also, it seems odd to her to ask women to protect culture and intellectual liberty when they have had little or no opportunity to exercise control over the institutions which organize and govern culture, and when their liberties have been so restricted (280f.). For Woolf, the only way to help men to defend culture and intellectual liberty, and here comes another irony, is for women to defend their own culture and intellectual liberty! Only in that way is culture and liberty more equitably distributed and established in society. However, Woolf is not opposed to donate a guinea if the barrister's society is really resisting dictatorship and protecting the 'democratic ideals of equal opportunity *for all*' (301, emphasis not in the original).

JULIA: However, it is when discussing this idea of resisting **dictatorship** that Woolf is at her most controversial.

KRISTEVA: Yes, just when Britain was on the verge of war against the Fascists Woolf, in a very courageous and deft twist, locates the evil seen as a threat to democracy, liberty and culture *within* Britain itself (303f.).

JULIA: Exactly, she makes the point that all those maligned women known as 'feminists' were actually the 'advance guard' of the barrister's own movement.

KRISTEVA: To appreciate the full force of what she was saying, her words are worth quoting. The feminists were fighting, and are still fighting, 'the tyranny of the Fascist state. Thus we are merely carrying on the same fight that our mothers and grandmothers fought' (303).

HÉLÈN: She says that the tyrant and dictator still exist in Britain, it is just that the 'monster has come more openly to the surface' in countries like Germany and Italy. Men now feel what their mothers felt when they were 'shut out' and 'shut up' (304).

CIXOUS: She also introduces a concept mentioned earlier that has become enormously important to cultural criticism dedicated to questions of marginalization, exclusion and inequality: **difference**.

KATE: As mentioned earlier, sexual difference is described in *Three Guineas* as something brought about by how society is structured. Woolf effectively asks, what is the point of women losing their difference if it only leads to their becoming like men? In this way no positive change would be possible. Society for women has been a question of exclusions at every level (305f.).

MILLET: She also asks if there is not something about the uniting of people into societies that 'releases what is most selfish and violent, least rational and humane in the individuals themselves' (307–8). Society, as it is, is a kind of conspiracy that deforms, limits and transforms the brother worthy of respect into a ...

THE VOICE OF VIRGINIA WOOLF: 'monstrous male, loud of voice, hard of fist, childishly intent upon scoring the floor of the earth with chalk marks, within whose mystic boundaries human beings are penned, rigidly, separately, artificially; where, daubed red and gold, decorated like a savage with feathers he goes through mystic rites and enjoys the dubious pleasures of power and dominion while we, "his" women, are locked in the private house without share in the many societies of which his society is composed' (308).

NANCY: Hardly surprising, then, that Woolf declines to join the society represented by the barrister, suggesting that women of her class begin an 'Outsiders' Society'.

CHODOROW: As outsiders, and by practising the kinds of suggestions Woolf has outlined above, they may be able to succeed where men have failed.

## Conclusions on method and practice

Let's leave the conversation there, even though there's much more that could be discussed and I haven't been able to reflect all its subtleties, twists, ironies, or all the questions raised. In the following chapter I shall take *Three Guineas* and use it to suggest how you might start thinking about probing the margins and remembering the forgotten not only in terms of gender but in terms of other categories like sexuality, race and ethnicity. The idea is that you can adapt these ideas to explore any subordinated group. Before moving on to the next chapter, let's summarize not so much what Woolf says but what she *does*. In the dialogue below a number of important voices within cultural criticism associated with race or postcolonial criticism discuss the relevance of Woolf's ideas to method and how they might be adapted to other contexts. Again, if you come across a name that is unfamiliar, you might do a little investigation of your own to find out more about that particular writer.

FRANZ FANON: We saw above that, within a dialectical method that explores gender issues, Woolf contextualizes the points she wants to make, offering evidence to support her claims. This means she doesn't fall into unsubstantiated generalizations. She is also very aware of the way political, economic and legal contexts have been organized through time to subordinate women. We can take this basic approach and apply it to any marginalized group. If the gay and lesbian community is in conflict with the sexual norms of the dominant heterosexual community, then it is important to ask *how* this situation has arisen in a particular geographical, political context. Equally, if a particular race or ethnic group feels itself to be subordinated, silenced or forgotten, again, the same questions can be asked. This approach can be summed up under **exploration of historical contexts**.

EDWARD SAID: In much cultural criticism you will see the term '**the other**'. It has been used so often that it is one of *the* clichés of much contemporary criticism. However, the reason it has been repeated so often is that it *does* help to think through how subordinated groups are constructed through dominant representations. Woolf, without using the term, tends to see the women of her class as a significant 'other' in the sense that the dominant group of men, who represent what she calls patriarchy, position women as subordinate to themselves.

GAYATRI CHAKRAVORTY SPIVAK: This idea of 'the other' can be adapted to any situation, whether we are talking about gender, race, ethnicity, class, sexuality or other concepts like age. Of course, 'the other' can be seen the other way round: how dominant groups are viewed or represented by the subordinate.

HOMI BHABHA: As we have seen in earlier chapters, the context of gender, race or class etc. may be analysed with relation to any of the others. We saw that Woolf confines what she has to say about women to those of her own class: she does not try to speak for all women. If we take the main categories of class, gender, race, ethnicity and sexuality each one of these may divide a community into smaller and more complex units. Here are just a few possibilities: you may be black, white or mixed race; working class, middle class; a man or a woman; heterosexual, gay, lesbian or bisexual. Further distinctions might be made in terms of religion, education, regional dialect, age, political affiliation, if you are waged, unemployed or semi-employed etc.

HENRY LOUIS GATES JR: This is an important point which relates to the idea of **difference** which, in turn, relates to identity and representation. Remember she raised the question of national identity when she claimed she had no wish to be 'English' and had no country because it had made women of her class wholly dependent on men who had repeatedly treated them like slaves. We saw that her identity as a woman was very much a product of cultural differences constructed by a society historically dominated by men. Sexual difference was not a question of something laid down by 'nature', but a product of how the sexes experience the world through the culture and opportunities available to them.

BELL HOOKS: (who always writes her name in lower case: bell hooks – you might reflect on this) Taking into account the concept of difference means that any simple approach to **identity** can be challenged. What does it mean to call someone American, Australian, French or Indian? If you return to the points made in the name of Homi Bhabha (above) the multiple contexts of difference should help to challenge the idea of identity as something straightforward. Even the useful concept of patriarchy, as the ways in which men dominate, subordinate and exploit women, ought to be used with relation to difference. As Strinati (1995: 198) has observed, 'not all men or all women are equally advantaged or disadvantaged. Other structures of inequality like class and race need to be taken into consideration'. We might add that difference would also require us to analyse the relations of power *between men* within patriarchy.

GLORIA ANZALDÚA: As has been suggested throughout this book, identity is not something just waiting to be discovered – it has to be constructed. Woolf's *Three Guineas* helps to teach us that **representation** is fundamental to how identity is understood. Men have represented women in certain dominant ways; Woolf challenges these representations and re-represents the women of her class in a different way. It could be said that she was involved in a counter-hegemonic struggle over representations and meaning. For example, we saw how she opposed the view of women as intellectually inferior and laughed at the idea that women were more obsessed by their physical appearance than men.

CORNEL WEST: This links to Woolf's interest in **signifying practices**. We saw that Woolf not only demonstrated how dominant culture could be related to its patriarchal basis but indicated how it manifested itself in ritual and symbol, and how men interpreted the world with relation to clothes and fashion. In this she was a like a feminist cultural anthropologist describing beliefs, attitudes and social relationships but reading these things through gender. We saw, when we looked at subcultures, that understanding the relation between objects, social rituals, places etc. and groups is very important to cultural analysis.

CHINUA ACHEBE: In the context of representation, one very useful approach in cultural analysis is to consider the question of cultural identity with relation to visual images. Stuart Hall, in an essay on cultural identity and cinematic representation, has distinguished between two ways of thinking about cultural identity.

TRINH T. MINHA-HA: The first model assumes that a **general collective cultural identity** can be discovered behind individual differences. Although Hall tends to favour the second approach mentioned below, he does see the first model as useful in so far that writers and film makers can try to re-represent groups or nations to challenge what they believe to be false representations of cultural identity.

NGUGI WA THIONGO: The second model accepts that identity is based, to some extent, on collective similarity but recognizes that 'there are also critical points of deep and significant *difference* which constitute "what we really are": or rather – since history has intervened – "what we have become"' (Hall, 2000: 706). Woolf seemed, in *Three Guineas*, very aware of the point that Hall makes about identity as '**production**', which is always incomplete, in process and 'constituted within, not outside, representation' (704). As Bennington has observed, the construction of nation is intimately bound up with its narration (1990: 132). These models enable critics to think about whether or not a representation is reinforcing or challenging existing models of identity, or whether a representation questions the whole idea of a stable identity. We saw that national identity for Woolf was severely compromised by questions of gender. Woolf showed how women are, and have been, subjected to subordinating forms of social, political, economic and legal power in order to perpetuate a system which preserves and perpetuates the status quo in favour of dominant male groups.

PAUL GILROY: This would fit into Hall's particular way of understanding popular culture that we looked at in chapter ten. This offers the possibility of analysing the **relations of power** with reference to different groups to see how they are subordinated, or have become subordinated within a given culture.

WOLE SOYINKA: Hey, this makes her sound like a Marxist, echoing themes explored with relation to Gramsci and Althusser!

MICHEL FOUCAULT: (interrupting) Yes, although she had no Marxist affiliations, you can see how radical criticism tends to explore the relations between culture and power. As it happens my work has proved to be particularly useful in this sense. Pity I died before I could complete all my projects.

AUTHOR: Hold on, I wasn't planning to list you under studies dedicated to the analysis of race and ethnicity or post-colonial criticism!

FOUCAULT: Maybe not, but you can't deny that my ideas have often proved to be of great value. Really, I can't believe you've not mentioned me more often in your book!

AUTHOR: Well, one might list Freud, or Marx, or many other writers who have been important to theorization in these areas. But then, I agree, I think you are important to so many different forms of cultural analysis concerned with the relations of culture and power, the history of sexuality, constructions of madness, punishment, imprisonment, discipline, surveillance, the rise of the human sciences and your work has often helped to highlight the kinds of subordination that have been discussed here.

FOUCAULT: So, how about throwing in a few references to my books like *The Order of Things* (1974), or *Discipline and Punish* (1977)?

AUTHOR: Well, you're so well known and easy to find that I'll leave it to my readers to find further references to you …

JACQUES DERRIDA: (interrupting) You keep mentioning the idea of difference, but I don't see any references to my deconstructive philosophy, which has generated an enormous amount of debate about identity (whether we're dealing with gender, sexuality, race, ethnicity, class, history, the self etc. etc.). Surely my *Of Grammatotology* (1976) or *Writing and Difference* (1978) might be of interest?

AUTHOR: Difficult for beginners, though … And how come so many men got in here? This chapter was supposed to be dedicated to women and feminism …

ROLAND BARTHES: (interrupting) Pardon me for intervening, but I would have thought my work has been of considerable importance to what you referred to as 'signifying practices'. Just look at the indexes to most books on cultural studies – I'll be there. You've already mentioned my *Mythologies* (1993), but what about my *Empire of Signs* (1983) and my *The Fashion System* (1985)?

AUTHOR: OK. I think you've earned a coupe of extra references …

JACQUES LACAN: (interrupting) It's all very well mentioning Freud but I think you'll find that my readings of Freud have had a huge impact on most of the areas you mention here.

AUTHOR: But your works are notoriously difficult for beginners! I'll drop in a reference to *Écrits* (1977) but readers might try a book like Slavoj Žižek's *Everything You Always Wanted to Know About Jacques Lacan (But Were Afraid to Ask Hitchcock)* (1992) before exploring your works.

JEAN-FRANÇIOS LYOTARD: (interrupting) And what about my *The Postmodern Condition* (1984)? Hasn't this work radically altered how we understand the identity of contemporary society?

FREDRIC JAMESON: (interrupting) Surely, if you're going to start mentioning contributions to postmodern thinking, what about my *Postmodernism, or the Cultural Logic of Late Capitalism* (1991)?

JEAN BAUDRILLARD: (interrupting) And my *Simulacra and Simulation* (1994)?

*At this point the author sneaks off, defeated by what's been left on the margins of his own text … (and by the way, he borrowed the idea of the margin of the text from Derrida, 1982).*

## *SUMMARY OF KEY POINTS*

This chapter has outlined some basic approaches to feminism, putting particular emphasis on what is known as the 'images and representations' approach. Virginia Woolf's *Three Guineas* has been used to give insights into a number of key feminist issues and to demonstrate what cultural criticism might look like from a feminist perspective. The chapter has also shown how Woolf developed a series of critical strategies to critique and challenge structures of patriarchal power and has introduced a series of key concepts (like 'difference', 'the other', representation and 'signifying practices') which can be used to explore other contexts of subordination. From the point of view of methodology Woolf's approach to can be seen as significant through:

- Providing a critique of patriarchal culture that probed the relations of power that helped to perpetuate the systematic subordination of women.
- Helping us to see (sexual) identity as a cultural construction and how representation functions with relation to repression.
- Showing how contexts of difference can challenge simple notions of identity and how culture can be seen as gendered.
- Making us aware of the role of what are now known as 'signifying practices'
- Demonstrating the importance of historical contexts and concepts like gender, 'difference' and 'other'.
- Providing an effective demonstration of a key area of resistance and struggle in contemporary culture.

## References

Althusser, Louis (1971) *Lenin and Philosophy and Other Essays*. New York: Monthly Review Press.

Barthes, Roland (1972) *Mythologies*. London: Jonathan Cape.

Barthes, Roland (1983) *Empire of Signs*. London: Jonathan Cape.

Barthes, Roland (1985) *The Fashion System*. London: Jonathan Cape.

Baudrillard, Jean (1994) *Simulacra and Simulation*. Michigan: University of Michigan Press.

Bennington, Geoffrey (1990) 'Postal Politics and the Instituion of the Nation', in H. Bhabha (ed.), *Nation and Narration*. London: Routledge.

Bhabha, Homi (ed.) (1990) *Nation and Narration*. London: Routledge.

Derrida, Jacques (1976) *Of Grammatology*. Baltimore: John Hopkins University Press.

Derrida, Jacques (1978) *Writing and Difference*. Chicago: University of Chicago Press.

Derrida, Jacques (1982) *Margins of Philosophy*. Chicago: University of Chicago Press.

Foucault, Michel (1974) *The Order of Things: An Archaeology of the Human Sciences*. London: Tavistock.

Foucault, Michel (1977) *Discipline and Punish: The Birth of the Prison*. Harmondsworth: Pelican.

Hall, Stuart (2000) 'Cultural Identity and Cinematic Representation', in R. Stam and T. Miller (eds), *Film and Theory: An Anthology*. Oxford: Blackwell.

Jameson, Fredric (1991) *Postmodernism, or the Cultural Logic of Late Capitalism*. London: Verso.

Johnson, Richard, Chambers, Deborah, Raghuram, Parvati and Tincknell, Estella (2004) *The Practice of Cultural Studies*. London: Sage.

Jordan, Glenn and Weedon, Chris (1995) *Cultural Politics: Class, Gender Race and the Postmodern World*. Oxford: Blackwell.

Lacan, Jacques (1977) *Écrits*. London: Tavistock.

Lyotard, Jean-François (1984) *The Postmodern Condition: A Report on Knowledge*. Minneapolis: University of Minnesota Press.

Moi, Toril (1989) 'Men Against Patriarchy', in L. Kauffman (ed.), *Gender and Theory: Dialogues on Feminist Criticism*. Oxford: Basil Blackwell.

*North by Northwest* (1959) dir. Alfred Hitchcock.

Rakow, Lana F. (1998) 'Feminist Approaches to Popular Culture: Giving Patriarchy its Due', in J. Storey (ed.), *Cultural Theory and Popular Culture: A Reader* (2nd edition). Essex: Pearson Prentice Hall.

Storey, John (1998) (ed.) *Cultural Theory and Popular Culture: A Reader* (2nd edition). Essex: Pearson Prentice Hall.

Strinati, Dominic (1995) *An Introduction to Theories of Popular Culture*. London: Routledge.

Saussure, Ferdinand de (1966) *Course in General Linguistics*. New York: McGraw-Hill.

Thompson, E.P. (1978) *The Poverty of Theory and Other Essays*. London: Merlin Press.

Turner, Graeme (1996) *British Cultural Studies: An Introduction* (2nd edition). London: Routledge.

Woolf, Virginia ([1925] 2000) *Mrs Dalloway*. Oxford: Oxford University Press.

Woolf, Virginia ([1927] 2006) *To the Lighthouse*. Oxford: Oxford University Press.

Woolf, Virginia ([1939] 1992) *A Room of One's Own, Three Guineas*. Oxford: Oxford University Press.

Žižek, Slavoj (1992) *Everything You Always Wanted to Know About Jacques Lacan (But Were Afraid to Ask Hitchcock)*. London: Verso.

## Further reading

Barker, Chris (2000) *Cultural Studies: Theory and Practice*. London: Sage. This book includes concise entries on a number of concepts mentioned in this chapter like race, ethnicity, hybridity, national identity, feminism and difference.

Storey, John (1998) see references above. We saw that Woolf put a lot of emphasis on biography and much feminism on popular culture uses the interview and autobiography in very productive ways. A good place to start would be to look at Storey's reader and read through the selections on 'Feminism'. You'll see that many studies have tried to understand romance and crime novels, soaps etc. through analyses which try to take account of reception: that is, how women respond to, use and evaluate popular cultural forms. Many of these studies do not denigrate these forms and recognize that popular culture, however good or bad it may seem, is a vital and important source of pleasure. You'll see that popular cultural forms help to articulate a personal sense of resistance, create powerful identifications and can be empowering; and they are not necessarily consumed in uncritical ways.

Walters, Suzanna Danuta (1995) *Material Girls: Making Sense of Feminist Cultural Theory.* California: University of California. A fairly accessible study which demonstrates how feminist cultural theory can be put into practice. The book introduces theory and illustrates it with case studies without losing sight of history.

Woolf, Virginia, *A Room of One's Own.* This essay is printed with *Three Guineas* in the edition cited above. It is also worth reading Morag Shiach's introduction to this edition which not only puts forward the main arguments with great clarity but, while sympathetic to Woolf's arguments, offers a number of criticisms. My own introduction is shaped by my overall intention to extrapolate useful ideas for practice; Shiach's introduction does more justice to the intricacies of Woolf's arguments.

# Adapting Theory to Explore Race, Ethnicity and Sexuality: the Case of *East is East*

## Introduction

Here we arrive at the second of the chapters on 'Probing the Margins, Remembering the Forgotten: Representation, Subordination and Identity'. As mentioned at the end of chapter twelve, here I shall show how the strategies explored in the previous chapter can be adapted to an exploration of questions of race and ethnicity. With reference to a simple heuristic I shall use the film *East is East* to offer examples of how the different concepts work in practice. I shall also show how the film itself may generate further ideas for heuristic thinking. Hints will be given on how some of these concepts might be adapted to discussions of sexuality and advice is given on further practice. To facilitate this, the chapter ends with some comments on the use of film and some annotated filmographies.

### MAIN LEARNING GOALS

- To see how a simple heuristic can help you to consolidate practice which focuses on themes of subordination on the grounds of gender, race/ethnicity, class and sexuality.
- To understand how the key ideas explored in the previous chapter (like awareness of historical context, resistance, identity, representation, the 'other', difference, 'signifying practices' etc.) can be adapted to new or related areas of study.
- To recognize how films (and other forms) can serve as useful heuristic devices in themselves to help thematize and theorize questions of subordination, gender and race etc.
- To be aware of possibilities for further study.

I'd like to start this chapter by presenting a simple heuristic which summarizes the main concepts explored in the previous chapter.

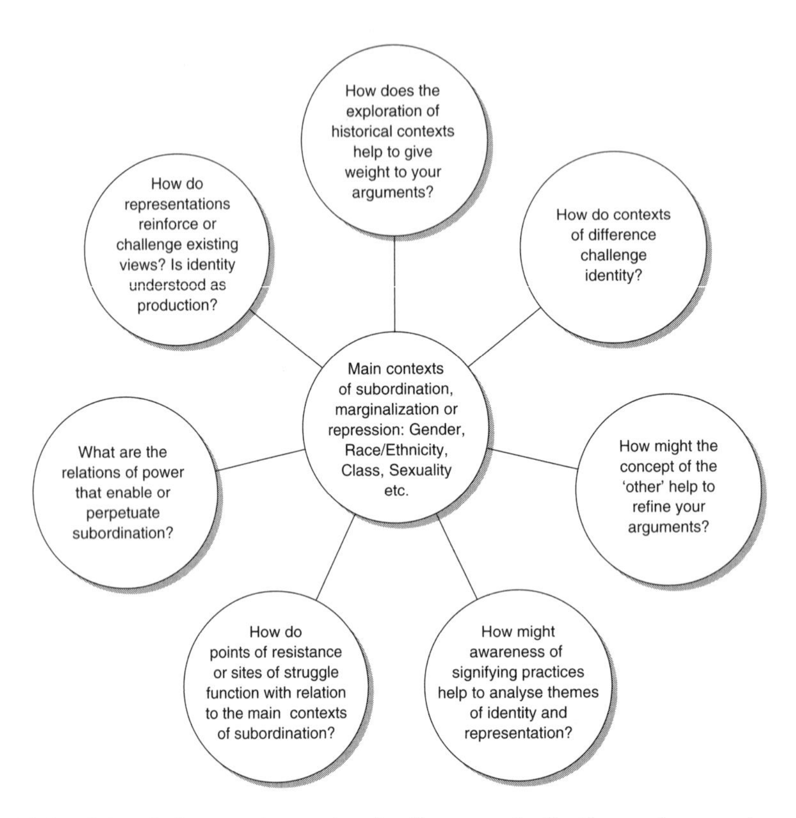


Figure 13.1 A heuristic to explore subordination, marginalization and repression

Let's take this heuristic device and see how you can use it in practice. As suggested in earlier chapters, film is a good place to start to practise your skills. I want to look at the British film *East is East* (1999) (based on Ayub Khan-Din's play of the same name) to demonstrate how you might go about exploring some of the themes we've been discussing. Although this film is advertised as a comic drama, it combines comedy with some scenes of disturbing violence. It's worth remembering that I'm using *East is East*, like I did *Quadrophenia*, not as a slice of life but as a convenient dramatization to explore simple forms of practice which require a minimum of preparation.

I'll illustrate how each of the categories in the heuristic might be used to address various forms of subordination, marginalization or repression. You'll find that separating the categories in this way is just a convenience and, in practice, they all interrelate. The strength of dividing them like this is that they help to raise a series of important questions that can then be developed into a series of arguments.

A review of the basic plot of *East is East* should demonstrate how relevant the film is to the exploration of these themes. The film is situated in Salford, England, and is centred on the members of the Khan family – the fruit of a mixed marriage between the Pakistani, George Khan, and his British wife, Ella. They all live under the same roof – in a chip shop. In an effort to inculcate his children with traditional Muslim values, George tries to educate his children as he sees proper to his beliefs. This is not an easy task with an eldest son who runs off during his arranged wedding ceremony, a daughter who prefers football to wearing saris, two sons who prefer discos to learning Arabic, and a young son who resists being circumcised. When George decides to try and arrange two further marriages, the whole family rebels and his plans end in disaster. I shall generally ignore the comedy and formal features, which means that my interpretation of the film will make it sound rather more sombre than it is, and I shall ignore the kinds of formal and aesthetic details that film criticism might emphasize. You may find this curious but in this chapter you will see no notes on practice. This is because the *whole chapter* is a series of notes dedicated to showing how theory can be put into practice.

## Historical contexts

The film takes place in 1971 in Salford, Manchester, where there are established Pakistani, Bangladeshi and Indian communities. One highly relevant question to ask is, how was it that communities of people from the Indian subcontinent settled in Britain? The answer would require some knowledge of Britain's imperialist past. Very simply put, India had been gradually colonized and exploited, as had many other parts of the globe, since the seventeenth century and rapidly came under British supremacy. By 1858 India was under full British colonial rule (Eldridge, 1978: 59). There were many uprisings and much conflict and resistance, but it wasn't until 1947 that Britain finally gave up its imperialist claims to India and the country was partitioned on religious lines into India (mainly Hindu) and Pakistan (mainly Muslim).

The partitioning of India led to long-term border problems between the two nations and *East is East* is set in 1971, the year when East Pakistan formally became Bangladesh, after a civil war and the defeat of Pakistan by India. George Khan, the father of the family, can be seen listening to his radio several times lamenting the fate of his homeland (India's greater military power enabled a swift victory). At one point in the film George asks a doctor, in a slightly disdainful way, if he's Indian. Without some knowledge of these historical contexts it would be hard to understand details like this.

George states that he arrived in England in 1937, before the main flows of immigration into Britain from the Caribbean and the Indian sub-continent, which took place from the late 1940s to the early 1960s. Let's come back to the question, how was it that communities of people from the Indian sub-continent settled in Britain? To answer this question more fully it is necessary to recognize that Britain was going through a phase of post-war prosperity and many citizens from the ex-colonies were invited to fill 'low-paid, low-status, dead-end jobs at the base of the employment structure' (Ramdin, 1999: 163). This was when the British economy 'demanded and got cheap black labour'; at a time when the British working classes were increasingly abandoning low-grade work (163).

Ron Ramdin outlines another important context that can be used to shed light on the historical circumstances of the film. He claims that the replacement of white labour for workers from the ex-colonies would lead to a weakening of working-class solidarity and 'increase the racist tendencies of white workers', something which seems to be reflected in the film. This can be illustrated by reference to one of the Khan's neighbours, Mr Moorhouse, a supporter of the Conservative politician, Enoch Powell.

The film incorporates into its narrative Enoch Powell's controversial discourses concerning repatriation. Powell gave what became known as his 'Rivers of Blood' speech (1968) in which he argued that immigration into Britain should be suspended and immigrants should be resettled in their countries of origin. He warned that their continued presence in Britain would end in serious conflict and bloodshed. His argument implied that England was for the English – that is, to be English was to be Anglo-Saxon and white. Even the leader of his party, Edward Heath (then in opposition) regarded his speech as racist and had him dismissed from the Shadow Cabinet. Although his speeches were seen as racist, responses to them were complex because he had supporters and detractors in both the 'white' and immigrant populations. There was an ever-growing community of 'Mr Moorhouses' but, at the same time, there were many from the ex-colonies who had dreamt of a better life in Britain and were disenchanted with the possibilities, disheartened by the conditions and wounded by the racial prejudice they encountered. Those who dreamed of a warm welcome to the British Isles were all too often confronted with the cold shoulder of the *Brutish* Isles. It was hardly surprising that some members of the immigrant communities looked at the possibility of repatriation in a positive way – even though they were, ironically, aligning themselves with what many regarded as the racist and reactionary Right.

The film helps to dramatize the way public opinion was, to some extent, shaped by important political voices. We see that racism, to become an important social political force, has to be marshalled. The figure of Mr Moorhouse, supporting Powell's ideas by organizing a meeting and putting up posters, helps to show *how* the 'racist tendencies of white workers' might be mobilized. This can be linked to an analysis of the forces of hegemony explored in chapter ten.

**Oversimplification**

**WARNING**

In the context of Gramsci and racism, Hall has recommended that racism be explored in particular situations, rather than be abstracted and oversimplified. Although it is always a 'deeply anti-human and anti-social practice' it is not always the same in all the various contexts in which it can be found (Hall, 1996a: 435f.). Thus, while using *East is East* to explore racism, we should recognize that it is helping us to understand a 'particular' manifestation of it and avoid over large claims.

By 1971, as can be seen in the film, the first generation of immigrants had settled and now had children of their own – a situation which would not only complicate what it meant to be British but also create tensions *within* the ethnic communities themselves. You might notice that, to some extent, by opening up these historical contexts, we're doing an Althusserian symptomatic reading.

## How do representations reinforce or challenge existing views?

The opening sequences of *East is East* can help to answer this question. The film begins with a Catholic procession through the streets of Salford. George and

Ella Khan's seven children participate by carrying the figure of Christ on the cross. However, when they realize their father is watching they have to make a detour and rejoin the procession further down the street. The identity of the Khan's offspring challenges any simple either 'white British national' or 'immigrant community' distinction. The Khan children, while not professing Christian beliefs, are seen to participate in, what is for them, a local festival. Their father may regard them as different, as does Mr Moorhouse, the symbol of Enoch Powell's ideas, but they pose a challenge to these polarized views.

If we ask if the film challenges more traditional models of national identity, or whether its representations question the whole idea of a stable identity, I think the answer would coincide with the latter. In *East is East* the representation of Britain in the 1970s is one where there are towns and cities where the traditional British way of life co-exists with cultural signs and practices associated with settled ethnic communities. Even the use of language can be seen to challenge polarized views. The Khan children all speak with a strong local accent and use typical regional phrases like 'our kid', 'Bloody Nora!' (an exclamation like 'Bloody hell!') and 'gobshite' (idiot). The same is generally true of dress: apart from Maneer, unless obliged by their father, they do not distinguish themselves in terms of traditional Pakistani dress.

However, Pakistani families have established important symbols in the community. George Khan regularly visits a mosque; he goes to a local market to buy clothes, fabrics and other goods associated with the Muslim way of life. It is possible to say, then, that the existence of families like the Khans poses a challenge to the towns and cities where they live and to traditional views about what it means to be English. In line with Hall's thinking outlined in the previous chapter, identity, from this point of view, can be understood not in terms of fixed entities but as identity in production.

## How do contexts of difference challenge identity?

From the previous points it is possible to see that significant immigration and settlement in a country will produce important changes. For this reason the terms **multiethnic** and **multicultural** are often used within cultural criticism. Although *East is East* focuses on the family of a local woman married to a Pakistani man it can be seen as a symbol of how Britain had become multiethnic and multicultural. Despite the groups who supported Enoch Powell's ideas, Britain's identity was, and is, forced to evolve.

Another interesting aspect explored in *East is East* is how the significance of difference may depend on the attitudes of those who perceive. Mr Moorhouse sees absolute cultural difference; his only reaction is to argue for exclusion. However, his granddaughter and grandson offer alternative responses. In the case of his granddaughter, Stella, she is attracted to one of the Khan sons, Tariq. For her there is no cultural or political divide. This latter point is also true of her brother, Ernest. They represent the more positive cultural forces of integration and fuller acceptance in the dominant community. Sajid, the Khan's youngest son, is Ernest's best friend and, more importantly, Ernest tries to communicate with Sajid's father in the terms he hears him speaking to other Muslim members of the community. Whenever he can Ernest uses the phrase 'As-Salaam-Alaikum' (peace be with you) or the reply 'Wa-Alaikum-Salaam' (peace to you, too). *East is East* balances prejudicial rejection with integration and acceptance where there is at least the possibility of a productive interchange of cultures.

## Main contexts of subordination

The main contexts of subordination in *East is East* are on the grounds of gender and race/ethnicity (before reading on you might review the section on 'questions of race' in chapter eight). One of the first scenes in the film shows how the Khan's oldest son, Nasir, resists an arranged marriage by escaping from the mosque during the ceremony. Six months later George Khan attempts to arrange further marriages for two of his other sons, Tariq and Abdul. It is George's attempts to impose his beliefs and values that threaten to destroy the unity of the family. Once George's wife, Ella, finds out that he plans to marry two of their sons without informing them, she expresses her disagreement and tries to persuade him that they have a right to know.

Things come to a head when Tariq and Abdul discover their father's plans and Tariq tries to destroy the traditional wedding garments. George, finding himself defied, loses control and ends up beating Ella and, ironically, Maneer, the son who most closely identifies with his Muslim beliefs. In this way, the film dramatizes the other context of subordination, that of gender.

By the end of the film, George is made to see that he has always put himself and his beliefs before the happiness of his own children. He has alienated his eldest son, considering him dead after his 'betrayal'; his son, Saleem, has to pretend he's studying engineering (when he's studying art) because he fears his father's reaction; he has behaved aggressively to all his children and exercised direct violence on Ella and Maneer. We see here that subordinating his family to his beliefs is intimately related to his exercise of patriarchal power. Religious subordination is exercised *through* the power he bestows on himself as head of the family. He only wants what *he* thinks is the best for his children, but without reflecting on the politics of his own actions. Only when he is defeated and bewildered, and it looks like he will lose everything, does he show signs of regret. At the end he has to confront his male *pride* and his cultural *allegiances*. Woolf might have taught him a thing or two.

The other context that the film explores is the attempt to repress, marginalize or exclude people on the grounds of race or ethnicity. Mr Moorhouse is depicted as something of a buffoon and racial violence is never practised on any member of the Khan family. However, George is subjected to direct insult by Moorhouse and the recognition of an atmosphere of pervasive prejudice is manifested in a number of less obvious ways.

Firstly, at one point in the film Tariq and Abdul go to a local disco. In the queue, waiting to get in, are two Asian men. They are turned away – no explanation is given but the reason is obvious when Tariq is allowed in because he doesn't look obviously Asian and calls himself Tony. Abdul is almost turned away but is saved by 'Tony' who says he's his brother. The bouncer on the door looks a little doubtful – until, that is, Abdul announces himself as Arthur. These points can be further highlighted by a consideration of in what ways a group can be seen as 'other'.

## Using the concept of the 'other'

Another way in which subordination and prejudice can be explored is with reference to the idea of the 'other'. George Khan and his children are seen by the Mr Moorhouse fraternity as an invading 'other' to be removed. Ella Khan is, for most of the film, the disempowered 'other' to her husband, George. However, the way most of the Khan children talk about members of the Pakistani community constructs another victimized 'other'. Some of the Khan children tend to speak about Pakistani people who try to live by their Muslim beliefs as 'them'. Tariq, in an outburst of rage, cries, 'I'm not marrying a fucking Paki' and Sajid, when the Shah family arrive to present their daughters to the Khan family prior to the second arranged marriage, shouts, 'Mom, the Pakis are here!'

At first, this might seem funny coming from children of a Pakistani man, but in this, they are perpetuating the kind of racist slogans that help to bolster up the racial superiority that characterizes Mr Moorhouse. As Étienne Balibar has argued, nationalist ideologies are dependent upon the differentiation between 'us' and 'them' as outsiders or foreigners (Balibar and Wallerstein, 1991: 86f.). There is, however, another variation on racism at the end of the film when the Shah family, feeling insulted by Saleem's 'work of art' (a rubber vagina that happens to land on Mrs Shah's lap), are thrown out by Ella, who feels she's been patronized. In the trading of insults, Mrs Shah calls Ella's children 'half-breeds', suggesting that racist language and attitudes are very deeply rooted in all communities. We see that cultural identifications produce their 'others' that can so easily be converted into groups or communities to be maligned, subordinated, marginalized or excluded.

## What are the relations of power that enable or perpetuate subordination?

We can see that the Khan family is dominated but, at the same time, almost dismembered by subordination on the grounds of gender. Patriarchy establishes the traditional right of the father (or eldest male) to establish the grounds on which family life will function. It is only the resistance of Ella and the Khan children that finally challenges the rights that George confers upon himself through his beliefs. (For further discussion of resistance, see the section on 'points of resistance or sites of struggle', below.)

Although *East is East* mainly explores the Khan family, and can be read as an indictment of patriarchal control as exercised through the Muslim faith (especially with relation to arranged marriages), it can also serve, as seen above, as a model for the ways in which relations of power are exercised *over* immigrant populations. Mr Moorhouse tries to exercise the same kind of power over his grandchildren as George does over his family: they are expected to reflect his own beliefs and opinions back at him. He rebukes Stella for smiling at Tariq and reprimands Earnest for being open and friendly to the Khan family. As mentioned earlier, Mr Moorhouse's support of repatriation also helps to show how immigrant populations were converted into marginalized 'others' and caught up in discourses which were ignorant of, or conveniently ignored, the exploitative character of Britain's immigration policies and its despotic colonial past.

## Signifying practices (reading cultural symbols)

We can see from the above points that culture is intimately bound up with signifying practices of different kinds. Things are made to mean by different people according to their values and beliefs or, as the cultural anthropologist Clifford Geertz has stated, according to the 'conceptual world' in which individuals live (1973: 24). Mr Moorhouse interprets the Khan's presence in the community in line with the ideas expressed by Enoch Powell; some members of the Khan family see other members of the community in similar ways to Mr Moorhouse, as 'Pakis'; they, in turn, are seen as 'halfbreeds'.

If we look at some of the dominant symbols in *East is East* we'll see things which are very much associated with what many might regard as typically British. The Khans run a chip shop, Meenah, Tariq and Abdul eat bacon and pork sausages (ironically, while they are watching Enoch Powell on TV), Sajid is addicted to wearing his parka coat (associated with Mod culture) and Meenah, Tariq and Abdul listen to the British pop music of the day. Yet, members of the community like Mr Moorhouse see the Khans as culturally different. In some ways they are. Most of the family members on George Khan's side are integrated into a British–Muslim way of life. The question is, how can this situation be described?

In much cultural criticism the concept of **hybridity** is used to discuss the cultural changes associated with the movement of peoples (or **diaspora**). The concept of hybridity describes all kinds of phenomena related to how the 'host' and new communities influence each other. Once new peoples establish themselves new identities, perspectives, experiences and cultural fusions and variations (hybrid forms) are possible (we might think of musical forms like Bangra and Bangla in Britain). In multi-cultural countries like Britain, the British-born and educated children of immigrant populations have the possibility of identifying with either cultural milieu, or moving between the two. As Chris Weedon has noted, it is the new generations that are 'producing new critical forms of hybrid culture which take issue both with British ethnocentrism and racism and the traditional cultures of their parents' (Weedon, 2000: 262). *East is East* is a product of hybrid culture – one cultural form among many dramatizing the often antagonistic space and divided loyalties *between* the dominant and ethnic cultures.

## **help** FILE: ethnocentrism and diaspora

Chris Weedon uses the term **ethnocenticism**, which describes the tendency of members of an ethnic or racial group to privilege themselves above other groups. We have seen that this is not necessarily confined to dominant groups. Another variation on this idea is **cultural centrism** where superiority is based on the privileging of one culture over another or others (Bolaffi et al., 2003: 103).

**Diaspora** is another important term within cultural criticism which concerns itself with the movement of peoples, usually entailing some measure of coercion or severe difficulty, such as poverty, slavery, colonization, eviction, political or ethnic persecution or war. As Bolaffi et al. argue, it is not only necessary to establish who travels 'but when, how and under what circumstances' (2003: 73). Hall (1996b: 447) has coined the term *diaspora-ization* which helps describe 'black experience' and processes of 'unsettling, recombination, hybridization and "cut-and-mix"' – the kinds of themes being explored here with relation to *East is East*.

The exploration of how new generations cope with the problems of living between cultural spaces, where their identifications and loyalties may be clearly in favour of one community, or divided or ambiguous, opens up the possibility of a rich vein of criticism that can be explored with relation to film, TV, music and literature. We have seen that *East is East* offers a dramatic symbol of how a family has to negotiate between different forms of ethnocentrism and cultural centrism and confront the problems of hybridity. At the end of this chapter you will find some references that you might take up to explore these ideas.

However, the exploration of ethnicity does not necessarily end here. Stuart Hall has put forward the idea that everyone has to speak from a particular place, history or culture. This suggests that the concept of ethnicity can be applied to *any* group in society, including the dominant group(s). Everyone is, then, '*ethnically* located' and this location is fundamental to a sense of identity (Hall, 1996b: 447). From this point of view, Mr Moorhouse's sense of identity as 'authentic' white English is dependent on his ethnic location, just as the Khan's children's hybrid, multicultural identity is dependent on their particular cultural location. It is from these locations that notions of community, identity and 'other' are made possible.

## Points of resistance and sites of struggle

How do points of resistance or sites of struggle function with relation to the main contexts of subordination? In terms of the struggle against subordination on the grounds of race or ethnicity, *East is East* does not explore resistance at this level, preferring to focus on *the circumstances* of why resistance may be necessary.

The main site of struggle is focused on how Ella and the Khan children resist George Khan's authority. Nasir, the oldest son and the first to escape the trappings of an arranged marriage, actually introduces another relevant site of struggle and that is subordination at the level of sexuality. Although no one seems aware of it at the begining of the film, Nasir is homosexual. Later it is evident that he has a male partner, his boss at a designer hat shop in Eccles.

Nasir's rejection of an arranged marriage can also be seen as a symbol of his taking a stance against the heterosexual assumption that men will naturally marry women. Although this is not explored in any depth in the film, it is there and may be listed under resistance. It would also be relevant to look at the representation of the gay world in the 1970s. Nasir and his boss are represented as florid examples of Glam-Rock, with Nasir and his partner very much in the affected camp style.

Ella, as mentioned above, confronts her husband on numerous occasions and while generally sympathetic to George's religious beliefs, tries to make him aware of his dictatorial and egoistic behaviour (as does Abdul). Meenah, the Khan's only daughter, is constantly being repressed for being self-assured, usually by Abdul and Tariq who suspect she will provoke her father, which she does towards the end of the film. She prefers non-traditional Pakistani clothes and plays football – failing to live up to her father's idea of a 'good' Muslim girl. Like the others, she does not express a political view, just displays moments of resistance. *East is East*, then, while incorporating resistance at an everyday level, does not put highly politicized discourses against racism or sexism in the mouths of its protagonists.

Other films, like Spike Lee's *Malcolm X* (1992), Richard Attenborough's *Gandhi* (1982), or Horace Ove's *Pressure* (1975), deal with black rights issues much more self-consciously. These films, which centre on the USA, India and Britain respectively, could be said to be much more about struggle and discourses of resistance and would also be useful starting points for essay work. Below you will find some more ideas.

## Possibilities for further practice: adapting the concepts to explorations of sexuality

However, it is as interesting to take sources which are not necessarily focused on class, gender, race, ethnicity or sexuality to examine what kinds of representations can be found in them. For example, Jean-Pierre Jeunet's popular film *Amélie* (2001) does not seem to self-consciously explore issues of gender or sexuality, yet it does feature a lesbian in one of its scenes. Other popular films like the *The Full Monty* (1997) and *Four Weddings and a Funeral* (1995) include characters who are gay. The question you might ask is, what kind of representations are they? Apart, then, from looking at what films self-consciously explore, it is also possible to look in these marginal spaces to examine popular constructions of races, ethnicities, classes, genders and sexualities etc.

In this chapter I have concentrated on how to open up issues of gender, race and ethnicity. I have hardly mentioned class because I have dealt with it in earlier chapters, although that would also need to be taken much more into account. I have only mentioned sexuality in passing but most of the main ideas outlined here can be used to explore repression or subordination on the grounds of sexuality. Some films are very useful to see how several of the main categories of subordination criss-cross within a single narrative. For example, Stephen Frears' film of Hanif Kureishi's *My Beautiful Laundrette* (1985) explores the gay relationship between the middle-class Anglo-Pakistani, Omar, and the working-class skinhead Johnny, bringing together issues which border on race, ethnicity, sexuality and youth subculture.

To start out exploring sexuality in a more detailed way you might choose one of the films listed below and work through some of the concepts introduced in this chapter. It should be remembered that these concepts are only designed as starting points to stimulate ideas. They are not specific enough to deal with every area of subordination, marginalization or repression in much detail. For this reason, if you want to explore sexuality, you might also look up and examine a series of further concepts like: queer, butch, drag queens, homophobia, representations of the body, sexual dissidence, gender bending, transvestism, transexuality, sexual transgression, bisexualism, masculinity, femininity, camp subculture, sexual stereotypes, perversion, fetishism, body politics, politics of pleasure, sexploitation, transgender, pornography, Stonewall and HIV. If you type these terms into a search engine on your computer, you will find a huge body of possible resources for research.

## Possibilities for further practice: the use of film

Here I shall offer a short list of popular films which might be of particular interest to begin an exploration of different contexts of subordination. It is in no way exhaustive (an exhaustive list could easily fill this book) and the vast choice means that I've had to pull these names more or less out of a hat. However, the choice is not entirely arbitrary in so far that, in my mind, they all have something interesting to say or suggest, and they are all either available on video or DVD and/or obtainable from a fairly well-stocked library. Also, because of some significant differences in terms of *how* they represent different groups, they can be used to do some useful comparative analysis. To help you with this I offer short observations to suggest areas of interest. To get a fuller idea of what's available, do the first exercise in the section 'Two further practice exercises' below.

## A short list of films that centre on or include gender issues, homosexuality or lesbianism as an important theme

*The Adventures of Priscilla, Queen of the Desert* (1994) dir. Stephan Elliot. This has become a classic variation on the road movie, depicting three transvestite gay men travelling through the Australian desert. A film useful for reflecting on sexual and national identities.

*Bad Education* (*La mala educación*) (2004) dir. Pedro Almódovar. This is just one of Almodóvar's films which might be used to explore representations or gender, camp, homosexuality, transvestism, transexuality, cross dressing etc. Although Almódovar's films are more often than not motivated by the exploration of homosexual desire, his films often feature challenging and, at times, controversial representations of women.

*Beautiful Thing* (1996) dir. Hattie Macdonald. A film based on the play by Jonathan Harvey in which two young working-class men fall in love. If you look at the working-class homosexual in the film *Wilde*, you'll see that he's a prostitute and on the wrong side of the law. The working-class gay in *My Private Idaho* is also a rent boy and a tortured delinquent. Harvey presents gay love in a working-class environment as something to some extent still taboo but more everyday and acceptable. This is a much more optimistic representation of the gay world.

*Bound* (1996) dir. Larry and Andy Wachowski. Drawing on the conventions of film noir and gangster films this film represents a lesbian couple. Worth reviewing to explore how the couple is represented and how it draws on the image of the 'butch woman' a lesbian type who cultivates a noticeably 'masculine' look.

*Boys Don't Cry* (1999) dir. Kimberly Peirce. This film is based on the true story of Teena Brandon who, born a girl, was so uncomfortable with her gender that she went to great lengths to disguise herself as a young 'man', changing her name to Brandon Teena. She was so convincing that she managed to get a young heterosexual woman to fall in love with her. Brandon was eventually brutally raped and murdered and it was only then that many who knew her as a man discovered that s/he was a woman. This is a suggestive (if disturbing) source for considerations of gender identity and a kind of what might be considered a variation of homophobia (it would seem her killers' rage was provoked by her gender bending). It would also be interesting to explore this film with relation to Judith Butler's idea that gender is 'performative' (see chapter eight).

*Brokeback Mountain* (2005) dir. Ang Lee. This film is based on an Annie Proulx's short story and explores the love between two men, one who accepts his sexuality, the other who finds it hard to come to terms with it. Neither, however, is able to 'come out' and the film traces their secret passion against a background of sexual prejudice, potential hostility and violence. A film which, like many focused on the gay world, explores the social realities (and tragedy) of what it means to be gay in a largely homophobic world.

*Maurice* (1987) dir. James Ivory. Based on E.M. Forster's novel of the same name, this film explores Maurice's journey towards recognizing and accepting his sexuality at a time when it was still prohibited (Forster did not publish his novel in his own lifetime). The film is also interesting because it also represents a relationship between men of different classes: Maurice is a member of the repressed Edwardian upper class who eventually finds emotional and sexual satisfaction in the arms of a gamekeeper. You might also note that Maurice, before accepting himself as he is, seeks a cure for his sexual inclinations, a detail which echoes how homosexuality was socially constructed and understood at the time (to follow this up, see the titles in the section on further reading).

*My Father is Coming* (1991) dir. Monika Treut. This film can be used to explore sexual difference and representation through the main protagonist's exploration of lesbianism and her relationship with a transsexual. Treut extends themes already explored in other films like *Virgin Machine* (1998).

*The Pillow Book* (1995) dir. Peter Greenaway. Set in Kyoto, Japan, an English translator gets passionately involved with a Nagiko, a young Japanese woman, who uses his body to write on. The film is interesting from the point of view of women as active agents (Nagiko starts as passive body to be written on) and gay representations (the translator, Jerome, is comfortably bi-sexual).

*My Private Idaho* (1991) dir. Gus Van Sant. This film draws on Shakespeare's *Henry IV* and centres on the relationship between two young men, one of whom is a homeless, male prostitute (suffering from narcolepsy), the other from a wealthy family. It is possible to explore how differences of class and sexuality operate.

*Queer as Folk* (1999) dir. Sarah Harding and Charles McDougall. This is a controversial British series tracing the lives of three gay men, one of whom is 15 years old. Very useful from the point of view of contemporary representations of gay life. There is also a North American version, which would be interesting to compare with the British series.

*Wilde* (1997) dir. Brian Gilbert. Based on Richard Ellmann's biography (1988), this film represents the life of the Irish writer Oscar Wilde in terms of a triumphant rise and ignominious fall. While concentrating on his relationship with the aristocrat, Lord Alfred Douglas (and not ignoring Wilde's life as husband and father), it also gives an insight into the homosexual subculture that Wilde became a part of and which helped to get Wilde imprisoned for two years with hard labour.

*Withnail and I* (1987) dir. Bruce Robinson. A British cult film set in the 1970s which, in many ways, centres round a secondary character, Monty Withnail. Monty is an ageing homosexual who has had to repress his sexuality. While the film creates much humour at his expense, it can be argued that he is not treated unsympathetically. The construction of Monty's gay identity (he's an upper-class product of the British educational elite) could be compared in useful ways to the other possibilities listed here.

## A short list of films that can be used to focus on race, ethnicity, multiculturalism, diaspora and national identity

*Ali* (2001) dir. Michael Mann. A biopic based on the life of Mohammed Ali, the former heavyweight boxing champion of the world. What makes this relevant to the themes of this chapter is his interest in Black Rights, his refusal to be subordinated on the grounds of race, his defiance of authority, his refusal to submit to military subscription to fight in Vietnam, and his conversion to Islam (which prompted him to change his birth name from Cassius Clay to Mohammed Ali).

*Anita and Me* (2003) dir. Metin Hüseyin. Based on Meera Syal's novel of the same name. Set in the 1970s and centred on the young Asian girl, Meena, this film (like *East is East* and *Bhaji on the Beach*) can be used to explore themes like multiculturalism and hybridity in Britain.

*Bhaji on the Beach* (1993) dir. Gurinder Chadha. As mentioned in the previous entry, Chadha's film can be used to explore many of the themes explored in this chapter. This film brings together different generations of Asian women who go on a trip to a seaside resort in Britain. This gives Chadha the opportunity to explore different kinds of Anglo-British identity but with the main focus being on Anglo-Asian woman. Chadha has re-explored some of the themes set out in this film in *Bend it Like Beckham* (2002) in which a teenage Anglo-Indian girl wants to become a professional footballer, much to her parents' dislike. Like *Anita and Me*, these films can be used to explore themes like multiculturalism and hybridity in Britain.

*Birth of a Nation* (1915) dir. D.W. Griffith. This enormously controversial film is still available. It is set during the American Civil War and depicts black people (white actors blacked up) as little more than unruly savages. Outrageous white supremisism comes in the form of the Klu Klax Klan as redeeming heroes. Interesting to study with relation to the history of negative and racist representations of black communities in the US.

*The Color Purple* (1985) dir. Steven Spielberg. Spielberg's adaptation of Alice Walker's novel of the same name. A young woman is raped by her father and forced to marry a brutal man she does not love. A narrative that links feminist issues with those of sexuality and race.

*Gandhi* (1982) dir. Richard Attenborough. This was mentioned above because it is a biopic which focuses on struggle and discourses of resistance – in this case Gandhi's role in helping India to free itself from British Imperial rule through his policy of peaceful non-cooperation which included fasting to death for the cause.

*Malcolm X* (1992) dir. Spike Lee. Another film mentioned above, based on the life of Malcolm Little who, while in prison (he had been a drug pusher, addict and burglar), turned to Elijah Muhammad's Black Muslim sect. Ousted from the Black Muslim movement (and shortly before he was murdered), he eventually formed the Organization of Afro-American Unity. The film follows him from young delinquent to being one of the most eloquent and controversial defenders of civil rights in the United States. Most of Spike Lee's films are worth exploring.

*To Kill a Mockingbird* (1962) dir. Robert Mulligan. Based on a work by Harper Lee, this film, a variation on the courtroom drama, is set in a small town in Alabama in the Southern States of America during the Depression. A black man is accused of raping a white woman with no real evidence to back up the accusation. It looks as if he will be unjustly convicted when no one steps forward to defend him. Eventually, an honest white attorney takes up the case and clears him. His defence, however, provokes much animosity in the community and Lee uses this to explore deep-rooted racism. You might compare this with other courtroom dramas like Spielberg's *Amistad* (1998) and Bob Reiner's *Ghosts of Mississippi* (1996) which deal with race. These films provide something of a counter balance in terms of representation to films like the *Birth of a Nation* in the way they understand North American history and its relation to slave populations.

*Pressure* (1975) dir. Horace Ove. This film was mentioned above because it focuses very directly on struggle and discourses of resistance. This film is set in 1970s Britain and has as its protagonist Tony, who has been brought up in Britain by Trinidadian parents. Tony is a second generation Black British 'immigrant' who identifies with his London environment and is accepted by his peers. However, once he starts looking for a job he realizes he is the victim of racial prejudice – he is intelligent but ends up having to accept the most menial jobs because of his colour, and he becomes increasingly alienated from the country in which he has been brought up. Ove explores racism, delinquency and the struggles of the Black Rights Movement (the Black Panthers), which is shown to be the victim of police repression. A film which effectively illustrates Hall's definition of popular culture.

*West is West* (1987) dir. David Rathod. *East is East* can be seen as a play on the title of this film. Whereas George from *East is East* settles in Britain from Pakistan, Rathod has his protagonist, Vikram, arrive in San Fransisco from Bombay, India. This film can be used to explore issues of multiculturalism etc. but in the US context.

## **practice** EXERCISES: online libraries, analysing roles and stereotypes

Before I sum up I'd like to recommend three exercises designed to help you research the themes explored in this chapter. Firstly, go into the online catalogue of a large library and scroll through the film collection. Film resources are often catalogued with relation to themes like Race, Ethnicity, Gay and Lesbian cinema etc. and include useful subsections. Entries often contain a brief summary of the film in question. Even if you do not have access to the libraries' resources, this is a good way to discover new materials. You might start by exploring Berkeley's online catalogue (www.lib.berkeley.edu) or use the British Film Insitute's online resources (www.bfi.org.uk) and make

*(Continued)*

a short list of titles you feel are particularly interesting from a particular point of view. You can do a similar exercise with relation to novels, plays or theoretical works.

Secondly, another way of exploring race and ethnicity is to choose an actor or actress you feel is representative of a particular group or minority and review the kinds of roles that s/he has performed. This exercise is inspired by a point made by Manthia Diawara that if you look at the characters Eddie Murphy has played in films like *Trading Places*, *48 Hours*, and *Beverly Hills Cop I* and *II* it is possible to see his characters evolve from being threatening to being contained or domesticated (Diawara, 1988: 71f.). You will often find that a single actor or actress has performed a great many different roles that involve very diverse kinds of representations. These can then be analysed from the point of view of whether or not they follow basic stereotypes or offer some kind of challenge to traditional representations.

Finally, one question you can ask yourself is, how do stereotypes function? Anneke Smelik has offered a very neat summary of how Richard Dyer approaches the question. Although Dyer's main focus is gays in film, the points can be adapted to any form of representation:

> Dyer argues that stereotypes have the function of ordering the world around us. Stereotyping works in society both to establish and to maintain the hegemony of the dominant group (heterosexual white men) and to marginalize and exclude other social groups (homosexuals, blacks, women, the working class). Stereotypes, then, produce sharp oppositions between social groups in order to maintain clear boundaries between them. They are also normative. Stereotypes of gays and lesbians such as the queen and the dyke reproduce norms of gendered heterosexuality because they indicate that the homosexual man or woman falls short of the heterosexual norm: that they can never be a 'real' man or woman. (Smelik, 2000: 134–5)

It is worth keeping in mind that stereotypes may not necessarily be negative (they may be playful, critical, parodic or celebratory). It is also worth remembering a point made in previous chapters, that a film which seems highly critical at one level (it may be particularly sensitive to multiculturalism) but may not be so at another (for example, gender or sexuality). Looking at materials in this way enables us to take account of difference in much more subtle ways.

## SUMMARY OF KEY POINTS

In this chapter I have looked at how we might use cultural forms which challenge the dominant political order through categories like gender, class, race, ethnicity and sexuality. To this

*(Continued)*

*(Continued)*

end I have outlined a number of ideas and shown how they might be used in practice, offering a detailed interpretation of the film *East is East*. This chapter has demonstrated how films (and this can be extended to books, TV series, music, theatre and other forms) can very often serve as useful heuristic devices in themselves to help thematize and theorize. From the point of view of methodological relevance we have seen that:

- Heuristic thinking can help consolidate practice by focusing on themes of subordination on the grounds of gender, race/ethnicity, class and sexuality.
- That a number of key ideas extrapolated from Woolf's *Three Guineas* (like awareness of historical context, resistance, identity, representation, the 'other', difference, 'signifying practices' etc.) can easily be adapted to new or related areas of study.

We have now come to the point where we can try to back off from all the themes and strategies put forward in this book and begin to sum up the image of cultural studies that has been conjured up in these pages. By now I hope you have begun to develop a sense of interpretive independence and you are now in a position to consolidate your skills. That is to say, you should now be ready for the final chapter of this book.

## References

*Amélie* (2001) dir. Jean-Pierre Jeunet.

Balibar, Étienne and Wallerstein, Immanuel (1991) *Race, Nation, Class: Ambiguous Identities*. London: Verso.

Bolaffi, Guido, Bracalenti, Raffaele, Braham, Peter and Gindro, Sandro (eds) (2003) *Dictionary of Race, Ethnicity and Culture*. London: Sage.

Diawara, Manthia (1988) 'Black Spectatorship: Problems of Identification and Resistance', Screen 29 (4).

*East is East* (1999) dir. Damien O'Donnell.

Eldridge, C.C. (1978) *Victorian Imperialism*. London: Hodder & Stoughton.

Ellmann, Richard (1988) *Oscar Wilde*. London: Penguin.

*Four Weddings and a Funeral* (1995) dir. Mike Newell.

*The Full Monty* (1997) dir. Peter Cattaneo.

*Gandhi* (1982) dir. Richard Attenborough.

Geertz, Clifford (1973) *The Interpretation of Cutlures*. New York: Basic Books.

Hall, Stuart (1996a) 'Gramsci's relevance for the study of race and ethnicity', in D. Morley and K-H. Chen (eds), *Stuart Hall: Critical Dialogues in Cultural Studies*. London: Routledge.

Hall, Stuart (1996b) 'New Ethnicities', in D. Morley and K-H. Chen (eds), *Stuart Hall: Critical Dialogues in Cultural Studies*. London: Routledge.

*Malcolm X* (1992) dir. Spike Lee.

Morley, David and Chen, Kuan-Hsing (eds) (1996) *Stuart Hall: Critical Dialogues in Cultural Studies*. London: Routledge.

*My Beautiful Laundrette* (1985) dir. Stephen Frears.

*Pressure* (1975) dir. Horace Ove.

Ramdin, Ron (1999) *Reimaging Britain: 500 Years of Black and Asian History*. London: Pluto.

Smelik, Anneke (2000) 'Gay and lesbian criticism', in J. Hill and P. Church Gibsons (eds), *Film Studies: Critical Approaches*. Oxford: Oxford University Press.

Weedon, Chris (2000) 'Goodness, Gracious Me: Comedy as a tool for Contesting Racism and Ethnocentrism', in M.J. Coperías Aguilar (ed.), *Culture and Power. Challenging Discourses*. Valencia: Servei de Publicaciones Universitat de València.

## Further reading

Abelove, Henry, Barale, Michèle Aina and Halperin, David (eds) (1993) *The Lesbian and Gay Studies Reader*. London: Routledge. This is a useful collection of some key texts to follow up issues of gender and sexuality.

Barker, Chris (2000) *Cultural Studies: Theory and Practice*. London: Sage. Chapter three is a highly accessible introduction to the difficult set of theoretical possibilities and problems associated with signifying practices. Barker also includes useful short sections on race, ethnicity, hybridity, national identity, feminism and difference. This is a useful book to dip into to clarify ideas.

Dollimore, Jonathan (1991) *Sexual Dissidence: Augustine to Wilde, Freud to Foucault*. Oxford: Clarendon Press. This is a classic study of how homosexuality has been constructed in Western societies and would also serve as an illustration of how theory may be put into practice. Although this is a difficult book for a beginner (and especially if your first language isn't English) it would repay close reading and illuminate how concepts like homophobia, sexual difference, camp, perversion and sexual transgression might be used in practice. A useful section of this study is printed in Munns and Rajan (1995), below.

Dyer, Richard (ed.) (1984) *Gays and Film* (2nd edition). New York: Zoetrope. This collection provides a rich source of critical insights into gay cinema and includes Dyer's critique of stereotypes mentioned by Smelik in the last practice section.

Hall, Stuart (1996a and 1996b see references above). These essays are much broader than my introduction may suggest and are well worth reading in great detail. It is also worth looking at Hall's 'Cultural Identity and Cinematic Representation', in Stam & Miller (2000).

Munns, Jessica and Rajan, Gita (eds) *A Cultural Studies Reader: History, Theory, Practice*. London: Longman. This reader has sections on Race Studies and Gender Studies and includes useful overviews of the areas. You might use the index to see how different authors use some of the concepts outlined in this chapter.

Stam, Robert and Miller, Toby (eds) (2000). *Film and Theory: An Anthology*. Oxford: Blackwell. A very useful reader which includes Hall's 'Cultural Identity and Cinematic Representation' (see References, above) and many contributions that touch on themes of race, social class, sexuality and race.

Woodward, Kathryn (ed.) (1997) *Identity and Difference*. London: Sage. This book looks at how concepts of identity and difference relate to the body, health and eating disorders, sexualities, motherhood and diaspora. This would be an excellent way of getting a more profound idea of how important these concepts are to cultural studies.

# PART V

## Honing Your Skills, Conclusions and 'Begin-endings'

# Consolidating Practice, Heuristic Thinking, Creative Cri-tickle Acts and Further Research

## Introduction

If you've got this far you've crossed the threshold of the fifth and final section of the book entitled 'Honing your Skills, Conclusions and "Begin-endings"'. Using creative critical techniques, I will offer a very brief résumé of the book and discuss ways of consolidating practice skills by considering the integration and development of models of analysis. Apart from reflecting on the identity of 'culture' and 'cultural studies', I will also consider the uses of creative criticism, comment on what's been omitted from this book, and offer advice on further reading and further research. Through scrambling up names, this chapter is designed to activate your memory and, through significant gaps, motivate you to think through its content in an active way.

### *MAIN LEARNING GOALS*

- To appreciate how cultural studies has evolved and how this complicates definitions of it.
- To understand how practice might be consolidated through integrating heuristic thinking and creative criticism.
- To see how these approaches can play a role in understanding sources, expressing ideas, and aid memory and learning.
- To become aware of some additional possibilities for further study and the further development of practical skills.

## Begin-ending 1 Summing up

In order to begin the work of consolidation, this first section will be made up of a conversation between Ivadd and Lawton and various writers whose work has been discussed. This is designed to summarize, in a very broad way, some of the important themes and general contours of the book. Here at the end, we will return to the beginning. The speakers will go back to the general conclusions from the chapter on Arnold to reflect on how they can be used to think about some of the ways in which cultural studies has developed. You'll notice that they are suffering from selective amnesia: the only writer's name remembered accurately is Matthew Arnold's. You'll also see that this amnesia has affected me in my spelling of my dramatis personae. If you cannot guess who a writer is from the ideas expressed, you need to go back and re-read the necessary sections. Just in case you need help recognizing a writer, the surnames are expressed in simple anagrams: these will unlock who the ideas belong to.

IVADD: Well, we've come a long way since the early chapters and it's time to sum up. I think an effective way might be to return to the end of chapter one where we described Arnold's importance in methodological terms and use it as a starting point to outline some of the ways cultural analysis has developed.

LAWTON: Yes, we emphasized there that, like so many cultural theorists, he was concerned with **the definition of culture**. This is something which has been of fundamental importance. As the definitions got wider then so did the possibilities for analysis.

IVADD: Arnold's idea of culture, while establishing a major way in which culture has been understood and discussed, has been seen as too restricted. The Aviseles, while condemning mass urban culture, at least discussed it, thereby opening up a space for discussion known as the Culture and Civilization debate. El Tío, while committed to the minority culture associated with Arnold and the Aviseles, helped to broaden the definition to include the culture of everyday life, and even cheese! In this he reflected the anthropological approach associated with the social sciences.

LAWTON: Then there was Nodora and his distinction between 'authentic' culture and the culture produced by the culture industry. Art Ghog saw working-class culture as meaningful (before the 1930s, that is) then there was ... Well, rather than rehearse all those arguments again here perhaps readers might want to go back and consider how each definition of culture has helped to open up new possibilities for cultural analysis and understanding.

ARNOLD: I see you noticed that my approach to the definition of culture couldn't be divorced from bringing about positive change. I also observed that you made the assertion that **cultural studies tends to share a sense of having a 'mission'**. I quite agree! But some of your writers had missions very different from my own. Just take Sill Wami, he wrote about cultural change in terms of a long revolution towards greater democracy and freedoms! That could hardly be more distant from my view.

IVADD: Quite! And look at Sam Gric's hegemony theory! It has, in the hands of critics like Lhal, helped to emphasize that one very important aspect of cultural studies is that not only could it be politically *informed* but could be linked to political *action*. This was the point of Folow's *Three Guineas*: the principal aim of the feminist tradition being to bring about social and political changes – interpretation, in itself, simply isn't enough.

LAWTON: Yes, the general point of being sensitive to questions of gender, class, race, ethnicity and sexuality is that in all these areas it is possible to expose forms of injustice, repression or marginalization. The assumption is that criticism just might make a difference. Remember we saw that what makes cultural studies attractive to many people is that there's the possibility of not only analysing the world but being involved in efforts to change it. And here I think I hear an echo of Karl Xarm! Readers might read through the chapters again to re-explore the idea of criticism with a mission.

LAWRENCE GROSSBERG: I'm glad you emphasize this because I believe that 'intellectual work matters, that it is a vital component of the struggle to change the world and to make the world more humane, and that cultural studies, as a particular project, a particular sort of intellectual practice, has something to contribute. Cultural studies also matters!' (Grossberg, 2006: 2).

IVADD: Remember how we argued that Arnold stressed **the importance of being able to recognize the relative value of different kinds of culture**? This was so that an informed minority could decide which cultural products make a positive contribution to society.

NODORA: While I entirely disagree with Arnold's politics, much of what he said about the value of artistic creation has to be taken very seriously. However, whereas Arnold *feared* the working classes; I *feared for* the working classes. Arnold was worried that political activism would result in anarchy; culture would help to subdue rebellion – that was part of its value. I feared that mass culture would stifle political activism; mass culture was achieving what Arnold thought high culture would achieve – the pacification of the masses!

ART GHOG: However, I tried to show that the cultural practices of working-class communities were full of meaning and were legitimate objects for cultural analysis.

SILL WAMI: Quite true, but if you showed a great appreciation of pre-1930s working-class culture and helped us to understand its value for those communities, you tended to valorize newer cultural tendencies in much the same terms as the Aviseles.

ART GHOG: How right you are. All that rock 'n' roll music! And those milk bars! What noise! What triviality! But one has to recognize the great contribution that works like your *The Long Revolution* made to how culture could be conceptualized and understood. Also, you did much to broaden our approaches to cultural analysis with your distinctions between culture as ideal, documentary and social, with your keywords, your structure of feeling and your magic formulas etc.

SILL WAMI: Thank you, and yet we saw that, for all his shortcomings, Arnold's version of cultural criticism included a broad analysis of different classes in society. He also showed an awareness of historical conditions and tensions between different classes, which I see as so important.

IVADD: Our readers might remember Moth Pons' contribution in this respect. For Arnold working-class demands for equality and representation were a threat to the healthy State; for Moth Pons the State could not be healthy unless it incorporated these demands. Arnold would have class struggle erased from history; Moth Pons made class struggle an essential part, and condition, of it. Dissent, then, was fundamental to a proper definition of working-class culture. Our heuristics have all emphasized the importance of considering historical contexts and we have tried to practise what we preach by showing how the ideas of many of the writers we have introduced can be illuminated by the historical contexts in which they lived. Again, readers might reflect on the general importance of a sense of history with relation to the different chapters.

LAWTON: We also saw, when reviewing Arnold's contribution, that **cultural criticism included the idea of resistance and that it could not be divorced from politics**.

IVADD: Resistance is a key term for many of the writers we have reviewed but it functions in very different ways. Despite differences in terms of politics and ways of understanding culture, we called the Aviseles, Nodora and El Tío 'high cultural gladiators', I wonder if readers can remember why. Then we saw how Art Ghog introduced the idea that the working classes were not simple dupes but adapted cultural forms to their own needs and tastes and thereby put up some resistance.

LAWTON: The idea of working-class defiance, however, really becomes dominant in Moth Pons work, which is full of stories of the bravery and resistance of men and women who risked their lives to promote the interests of working-class communities. While the spirit of resistance is very much alive in Sill Wami's work it comes into prominence again when we look at the writers influenced by Sam Gric. Lhal co-edited a book called *Resistance through Rituals*, and I wonder if our readers can remember how the idea of resistance was mobilized with relation to youth subcultures?

IVADD: I also wonder if they can remember how Sam Gric's notion of hegemony as resistance related to Lhal's definition of popular culture?

LAWTON: And this brings me to the idea that different ideas of resistance reflect distinct forms of politics. Arnold's politics can be found in how his notion of culture relates to the good society and the State. Culture is the antidote to anarchy: in his model there is no room for working-class resistance, quite the contrary. Resistance is a question of cultural' elites combating the forces of barbarism. Similar ideas are found in the work of the Aviseles and El Tío, who can also be seen to be elitist in their support of the role of enlightened minorities who put themselves above the masses and establish and preserve what they regard as possessing particularly significant cultural value. Although Arnold thought himself above class, we can see that his notion of culture tends to stifle political demands that come from the working classes. Change can only come from the classes already in power.

IVADD: As mentioned above, we also saw that political resistance was a key factor in Moth Pons' work, and the class basis of cultural forms and the importance of social and political rights is fundamental to the way Sill Wami understood culture. Or, take the work of Althusser, concepts like 'interpellation', the 'problematic' and 'symptomatic reading' help to read the surface of things and then examine the gaps and silences which reveal hidden ideological structures. And this leads us to repressive structures and subordination: in short – politics! Look at Nodora, Lhal, Sam Gric and Folow, at all those interested in subcultures and marginalized communities – they can all be said to practise highly politicized forms of cultural analysis.

### **short** practice exercise

This is just one way of tracing paths through this book. Pause for a moment to see if you can think of others. What might these multiple paths suggest about the work of writing history and the writing of this book?

## Begin-ending 2 Consolidating practice: heuristic thinking and integrating models of analysis

Here our two speakers are replaced by Vidal and Tandow, who will sum up the heuristic approaches to practice and comment on how they maybe integrated, adapted and extended. In section three, they will reflect upon the identity of culture and cultural studies. They are not suffering from amnesia.

VIDAL: If you look at the general shape of this book, you'll see that the early chapters outline a number of important themes that would be extended or questioned by later critics. Thus, the themes explored in the Culture and Civilization tradition gradually give way to the approaches associated with the writers listed under Culturalism. The practice sections in these early chapters are designed to get you to take these ideas seriously but also to think about them critically. However, with the introduction of Adorno's ideas heuristic thinking was introduced.

TANDOW: As you saw, these heuristics are designed to help you learn and as a tool for generating ideas by asking specific questions as well as serving as an aid to thinking, independent thought, interpretation, analysis and research. They have also been designed to help you to structure your thoughts and experiment with ideas. By now we hope you have developed a certain interpretive independence and that you feel encouraged to think things through before examining what others have written. In short, you should now feel confident to *practise* simple forms of cultural studies for yourself. Here we would like to suggest further ways you might develop your heuristic thinking.

VIDAL: You may have noticed that the later heuristic devices incorporate ideas from earlier ones. However, not all the possible combinations have been explored. As suggested in the last chapter, it is possible to adapt concepts used in any of the heuristics to see how they might produce useful ideas for new contexts. We also saw how you can use a source, like Woolf's *Three Guineas* (which doesn't have much to say about method), and read it with the aim of developing a series of ideas which can be used in heuristic form. Any essay or book or article, even if it does not address the question of method, can be assessed for its heuristic possibilities. Notice how *East is East* was interpreted using the heuristic but actually helped to generate further ideas itself.

IVADD: The idea that's being put forward here, then, is that *you* can be the ruler of your own heuristic thinking. Up to now you have been encouraged to experiment with heuristic forms that have been designed for you. We hope this has helped you become more aware that interpretations and analyses are dependent on *ways of looking*. From now on you should be in a position to start making choices about which concepts and methods will best suit your own projects so that you can hone your own methodological skills. This will be greatly assisted by any further reading you do. Here we insist on the three 'Es': the hope is that this book will have encouraged you to experiment, explore and evaluate ideas, rather than just read about them and move on. As suggested in the introduction, if you do not live in Britain, or you do not intend to analyse British culture, you will need to adapt the concepts to the appropriate cultural contexts of your study.

LAWTON: This book will have served its purpose if you can use it, learn from it, be motivated to experiment with the ideas developed within it and, in the long term, grow out of it. This movement towards independence was symbolized in the chapter on Williams when Ladvi helped Vidal but encouraged him to take things into his own hands. Now we shall move onto some reflections on the identity of cultural studies.

## Begin-ending 3 Defining culture and cultural studies

### Learning from Gollum: the importance of recognizing plurality and difference

VIDAL: At the beginning of this book it was stated that general definitions of 'culture' and the identity of 'cultural studies', would be left to one side. The approach adopted here has been to assume readers would get a gradual idea of how these might be understood by being exposed to some of the most important contributors to the area and encouraged to experiment with a number of important concepts and strategies.

TANDOW: So, to begin the general question of what cultural studies or culture *is* (can be, or has been), it is necessary to take into account the institutional contexts in which cultural studies has come to be recognized. It is common to assume, when speaking of culture and cultural studies, that these phenomena exist prior to analysis, however, we hope that this book has helped to show that when words like cultural studies or culture are used they aren't 'fixed categories'.

VIDAL: This means that at any one moment there may be considerable disagreement about what constitutes the subject of study, or how the objects chosen should be analysed. Within educational institutions, there are hegemonic forces at work which establish dominant ways of looking (aided and abetted by publications like this one!). These factors influence not only *how* things are understood in terms of the concepts that are used to produce knowledge but also help to complicate the question of the identity of cultural studies. From this we might learn from the typical speech patterns of J.R.R. Tolkien's schizophrenic creature, Gollum, from *The Lord of the Rings* (1954–55). As Gollum habitually stutters and adds the letter 's' to many words, we can imagine the subtitle of this section being spat out of his mouth as 'Identitititifying 'cultures's's's' and 'cultural studies's's's'.

TANDOW: I presume here that you are using the term schizophrenic in the informal sense of a subject that *appears* to be divided in itself or may be motivated by contradictory or conflicting principles?

VIDAL: Of course! As I hope is clear from the previous chapters, contemporary approaches to identity tend to emphasize plurality and difference. In this sense, it is useful and instructive to see all phenomena through Gollum's eyes: in Gollum's mouth 'identifying' isn't a smooth, uncomplicated process – it trips over itself. 'Culture', as 'cultrures's's's', is no longer a singular noun: it breaks down into pluralities; as does 'cultural studies's's's' – the very form and sound of the words suggest division, and further divisions. Now, whereas Gollum might be diagnosed as psychotic, in the world of contemporary cultural analysis, the *conscious* refusal to see things in a simple, undifferentiated way is regarded as both healthy and desirable. Why? As I hope this book has demonstrated, this tendency helps us to see the world in much more intellectually complex and challenging ways. You might turn back to the last chapter and look at the way the notion of difference helps to achieve this more complex way of looking.

TANDOW: What is now called cultural studies, then, has as its subject culture but neither 'culture' or 'cultural studies' is, as emphasized earlier, a 'fixed category': that is to say, it is possible to offer definitions of 'culture' and 'cultural studies' but we cannot expect them to be like indestructible figures carved out of stone. Like other concepts and academic subjects, these will be subject to change, transformation and evolution.

VIDAL: Other aspects which tend to complicate fixing identity are concerned with what can be called *synchronic* and *diachronic* factors.

## **help** FILE: synchronic versus diachronic approaches

- A *synchronic* analysis tends to ignore longer historical transformations in order to concentrate on a specific period of time. So, if it's possible to focus on particular stages of development, then it is possible that the identity of something will alter not only with relation to *how* we look but *when* we look.
- A *diachronic* approach has to take into account longer historical transformations which demands that the specific findings of a *synchronic* approach are appreciated with relation to a wider chronological view. One way of understanding the two mutually correcting strategies is to see one like a detailed photo' which is a close-up, made possible by a powerful zoom, and the other like a wide-angle lens that takes in as much of the landscape as possible.

You might think about how these approaches could relate to planning your own projects.

TANDOW: To put these concepts into the immediate context of this book, the two approaches have been combined. The *diachronic* approach is like the individual chapters which

Figure 14.1 In Gollum's mouth identifying isn't a smooth, uncomplicated process

tend to focus on a particular moment of cultural studies and shows how different themes and concepts have been introduced and handled. However, if we step back from the individual chapters and view them together we have the *synchronic* view which gives *a sense* of historical development and change.

VIDAL: Of course, when taking photos, all manner of lenses, filters and film types are available and not every photographer will focus on the same area of landscape, or agree on how the image is to be constructed. Again, this affects the 'identity' of the things that are to be represented. This may be further complicated by the fact that, although different photographers may appear to be looking at the 'same' landscape, the results of their work may appear radically different.

TANDOW: For the purposes of this book, it should be emphasized that the *image* of cultural studies that is conveyed here (or in any study) is the product of:

- choices about what to put in and what to leave out
- preferences about what to foreground (focus on) and what to leave in the background
- how the materials made visible are structured and interpreted.

VIDAL: Thus, the sense of historical narrative constructed in these pages (or any book) will always be open to question and revision. As this book has tried to demonstrate, cultural studies is characterized as being multidisciplinary and draws on many theoretical perspectives to offer interpretations of cultural phenomena, and this makes the task of defining it particularly difficult. This difficulty also extends to the definition of 'culture'.

## Some notes on institutional consolidation: from identifying to 'Identity-defying' culture and cultural studies

TANDOW: So, the possibilities for the definition of culture within cultural analysis are enormous and many books have traced the institutional fortunes of the concept, see particularly, Jenks (1993), Turner (1996), Tudor (1999), Barker (2000) and Hartley (2003). Also, there are many academic subject areas which have an interest in 'cultural factors' and have developed their own responses to what constitutes culture and how it is to be analysed and understood. This book has only been able to hint at some of the links with approaches associated with the social sciences. However, if you are curious about other approaches you can consult the bibliographies of further reading and further research that conclude this chapter.

VIDAL: It might also be noted here that there isn't always a very clear line between disciplines or areas, especially where cultural studies is concerned, because one of its features is that it is inter-disciplinary. A good example of this uncertainty is to look at *who* new books are aimed at. For example, on the back of the dust jacket of Elaine Baldwin's *Introducing Cultural Studies* (Baldwin et al., 2004) you will find the following (not unusual) comment: '*Introducing Cultural Studies* provides undergraduates and postgraduates in a variety of disciplines – including Cultural Studies, English, Geography, Sociology, Social Studies, Communication and Media Studies – with a clear and comprehensible introduction to the field.' Apart from those subjects mentioned on the dust jacket other academic areas where the concept of culture has been elaborated are: Anthropology, Literary Criticism (including studies dedicated to Feminism, the Post-colonial, Gender Studies, Gay and Lesbian Studies), Language, Linguistics, History, Philosophy, Business Studies, Film Studies and Translation Studies – and this by no means exhausts all the areas in which meanings of the concept of culture are negotiated and deployed.

TANDOW: In these pages cultural studies has been referred to as 'an area'; however, it might be more effective to see it as a *space* in which a very diverse set of analytical practices take place. In a loose sense, this also involves the idea of it as a discipline, or more accurately, as a set of disciplines, in so far that whatever constitutes cultural studies in the academic context is part of a set of programmes of instruction and learning. These programmes involve forms of intellectual training, and it is one of the main aims of this book to help you to start that training.

VIDAL: The more or less accepted 'official' (i.e. often repeated) history of the origins or rise of cultural studies is that it developed out of a number of key studies that came out of Britain in the late 1950s and early 1960s: that is, the work associated with

Richard Hoggart, E.P. Thompson and Raymond Williams. It was then developed in institutions like the Birmingham Centre for Contemporary Cultural Studies and in other parts of the world, particularly the United States and Australia. This is the story of cultural studies that informs this book.

TANDOW: However, while it is hard to deny that the writers just mentioned are of great importance to the development of the forms of cultural analysis that have coalesced into 'cultural studies' (and for that reason are explored in this book), the origin of cultural studies is now being seen in terms of 'multiple births' with relation to distinct areas of practice around the world. For example, both African and South Asian scholars have pointed out the importance of their own traditions of analysis (Jordan in Walton and Scheu, 2002: 147f.), Australian practitioners are not always content with the Anglo-centric model (Frow and Morris, 1993), and even the Hoggart-Thompson-Williams model has been questioned (Tudor, 1999: 20f.).

## Oversimplification

**W A R N I N G**

Even if we only limit ourselves to the rise of British cultural studies, there are many writers who might be included in the tradition (like Virginia Woolf) but who are usually excluded. Chris Jenks has pointed out that there are many neglected antecedents to British cultural studies in the shape of writers like Charles Dickens, George Orwell, Henry Mayhew, Jack London, Walter Besant, Henry James, Friedrich Engels, William Foot Whyte, the neo-Chicago school and many more who 'gave voice to the outcast and inarticulate culture of a working class delineated and ghettoized morally, politically, economically, and even geographically and architecturally' (Jenks, 1993: 156–7).

VIDAL: Because of the kinds of problems discussed above, cultural studies is often written in lower case (even in Britain, the USA and Australia where it is much more fully established) to divest the area of fully-fledged, unproblematic capital-letter identity. This has reinforced the idea of it as an 'antidiscipline':

JOHN FROW: 'Cultural studies has always defined itself as an antidiscipline, and, even if we take this with a grain of salt, as a self-validating claim, it remains true that it doesn't have the sort of secure definition of its object that would give it the thematic coherence and the sense of a progressive accumulation of knowledge that most established disciplines see, rightly or wrongly, as underlying their claim to produce and to control valid knowledges. Cultural studies exists in a state of productive uncertainty about its status as a discipline' (1995: 7). If you want to read more on this check out my article 'Discipline and Discipleship' (1988: 307–23).

TANDOW: So, the difficulty of defining 'culture' and that elusive domain called 'cultural studies' can leave the beginner in a state of bewilderment about:

- what the area's status is as a form of knowledge
- what exactly its objects of analysis are
- whether or not it's possible to reduce it to a set of theoretically ordered practices.

However, if you see yourself as a budding cultural critic you need not throw your arms up in despair and abandon the area as a lost cause. There are three main reasons that can be given for this:

1. Whatever the disagreements about what culture may mean or what cultural studies is, as Frow has observed, there has been an institutional consolidation of the subject area (Frow, 1995: 7). That is, there is sufficient agreement among groups of what might be called, following literary theorists like Stanely Fish (1980), *interpretive communities* who willingly group themselves under the label 'cultural studies'. However, I'm not using this term in exactly the same way that Fish uses it because he tends to see the composition of interpretive communities as fixed (his main point of reference is Literary Studies). What I'm arguing here is that in cultural studies there is more of a sense of practitioners 'positioning' themselves or aligning themselves with relation to the area. This makes the community more negotiated or provisional.
2. As the psychologist Jean Piaget has written, mathematicians do not need to define the concept of number or space, any more than the biologist is required to explain the nature of life, before beginning work (1972: 68). It would be unfair to ask cultural studies to be more coherent or assume that lack of agreement rendered its analyses, interpretations and findings useless.
3. It is probably rarer to find an institutionalized subject area in the Humanities that is *not* riven by conceptual and methodological disputes. These disputes may, in fact, be seen to be the life-blood of a discipline, or provide the necessary dynamic for a discipline's continued development.

VIDAL: So, the implications of the approach adopted here to the definition of culture and cultural studies is to make a virtue of the complexity of the terms and build self-aware discussion of them into forms of practice.

TANDOW: Because of the extent of possible definitions of culture and the complexity of the range of studies that have been offered as forms of cultural studies, it could be said that while it's possible to identify forms of culture and make a case for a coherent, evolutionary set of practices that have cohered into cultural studies, it would be as easy to speak of *'identity-defying' culture and cultural studies.*

VIDAL: Thus, our author, faced with writing an introductory volume of modest length, has tried to construct, openly and self-consciously, a pedagogically useful version of cultural studies that he feels will provide a starting point for further study and development. To conclude this brief meditation on identity, let's refer to a recent animated film to bring out a series of further points about identity which might help to develop a particular 'attitude' towards intellectual work.

## Making yourself an ass: *Shrek* and the value of the multi-layered model of identity

TANDOW: In the Dreamworks' film *Shrek* (2001), the eponymous (anti)hero, describes himself to others as an ogre. In doing so he deliberately stereotypes himself as others see him in order to preserve a sense of privacy. That is, he perpetuates the fiction of the ogre as violent, inhuman beast – merely to keep others at a distance. This blurring of appearance and reality, where things are not what they seem at first glance, is constantly repeated in this narrative that both uses and challenges the conventions of the (Disneyfied) fairy tale: an ogre is far from the violent inhuman monster he's taken to be; the beautiful Princess Fiona is hiding the secret that she's an ogre; a fire-breathing dragon is capable of romantic love etc. The film can be seen as challenging in so far that it doesn't allow the viewer to accept things at face value. One of the things that this book has tried to stress is that what *Shrek* seems to require of the viewer is also something that is required of the cultural critic. You might go back to the chapters on ideology and hegemony to revise these aspects of the book.

VIDAL: There is one being in *Shrek* who does not allow himself to be overwhelmed by the convenient, fairy-tale myth of the ogre. This is Donkey, the loquacious, irritating ass. One of the reasons Shrek finds him so annoying is that he is forever rehearsing ideas, giving opinions, and trying to peep over the wall Shrek has constructed to protect his inner self from the outside world. Once Shrek has taken Donkey into his confidence, he tries to do justice to what he sees as the complexity of his identity. He chooses to describe himself as an onion because he sees himself as 'multilayered' – he looks like a monster to others but, although very down to earth, is a being capable of gentleness, love and sensibility.

TANDOW: This, albeit clichéd, image of identity as an onion, which is made up of multiple layers, is a useful metaphor when trying to define difficult concepts like culture, or understand cultural phenomena. This is because it makes us realize, like Shrek, that the simple façade of a concept, thing or process is only a convenient cover that requires a critical effort on our part to see it as a multiple-layered phenomenon. In a way we could say that the task of the cultural critic is that of the enquiring ass: we should look beyond obvious external images to attempt to appreciate the complexity of things.

VIDAL: So, the critic as 'ass' takes the onion of cultural phenomena and peels away the layers as carefully as possible. There are, incidentally, a number of approaches to culture which use the multi-layer model (Hofstede, 1991; Trompenaars, 1993) where culture is seen as being made up of fixed levels. Here, however, I am applying the idea not to fixed levels but to a general understanding of cultural forms. Where my usage coincides with theirs is in distinguishing between the visible and that which is hidden from immediate view. Another important point I'd like to make here is that Shrek's identity is, to use a common word used in cultural analysis, 'negotiated': that is, it only makes sense with relation to the community in which he lives. At the beginning of the film Shrek is able to preserve his privacy by exploiting the stereotypical identity that is imposed on him from outside: the men from the nearby village live in awe of him partly because they are victims of their own stereotypical thinking.

Figure 14.3 The critic as 'ass'

Later they have to revise this. Identity, from this point of view is constantly open to negotiation – Donkey, and later Princess Fiona, see him in other terms and, thus, identity is not self-enclosed but dynamic. This is something that was emphasized in the chapter on Williams and you might go back to it to revise this idea.

TANDOW: One conclusion that you may draw from this is that, having peeled away all the layers, there is nothing left inside – which ultimately suggests that there may be no fixed essence at the centre of things, a conclusion which Trompenaars and Hofstede do not consider and which Shrek conspicuously avoids. Again, this is a useful symbol given that much contemporary cultural criticism questions things as 'fixed categories' (as we saw above). Sometimes this way of thinking makes students feel discouraged because, after so much mental effort, they aren't left with much of a sense of certainty – there's the unsettling sensation that there doesn't seem to be anything at the centre of things. However, we can avoid this disheartening feeling if we remember Frow's point about institutional consolidation and that it is in the constant questioning of phenomena that the value of cultural analysis can be found. One way of representing cultural studies, then, is to see it as a knowledge-producing set of practices or strategies which, rather than search for certainties, produces knowledge and diverse forms of understanding which are constantly open to further questioning.

## Cultural studies: some basic assumptions

VIDAL: As a conclusion to this section here is a list of attributes that characterize some of the principal assumptions behind the *version* of contemporary cultural studies presented in this book:

- Contemporary cultural studies defines culture in very broad terms and is multidisciplinary in approach. It takes concepts and ideas from many fields of research, adapting them to its needs. In books dedicated to cultural analysis you will find everything from Punk, pubs and Pavarotti to game shows, Greta Garbo and gangland violence. This often blurs the boundaries between cultural studies and other knowledge-producing domains like Sociology, Communications, Film Studies, Literary Studies, Ethnology and Anthropology etc.
- As we have seen, it *generally* challenges definitions which downgrade the products of urban mass culture and argue that only High art or traditional folkloric forms of culture are of intrinsic value. As Chris Jenks has emphasized, culture 'cannot be viewed as a unifying principle, a source of shared understanding or a mechanism for legitimating the social bond'. This point is taken from Chris Jenks (1993: 157–8) who put together another list based on another inventory by B. Agger. Some of my points resemble Jenks' hybrid list but I have completely re-framed them.
- Cultural studies *politicizes* all aspects of culture (popular, or otherwise) and does not assume that popular mass forms of culture are meaningless, dehumanizing and debased. Working-class forms of consciousness and ways of life are taken seriously and not treated as inferior to those of other classes or social-intellectual elites, and great emphasis is put on the analysis, interpretation and understanding of popular culture.
- While the rhetorical power of the media and advertising is recognized, the working classes are not assumed to be the passive victims of commerce. They are generally considered to be actively involved in creating, adapting and resisting cultural forms.
- The politics of contemporary cultural studies generally leans towards the political left, especially given that Marxist forms of thinking have been of fundamental importance to its ways of seeing. The work of Antonio Gramsci on hegemony is of particular relevance (especially to British cultural studies). However, its politics cannot be restricted to revolutionary communism and would be better described as post-Marxist, given that Marxist thought is fundamental to its forms of critique but is complicated through revision and fusion with other theoretical trends.
- The proponents of cultural studies generally try to be aware of the theoretical implications of their work and avoid presenting their analyses, findings and interpretations as 'objective' or beyond question. There is wide-spread recognition that one's own position (in terms of factors like class, gender, race, ethnicity, sexuality etc.) influences all kinds of academic research. One's own cultural context, education and ideological leanings must always be recognized as important factors in the production of knowledge or meanings.
- As emphasized above with relation to *Shrek*, neither cultural studies nor culture should be viewed as static. Culture is never already 'there', it is the product of ways of looking

and bound up with dynamic processes which are continually challenging critics to expand their conceptual horizons.

- Cultural studies is particularly interested in the way groups of people behave, think about, adapt to, and experience the world around them. Questions of representation, resistance, ideology and the way culture is related to politics and power could be said to be part of the staple diet of the cultural critic.
- Cultural studies is not only interested in identity and representation but investigates the material and ideological contexts of production, distribution, consumption and reception.
- These contexts can be seen as the 'circuits' of culture (du Gay et al., 1997: 3f.) and these will be intimately related to how members of particular groups interpret and understand the 'worlds' they live in and how they interact with one another, and members of other groups. This involves not only using concepts and methods to interpret the world but trying to understand how meanings are available to, or are made by, groups and individuals within distinct social groups.
- To adapt and modernize a passage from Clifford Geertz, the concept of culture within sociology and cultural studies is often regarded as *semiotic*. This relates to the idea of *signification* that we explored in the last two chapters and assumes that culture cannot be fully understood without taking into account the importance of signs and symbols. From this point of view groups of people have to be seen with relation to complex 'webs of significance' which they themselves have spun (Geertz, 1973: 5) or, to bring Geertz's valuable notion more up to date, which they may inherit, negotiate, challenge, resist, adapt, make, re-make or surpass.
- Certain themes and approaches have become so dominant that to leave them out would lead to the question of whether the study in question could be considered a 'cultural studies approach': e.g. themes like, gender, sexuality, race, class, frontier, diaspora, ideology, high verses mass, low, or popular culture.
- The theoretical, thematic and conceptual limits of cultural studies are dynamic and thus subject to constant (re)negotiation.
- Cultural studies practitioners generally adhere to Marx's maxim that 'The philosophers have only interpreted the world, in various ways; the point is to change it'.

**practice** EXERCISE

Some of these characteristics have been explored more fully than others. Which assertions do you think are backed up by the content of this book? Which ideas do you feel need to be explored further?

## Begin-ending 4 The creative 'critickle' approach

The aim of this section is to help consolidate the creative critical facets of this book. Here is a conversation between Vidal and Tandow, Daliv and Downat (and a few miscellaneous 'others'), and a number of writers who can be said to have used creative criticism, or theorized it, in different ways.

VIRGINIA WOOLF: You can see how the author of this book draws on my *Three Guineas*, which can be seen as an example of creative criticism. Although the form is governed by responses to imaginary petitions, the content is very much 'of this world'.

PLATO: Firstly, I don't think our author can be said to be exactly original in his use of what he calls creative criticism. I am known as one of the greatest philosophers in the tradition of Western thought and yet it might surprise some readers that I put forward many of my ideas in the form of dialogues. I believe this is a very effective way of communicating difficult ideas.

AUTHOR: Thank you for pointing out my lack of originality!

OSCAR WILDE: Who cares about originality? Only the unoriginal. I believe I perfected the art of the critical essay as dialogue in works like 'The Decay of Lying' and the 'Critic as Artist' (Wilde, 1978) – I think you'll find considerably more wit in these than in Plato and in the book you are now reading.

JEAN-FRANÇOIS LYOTARD: But don't forget my *Just Gaming* (1985) a long theoretical dialogue very much in the Platonic tradition, but only in terms of form …

VIDAL: Thank you. What I wanted to say was the idea of the 'creative' in the 'creative critickle' is that the dominant conventions of critical, intellectual work can be combined with creative techniques associated with literary (and other) forms. Although it's not our intention to get into this debate here, it is possible to challenge the simple opposition between creative and critical work.

DAVID LODGE: (interrupting) I agree and I think you might find some of my novels, like *Changing Places* (1978), *Small World* (1985) and *Nice Work* (1989), play around with the conventions of the novel and academic writing. Take Jostein Gaarder's *Sophie's World* (1996), is it a novel that introduces philosophy, or an introduction to philosophy in novel form?

TANDOW: Thank you. Now, the idea of the 'tickle' in the 'creative critickle' is that the preparation and writing of academic essays does not have to be a boring, painful exercise. The argument here is that you can develop your interpretive and analytical skills – and have fun! For example, imagine you are reading a difficult text and can't seem to make sense of it. One possibility is to imagine someone has asked you to give them some help with it. You can then write a dialogue using the parts of your name or anagrams of it etc. to try to make sense of what you are reading (you might also try a letter to a friend or an imaginary person etc.). Criticism, then, can be an enjoyable as well as an enriching experience. Read 'critickly': if you don't understand something adopt a creative critical attitude – asking yourself, what does this mean? Does it make sense? Could I help myself to understand it by imagining a dialogue where someone is asking me to make sense of it for them?

VIDAL: This technique can also be used to develop your ideas. How many times have you done your background reading and found yourself in front of a blank sheet of paper, vainly hoping that you'll be inspired to write an essay or project? One possibility is to stare into open space hoping everything, by some miracle, will eventually make sense, another is to adopt the creative critickle approach – find a form to help you start: write a letter, an exchange of e-mails, a dialogue, a song, even a video game, a short story, or a script for a TV play – whatever comes to mind. Just choose a form and start writing. If you think your tutors will not accept your ideas in this format, later you can rewrite your ideas cutting out all the colloquialisms and signs of the literary, TV or song form etc. to conform to the demands of standard essay writing. Some students we know once wrote an essay based on Harold Pinter's play *The Birthday Party*. They used a number of relations between characters to provide a framework for understanding George W. Bush's military policies and relations with Europe and the Arab world.

TANDOW: This approach goes beyond the simple dialogue, but the dialogue, as Plato discovered, offers a very effective way of creating a dialectical approach to writing. What this means is that you are encouraged to take account of two sides of an argument (or several approaches at once). The group conversation or dialogue is a very useful tool when trying to compare writers or ideas. You'll also find that the dialogue can help you to create argumentative flow. You might look back at earlier chapters to see where and how this has been done. Remember the rap in the chapter on Adorno? You may find that imposing a form on your ideas actually creates new ideas. Being forced to find a word to a rhyme with another just might suggest something you hadn't thought of.

VIDAL: Thus, we hope that this book will not only serve to suggest these techniques to you but show how this might work *in practice*. The hope is that you will be motivated to try some of these techniques for yourselves. Actually, as stated in the introduction, this book has been conceived as a metaphor for cultural studies as a huge, continuing dialogue.

TANDOW: However, it must be kept in mind that this dialogic approach *is a way of understanding* some of the important contributors to British cultural studies. It might give the impression that the history of British cultural studies is a set of smooth transitions from one author to the next – but this is largely an effect of structure and style (you might keep this in mind when reading any introduction).

DALIV: As outlined in the introduction, this book has also worked towards the combination of heuristic thinking with creative-critickle approaches. We hope to have shown that the combination of the two can be very effective, engaging, and fun. So, another way of tracing a path through this book would be to concentrate on the possibilities it illustrates for creative approaches or for heuristic thinking.

DOWNAT: You may have noticed another creative element and that is the use of plays on words. If you look back on the sections on E.P. Thompson and Virginia Woolf you'll see we used the phrase 'the Brutish Isles' for the British Isles. When writing, you might experiment with neologisms as an aid to creating concepts to help you think. You'll see that I've exploited punning more in this section to suggest how puns may relate to the themes that are explored.

GREGORY ULMER: The play on words, then, can help us to conceptualize. This is what I've called the 'puncept' and it might help us to develop a more open pedagogy which allows in things like 'the pleasure of surprise' (1985: 309). If you're interested in the further implications of this, follow up my work in the references.

ROBERT RAY: As I have said, critics might experiment with the common *forms* of criticism to challenge what counts as legitimate knowledge (Ray in Naremore and Brantlinger, 1991: 234–5).

DALIV: You might consider how the following puns may help you think. In the context of subjugation of minorities and national identity, you might write of *repress*enting marginalized communities or people and exploring their *indigNation.* A study tracing the importance of cultural memory to radical politics might explore the possibilities of *black to the future.* Imagine writing of *identdirty* politics; the violence of linguistic forms as *axepressions* of insulting language, or a history of the *war*king classes. What might vegetarian politics as social *meatamorphosis* or mobil phones as *space invaders* suggest? How might *conqueering* the gay world be applied to affirmative representations of the self within homosexual communities? Notice that in chapter nine in a section on practice I suggested the possibility of an ethnographic study on Hip Hop in one word: ethnogRAPhy. I developed the idea of the 'creative-critickle' in a chapter that I called 'Creative-critickle Acts and the Theo-heretical Magnidefying Glass: a Foolosophy of the Uncannyscious …' If you think about that title you'll see all kinds of playful and suggestive 'puncepts' (Walton and Scheu, 2002; see also Walton, 1998).

SIR GEST: A play on words
can be productive and fun;
it absorbs more meaning
– like a sPUNge.

WALTER REDFERN: Yes, the pun, 'like the contraceptive, is a labour-saving device' – 'two meanings for the price of one' (1984: 26).

DALIV: The question is, how far can you exploit these meanings or ambiguities for the sake of developing ideas? Again, how much you use these creative devices largely depends on whether or not they are acceptable to your tutors.

DOWNAT: These devices not only echo the themes being discussed but may serve, like the illustrations, as mnemonic devices. That is, because they are so striking, they can aid memory. For example, this chapter is organized around the idea of 'begin-ending' to draw attention to the preliminary character of this book; part of the last section played on the idea of identifying and *identity-defying.* To aid memory the two terms difficulty and cultures might have been fused into 'difficultures'. The simple drawing or cartoon may also be used as a mnemonic device. Imagine you had to remember the basic contents of this book. One thing you could do to map your way through is remember the cartoon illustrations – these can serve as little symbols of the themes and ideas discussed. Writing in the form of raps, songs or poems can also serve as mnemonic devices to help you memorize for tutorials or exams.

SIR GEST: If you find it hard to retain the ideas you have explored, you might find it useful to draw your own mnemonic cartoons – the more humorous and outrageous the better. José María Campoy Ruiz has given you some idea about how abstractions or ideas might be turned into humorous images. You might even invent outrageous lies or inaccuracies to generate ideas. The author of this book once started a class with the statement, 'Today I'm going to talk about one of the greatest British philosophers of all time – Plato'. The idea was not only to attract the listeners' attention but to explore the implications of the inaccuracy (that there is an important Platonic tradition of thinking in Britain which has 'written' Plato in very significant ways).

JOHN HARTLEY: (interrupting) I reckon if you want to see how playful language can aid academic writing within cultural studies you might look at some of my books like *The Politics of Pictures* (1992a), where you'll have to get your mind round things like 'Altering the book' (109) and 'Aesthletics' (136). You might also try my *Tele-ology* (1992b) and *Popular Reality* (1996).

## A note from Omission Control

MS REPRESENTATION: But enough of these plays on words and about what's *in* the book, to sum up we could ask, not so much what's included in it, but what's been left out!

DAVOID NOTLAW: I've tried to suggest that this book is far from fully representative by having writers complain about their exclusion or have them interrupt – techniques which suggest that much has been left in the margins. The idea behind this book, as outlined at the beginning, is that the exploration of a limited number of authors and ideas would be better than trying to introduce a lot of material but without reference to practice or detailed examples of it.

MS ADVENTURE: I notice that you hardly mention structuralist approaches to cultural analysis, or what's known as the postmodern.

DAVOID NOTLAW: I've not concentrated on these because I've tried to limit this book to ideas that I feel can be explained and practised by readers with no previous knowledge of cultural theory or cultural studies. I've given some hints on structuralism but see it, like postmodernism, as the next stage on. I think the chapters on ideology, hegemony and marginalization will have stretched my readers quite enough for an introduction. Structuralism and postmodernism will have to wait for another book! However, readers might look up these approaches in introductions like Storey (2001) or Strinati (1995) to get a basic idea of their importance. This brings me back to the idea of the begin-ending. Where should readers go from here?

## Begin-ending 5 Cultural criticism and further reading and further research

DAVOID NOTLAW: Given what has been left out and the huge range of themes and approaches available to cultural criticism, the motto of this chapter should be the cliché, 'this is not the end, it is just the beginning'. In this section I shall outline some possible ways forward.

WILL SHAKESPEARE: One might quote my play *The Tempest* and assert that 'What's past is prologue' (Act II, scene i).

DAVOID NOTLAW: Hey, who let *you* in? But yes, that's not a bad alternative motto for this begin-ending. Another one might be 'welcome to infinity'. If you've enjoyed this book, the good news is that there's much more to explore. If you've found it a bore, then I hope you'll choose another title from those that follow. In this final section I will recommend materials which I believe can help you to develop your knowledge, ideas and skills further. There are many publications available and this section cannot do more than scratch the surface. I have limited myself to recommending:

- some basic introductions which are wider in scope than this book
- some general readers which will help you to get a fuller idea of what other approaches are available
- studies to help further develop your practical skills, including some which introduce methods associated with the social sciences
- a short list of academic journals to give you an idea of the work scholars are producing at the moment
- a short list of websites which you may find useful

## Basic introductions to cultural studies

There are many introductions to cultural studies on the market and it can be very hard to choose between them. I have found the following titles particularly useful for students wishing to get a basic idea of what cultural studies (especially the British variety) is all about. The following represent a small selection of what's available; the ultimate test is to go into a bookshop or library and browse. Firstly, there is Storey's *Theory and Popular Culture: An Introduction* (2001) (which has a back-up website) and Strinati's *An Introduction to Theories of Popular Culture* (1995) both cited in the references below. Other books you might consider, not cited in this chapter, are:

Barker, Chris (2000) *Cultural Studies: Theory and Practice*. London: Sage.

Grossberg, Lawrence, Nelson, Cary and Treichler (eds) (1992) *Cultural Studies*. London: Routledge.

Hartley, John (2003) *A Short History of Cultural Studies*. London: Sage.

Jenks, Chris (1993) *Culture: Key Ideas*. London: Routledge.

Johnson, Richard (1986) 'What is cultural studies anyway?' *Social Text* 6. This short article gives a very useful overview of the area and is included in

J. Munns and G. Rajan (eds) (1995) *A Cultural Studies Reader: History, Theory, Practice*. London: Routledge.
Tudor, Andrew (1999) *Decoding Culture: Theory and Method in Cultural Studies*. London: Sage.
Turner, Graeme (1996) *British Cultural Studies: An Introduction* (2nd edition). London: Routledge.

## Cultural studies readers

There are a number of very useful readers available. Here I recommend those of a general kind, but there many which focus on specific thematic areas like subcultures, visual and media cultures etc. The value of these is that you can dip in and get a taste of a writer's approach before moving on to a full book-length study. All of the readers are well structured and contain useful introductions and well-chosen selections; however, Storey's would be the most practical to use in conjunction with this book because it contains excerpts from many of the writers I review.

During, Simon (ed.) (1993) *The Cultural Studies Reader*. London: Routledge.
Munns, Jessica and Rajan, Gita (eds) (1995) *A Cultural Studies Reader: History, Theory, Practice*. London: Routledge.
Storey, John (1998) *Cultural Theory and Popular Culture: A Reader* (2nd edition). Essex: Pearson Prentice Hall.

## Titles to help you develop your practice skills

Here are a number of titles which emphasize and offer advice on method and the practice of cultural studies. All of them focus on how research may be done and explore theory and practice in considerable detail. They all offer extensive bibliographies that can be followed up (Giles and Middleton; Johnson et al. are particularly strong here). In terms of difficulty, all but one is written with the beginner in mind. McRobbie's title makes more demands on the reader, and if English is not your first language, you might try one of the others before moving on to her book.

du Gay, Paul, Hall, Stuart, Janes, Linda, Mackay, Hugh and Negus, Keith (1997) *Doing Cultural Studies: The Story of the Sony Walkman*. London: Sage. This book is useful because it takes a specific object, the Sony Walkman, and shows how cultural studies might approach it from five perspectives, all important to cultural studies: representation, identity, production, consumption and regulation (see the reference to du Gay in the section 'cultural studies: some basic assumptions', above).

Giles, Judy and Middleton, Tim (1999) *Studying Culture: A Practical Introduction*. Oxford: Blackwell. A very wide-ranging and accessible introduction which includes extracts and useful questions to get readers to consider the ideas put forward for discussion.

Johnson, Richard, Chambers, Deborah, Raghuram, Parvati and Tincknell, Estella (2004) *The Practice of Cultural Studies*. London: Sage. Another very wide ranging book which explains different 'agendas' associated with cultural analysis and discusses available methods, gives advice on how to do detailed research and how to integrate the various methods.

McGuigan, Jim (ed.) (1997) *Cultural Methodologies*. London: Sage. This is a book which helps the reader to think through some of the available methods and gives practical advice on how to go about research. The last chapter offers some useful suggestions concerning working practices.

McRobbie, Angela (2005) *The Uses of Cultural Studies*. London: Sage. This book, rather than describe how to do cultural studies, takes six important theorists who have become important to cultural studies and discusses what they do and what contribution they have made to the area. This book gets under the skin, as it were, of each theorist and helps readers understand, in a critical and very appreciative way, how their theories work in practice.

## Studies which emphasize or include social sciences approaches and method

This book has indicated where some approaches resemble techniques associated with the social sciences, although it has not put its main emphasis on these. The following references are here for those who would like to think about method with relation to areas like Anthropology, Ethnology and Sociology. However, while each one is rooted in the social sciences, most of them challenge any simple distinction between social sciences and non-social sciences books (a distinction already weakened by Johnson et al. and McGuigan in the previous section whose books challenge this simple classification). There's a lesson to be learnt here ... However, my classification is based more on emphasis than absolute difference.

Gray, Ann (2003) *Research Practice for Cultural Studies*. London: Sage. This book is an introduction to ethnographic approaches to cultural studies and gives the reader very useful advice on how to go about starting research.

Saukko, Paula (2003) *Doing Research in Cultural Studies: An Introduction to Classical and New Methodological Approaches*. London: Sage. Saukko introduces the reader to traditional and contemporary approaches and shows, with examples, how various trends can be woven together to create innovative research.

Seale, Clive (ed.) (2004) *Researching Society and Culture* (2nd edition). London: Sage. This is a very comprehensive introduction to how to do research in the social sciences with case studies and discussion exercises.

Stokes, Jane (2003) *How to do Media and Cultural Studies*. London: Sage. Another book which challenges my neat binary classification but it is included here because of its emphasis on quantitative and qualitative methods. It includes advice on how to approach media and cultural texts, industries and audiences.

White, Mimi and Schwoch, James (eds) (2006) *Questions of Method in Cultural Studies*. Oxford: Blackwell. This is a wide-ranging collection of essays which reflect the multidisciplinary character of cultural studies. The book focuses on how method relates to the analysis of objects, space and time, and considers questions of reception and the politics of knowledge. It also includes a very useful first chapter on the emergence of cultural studies within the context of intellectual history.

Williams, Noel (2004) *How to Get a 2:1 in Media, Communication and Cultural Studies*. London Sage. This is a very useful book which focuses on the kinds of skills students need to do well in the areas stated in the title. It defines the fields of study, discusses communication skills and provides tips on learning and thinking about your chosen subject. It also includes 50 key ideas and 40 key thinkers to help students into their chosen subject(s).

## Academic journals and webpages dedicated to cultural studies

If you wish to get a fuller insight into the multiple approaches to cultural studies, or if you are seeking further clarification, materials, resources or new ideas, you might explore journals and websites. You may remember that in the chapter on the Leavises I suggested you look at academic journals dedicated to cultural studies to explore how different articles might be related to consciousness raising. I also recommended some websites. Here are the lists, with a few additions (and which are by no means exhaustive). There are many more specialist journals (which cover areas from TV and crime to globalization and interactive media), but here I have limited myself to recommending those with a fairly broad thematic base. It is worth going to a library, or keeping an eye on the webpages of the major publishing houses, to see what new journals appear and to see if they publish a specialized journal that might particularly interest you. Most major journals offer the possibility of signing-up for electronic tables of contents. That way you get notification when new issues appear and can check to see if anything is of interest to you.

*Journals*

*Australian Journal of Cultural Studies*
*Continuum: Journal of Media and Cultural Studies*
*Cultural Studies*
*Cultural Studies: Critical Methodologies*
*European Journal of Cultural Studies*
*French Cultural Studies*
*Gender, Place and Culture*
*International Journal of Cultural Studies*
*Journal of Intercultural Studies*
*Journal for Cultural Research*
*Journal of Popular Culture*
*Media, Culture and Society*
*Theory, Culture and Society*

*Webography*

All these addresses were accessible at the time of writing (if you have a problem with the address, try typing the website name into a search engine):

*Cultural Studies and Critical Theory Collection:* http://theory.eserver.org/
*Cultural Studies Central*: http://www.culturalstudies.net/
*Cultural Studies-L Page:* http://comm.umn.edu/~grodman/cultstud/
*David Chandler's Media and Communication Studies Site:* http://www.aber. ac.uk/media/index.php
*Media and Cultural Studies Arena*: http://www.culturalstudiesarean.com/mediastudiesarean/about.html
*Popular Culture Association/American Culture Association:* http://www.h-net.org/~pcaaca/

*Sarah Zupko's Cultural Studies Center*: http://www.popcultures.com
*University of Iowa online communication studies resources:* http://www.uiowa.edu/~commstud/resources/culturalStudies.html
*University of Iowa online popular culture resource:* http://www.uiowa.edu/~commstud/resources/POP-Culture.html
*Voice of the Shuttle's Cultural Studies Page*: http://vos.ucsb.edu/browse.asp?id=2709

These are just some websites of a fairly general kind; there are many which are more subject specific. Most major thinkers (Marx, Gramsci, Althusser, Thompson, Williams, Hall etc.) have webpages dedicated to their lives and ideas. Just typing their names into a search engine will reveal the wealth of material available. If you check out university webpages (where there are departments of cultural and media studies, Sociology etc.) you will find that they often contain useful bibliographical information on themes and authors and sometimes have online articles. Major book publishers also have webpages which are useful for research. Again, you can also get publishers to put you on their subscription lists to receive information about publications in areas that are of particular interest.

## SUMMARY OF KEY POINTS

The first part of this chapter suggested ways this book might be summed up by going back to Arnold's importance in methodological terms. This has been used as a starting point to outline some of the ways cultural analysis has developed since. Part two summed up heuristic approaches to practice and commented on how they may be integrated, adapted and extended. Part three reflected on 'difficultures' - on the problems of defining culture and cultural studies and included notes on institutional consolidation. Part four summed up and discussed creative 'critickle' approaches, emphasizing how they might be used to assist understanding, develop ideas and analytical skills. Part four also outlined how creative approaches might help cultivate a dialectical style and discussed plays on words and the use of illustrations in the development of learning and memory skills. Part five spotlighted the limits of the book and what's been left out, while the final part zeros in on the final context of this begin-ending: possibilities for further reading and research. From the point of view of methodological relevance, the idea is for you to take things into your own hands. This leads me to a final practice exercise.

### **practice** EXERCISE: evaluating this book

In line with the aims expressed in the introduction, you might ask yourself how far this book has:

- Given you a basic idea of the historical development of cultural studies, using Britain as the main focal point?
- Made you familiar with some of the most important critics that have been drawn into the British cultural studies tradition?
- Given you a concise, reader-friendly, but critically aware, introduction to some of the key concepts that have been used within cultural studies?
- Made you conversant with some of the main areas of interest to cultural studies?
- Developed your awareness of how theory can be transformed into practice?
- Helped you to acquire ways of thinking with important concepts to help stimulate ideas and ask relevant questions in order to develop the skills required to produce well-argued and informed projects (heuristic thinking)?
- Offered you guidance on *how* concepts may work in practice from numerous practical examples?
- Helped you to appreciate the value of the different approaches and, by following up the numerous practice exercises, given you the confidence to begin practising simple forms of cultural studies for yourself?
- Given you a helping hand to recognize how creative critical techniques might play a role in understanding sources, expressing ideas and aid learning?
- Provided you with an idea of how you might go about further developing your knowledge and practice skills?
- Given you detailed advice on further reading and study?
- Indicated to you what's been left out of the version of cultural studies offered in these pages?

Finally, how far has the book convinced you of the value, interest and relevance of cultural studies?

## References

Baldwin, Elaine, Longhurst, Brian, McCracken, Scott, Ogborn, Miles and Smith, Greg (2004) *Introducing Cultural Studies* (2nd edition). London: Pearson Prentice Hall.

Barker, Chris (2000) *Cultural Studies: Theory and Practice*. London: Sage.

du Gay, Paul, Hall, Stuart, Janes, Linda, Mackay, Hugh and Negus, Keith (1997) *Doing Cultural Studies: The Story of the Sony Walkman*. London: Sage.

Fish, Stanley (1980) *Is There a Text in this Class? The Authority of Interpretive Communities*. Cambridge, MA: Harvard University Press.

Frow (1988) 'Discipline and Discipleship', *Textual Practice*, 2(3).

Frow, John (1995) *Cultural Studies and Cultual Value*. Clarendon: Oxford.

Frow, John and Morris, Meaghan (1993) (eds) *Australian Cultural Studies: A Reader*. Sydney: Allen and Unwin.

Gaarder, Jostein (1995) *Sophie's World*. London: Weidenfeld and Nicholson.

Geertz, Clifford (1973) *The Interpretation of Cultures*. New York: Basic Books.

Grossberg, Lawrence (2002) 'Does Cultural Studies have Futures? Should it? (And what's the matter with New York?)', *Cultural Studies*, 20(1).

Hartley, John (1992a) *The Politics of Pictures: The Creation of the Public in the Age of Popular Media*. London: Routledge.

Hartley, John (1992b) *Tele-ology: Studies in Television*. London: Routledge

Hartley, John (1996) *Popular Reality*. London: Routledge.

Hartley, John (2003) *A Short History of Cultural Studies*. London: Sage.

Hofstede, Geert (1991) *Cultures and Organizations: Software of the Mind*. London: McGraw-Hill.

Jenks, Chris (1993) *Culture: Key Ideas*. London: Routledge.

Lodge, David (1978) *Changing Places*. Harmondsworth: Penguin.

Lodge, David (1985) *Small World*. Harmondsworth: Penguin.

Lodge, David (1989) *Nice Work*. Harmondsworth: Penguin.

Lyotard, Jean-François (with Jean-Loup Thébaud) (1985) *Just Gaming*. Minneapolis: University of Minnesota Press.

Naremore, James and Brantlinger, Patrick (eds) (1991) *Modernity and Mass Culture*. Bloomingon: Indiana University Press.

Piaget, Jean (1972) *Psychology and Epistemology: Towards a Theory of Knowledge*. Harmondsworth: Penguin.

Ray, Robert B. 'The Avant-Garde Finds Andy Hardy', in Naremore, James and Brantlinger, Patrick (eds) (1991) *Modernity and Mass Culture*. Bloomington: Indiana University Press.

Redfern, Walter (1984) *Puns*. Oxford: Basil Blackwell.

*Shrek* (2001) dir. Andrew Adamson and Vicky Jenson.

Storey, John (2001) *Cultural Theory and Popular Culture: An Introduction* (3rd edition). Essex: Pearson Prentice Hall.

Strinati, Dominic (1995) *An Introduction to Theories of Popular Culture*. London: Routledge.

Tolkien, J.R.R. (1954–55) *The Lord of the Rings*. London: Allen and Unwin.

Trompenaars, Fons (1993) *Riding the Waves of Culture*. London: The Economist Books.

Tudor, Andrew (1999) *Decoding Culture: Theory and Method in Cultural Studies*. London: Sage.

Turner, Graeme (1996) *British Cultural Studies: An Introduction* (2nd edition). London: Routledge.

Ulmer, Gregory (1985) *Applied Grammatology: Post(e)-Padagogy from Jacques Derrida to Joseph Beuys*. Baltimore: John Hopkins University Press.

Walton, David (1998) 'Theme-Antics and the The-Eerie Class: CrWit(t)icism in Wrap', *Miscelánea: A Journal of English and American Studies*, 19.

Walton, David and Scheu, Dagmar (eds) (2002) *Ac(unofficial)knowledging Cultural Studies in Spain*. Bern: Peter Lang.

Wilde, Oscar (1978) *The Complete Works of Oscar Wilde*. London: Collins.

# Index